THE SUN
SHINES
BRIGHT

THE SUN SHINES BRIGHT

A Memoir

by Robert Whitridge Estill

Illustrated by the Author

FULL-SERVICE   BOOK-MAKERS

ESTD.   1999

*Grateful acknowledgement to all copyright holders who granted
permission for reprint, including the following:*

Excerpt from *New Interpreter's Bible Vol -12,* commentary by Lynn Harold Hough. Copyright © 1998 by Abingdon Press, an imprint of The United Methodist Publishing House. Used by permission. All rights reserved.

Several excerpts from the *Episcopal News Service.* Reprinted with the permission of The Archives of the Episcopal Church.

Excerpt from "The Right Reverend Will Scarlett," *The Church Awakens: African-Americans and the Struggle for Justice,* 2008. Reprinted with the permission of The Archives of the Episcopal Church.

Excerpt from the "Italo-Ethiopian War," *Encyclopedia Britannica,* December 29, 2015. Reprinted with permission from the *Encyclopedia Britannica,* © 2017 by Encyclopedia Britannica, Inc.

Excerpt from *The Long Loneliness,* by Dorothy Day. Copyright © 1952 by Harper & Row, Publishers, Inc. Copyright renewed © 1980 by Tamar Teresa Hennessy. Courtesy of HarperCollins Publishers.

Excerpt from *Means of Ascent,* by Robert Caro. Copyright © 1990 by Robert A. Caro, Inc. Published originally by Alfred A. Knopf, Inc. now an imprint of Random House, Inc. Reprinted with permission. All rights reserved.

Excerpt from *Let Them Call Me Rebel: Saul Alinksy, His Life and Legacy,* by Sanford D. Horwitt. Copyright © 1989, published by Alfred A. Knopf, Inc. now an imprint of Random House, Inc. Reprinted with permission. All rights reserved.

Excerpt from Reeve Lindbergh's introduction to *Against Wind and Tide: Letters and Journals 1947-1986,* by Anne Morrow Lindbergh. Copyright © 2012 by Lindbergh Literacy LLC. Published by Pantheon Books a division of Random House, Inc. Reprinted with permission. All rights reserved.

Excerpt from *Journals: 1952-2000,* by Arthur M. Schlesinger Jr. Copyright © The Estate of Arthur M. Schlesinger, Jr., 2007. Published by The Penguin Press, a member of Penguin Group, Inc. Reprinted with permission.

Excerpt from Kurt Vonnegut, "Requiem" from *A Man Without a Country.* Copyright © 2010 by Kurt Vonnegut. Reprinted with the permission of The Permissions Company, Inc., on behalf of Seven Stories Press, www.sevenstories.com

PUBLISHED BY
The Chapel Hill Press, Inc., Chapel Hill, NC

———

ISBN 978-1-59715-145-0
Library of Congress Catalog Number 2016945906

Second Printing
Printed in the United States of America

To the love of my life for more than sixty years,

Joyce Haynes Estill, and our children, Helen E. Adams,

Robert W. Estill, Jr., and Elizabeth E. Robertson.

Contents

Acknowledgments

This memoir starts where I started, in Lexington, Kentucky. It never would have happened without the help and encouragement of my dear friends, Joe Graves, author of *Cumberland Island: How the Carnegies Helped Preserve a National Treasure,* and his wife Hart. Joe's secretary, Norma Reynolds, dealt with my poor handwriting and numerous changes.

When the last draft was finished, I was fortunate to find John Sharpe, retired Duke University Curator of Rare Books. John's careful editing, his work and research on the footnotes, and his amazing skill with computers made possible what, for me, would have been impossible.

I am grateful, too, for our Director of Programs at The Cypress of Raleigh, Brian Strausbaugh. At one point Brian downloaded my entire life on a flash drive the size of my pinky finger! Thankfully we found Edwina D. Woodbury, CEO and President of Chapel Hill Press, as our publisher.

My hope is that as you read this memoir, the sun will shine bright in your life, too.

Preface

by Joe Graves

While reading this memoir, this life story, your heart will be touched. Pages later you will laugh out loud. Occasionally, your eyes will tear up.

What will you decide about the author after reading this story? Even if you already know him, I believe this very personal story will be a touching experience for the reader.

I wish each reader of this memoir could share thoughts with all other readers about which writings were especially touching, perhaps especially helpful.

Before writing this Preface, I spent all of one Saturday in a room alone reading the entire manuscript. For me, it was a very moving experience. Indeed, my heart was touched. Often I laughed out loud. There were times my eyes teared up.

With other memoir readers I share these findings:

- Bobby Estill "grew up being read to" by his mother. He would lie on the sofa with his head in her lap while they went through book after book while his father sat in his chair reading: "I must have soaked up a love for books there in her lap, because I still have that love."
- While visiting the Cincinnati Zoo as a boy, Bob listened to that zoo's opera, learning to love opera.

- While rector of Christ Church Episcopal in Lexington, Kentucky (1955–1964), Bob became very active in the civil rights movement. Then governor Bert T. Combs recruited Bob to become chairman of the newly created Kentucky Commission on Human Rights. Bob's memoir does not mention that, decades later, both former governor Combs, then deceased, and Bob were among the first to be elected to the newly created Kentucky Civil Rights Hall of Fame.
- The Continuing Education Center had been started to answer the mid-career crisis that many clergy have. Bob agreed to be its director.

This quotation is from Bob's journal:

Two years later, I'm convinced I am doing more in the Seminary than I could be doing anywhere else right now. To have a deep sharing in the lives of the men who come through our program and to share in strengthening their ministry all over the Church in the USA, in Britain and Japan and New Zealand, is really rewarding. My own continuing education is part of the experience of each term.

I've always considered myself under orders. My task is to discern what God is telling me to do.

Bob writes now that after meeting Joyce Haynes, "From that moment on she became and still is the love of my life." As of this writing they have been married sixty-four years. The pages of this memoir disclose the inspiring story of how Bob and Joyce have worked together while loving their three children, six grandchildren, and one great-grandson.

Robert W. Estill loves horses.

In Kentucky, where the sunshine is often bright, those who know about and care for Thoroughbred horses use a term very, very sparingly to describe only a truly great horse. I truly believe Robert W. Estill deserves this very description because he has a "touch of greatness."

Robert Estill has many gifts.
Would you agree that one of his greatest gifts is a marvelous sense of humor?
How many people do we know who have even a comparable sense of humor?
Is he a better teacher and preacher and bishop because he can tickle our funny bone?
Is there a message here for each of us?
Should we lighten up?
Should we try to create more smiles?
Bishop Estill,
Thanks for creating smiles and laughter.
Thanks for touching each of our lives in such a meaningful way.

—Remarks by Joe Graves during reception at
Christ Church Cathedral for Robert Estill at the
end of his term as interim, December 15, 1996

471 West Second Street

The number 471 means something to me. I was born "at home" on September 7, 1927, at 471 West Second Street in Lexington, Kentucky.

471 West Second

Fifty-two years later, my "number" in the American succession of the episcopate was 741.

Four hundred seventy-one was a large white brick house my mother had fixed over from an old roadside inn. It had six bedrooms, a large "sleeping porch" where the whole family slept in the summer, a large entrance hall with a bay window accommodating a window seat, a "drawing room" with a baby grand piano, a living room/library, dining room, sun porch, kitchen, pantry, and "maid's room." My favorite part of the house was the attic with its access to the roof, where one could observe the street below while unseen, and scramble up to the top holding onto the chimney.

I loved to climb out on the roof at 471 West Second Street.

My mother, Elizabeth Pierpont Whitridge, had been previously married and had two children: Taylor and Sara Revell. When she came to Lexington, she brought them as patients to my father, Robert Julian Estill, a forty-nine-year-old unmarried pediatrician in Lexington. But soon my mother and Dr. Estill were married, and into the household my mother brought with her my grandmother Sarah Wilson Whitridge, her maiden aunt Edith, the two children, and in a year, me.

Taylor and Revell's father was Oscar Taylor Hinton. He was from Kentucky and practiced law in the mountains in Hazard, Kentucky. The Hintons were all from Paris, and my grandmother, after her husband died, moved to Paris to be near *her* relatives—not the Hintons. Very likely my mother met O. T. Hinton in Paris.

When my mother and father were married, Taylor was thirteen, and Sara Revell, nine. My relationship with Revell was much closer than with Taylor, until later we became close friends when I was at Great Lakes in boot camp and he was teaching at Northwestern. He went away to college when he was sixteen and attended several colleges before earning his PhD from Columbia University at twenty-three years old. Revell went to the University of Kentucky and then got a master's at New York University.

Marriage with a divorced person was not as acceptable in that day, and I was told that my father's two sisters were hardly accepting, to say the least. It took my mother at least a couple of years to establish herself in the close-knit Estill family.

My Grandmother Estill[1] died before I was born. However, my grandfather Robert Christopher Estill was alive, and when I came along, he was very proud of the only male Estill—and very attentive. I always looked forward to his visits and to a strong-tasting root he carried in his pocket. I found out years later it was ginger root that was chewed and deposited up the rear of show horses to make their tails stand up! Another favorite visitor was Uncle Dan Estill. As I'll relate later, he made sure I could "defend

---

1. Naomi Wierman Sheffer Estill.

myself with my fists." He also taught me to shoot skeet and handle guns responsibly. He was unmarried until late in life.

Mother had dark brown hair and eyes, and was petite and energetic. I'm sure she turned my father's life upside-down. He had been a very eligible bachelor, lived in an apartment on Upper Street with his father, and ate his evening meal at the Lafayette Hotel with such regularity that the waiters would bring him dinner without waiting for him to read the menu. The Lafayette Hotel was just two doors from my father's office and a few doors from Christ Church, where later I was rector.[2] My father had a large medical practice, played golf on the weekends, was an active member of Christ Church, and spent his vacations abroad—especially in France. He was fluent in French.

He had volunteered in the first expeditionary force in World War I and had been in the trenches and commanded Base Hospital 8 in Savenay, France.[3]

Lexington, Kentucky, of all places, was very aware of its French ties. After all Lafayette was the name of both the major hotel and the county—Fayette County—and lots of French architecture. We actually had a woman come live with us—and other families—to teach the children French. Every summer my father, proud of his French Huguenot background, traveled to France. His family owned a large farm in Kentucky and were part owners of what was then the First National Bank of Lexington. Until I came along and became a "preacher," a male Estill was always on the board. That bank eventually through several mergers ended up as a branch of J. P. Morgan–Chase.

---

2. For a description of Christ Church, see www.nps.gov/nr/travel/lexington/cce.htm.

3. Base Hospital No. 8 was organized in November 1916 at the Post-Graduate Hospital, New York City. The unit was mobilized at Fort Jay, New York, July 18, 1917. After ten days of drilling and equipping, the organization embarked July 29, 1917, on the *Saratoga*. On July 30, shortly after midday mess, the *Saratoga*, while at anchor in New York harbor, was rammed by the *Panama*, and so badly damaged that all passengers were disembarked and transported back to Governors Island. The unit lost most of its equipment and personal property on the *Saratoga*, but after a week of reequipping embarked again on August 7, 1917, and sailed the same date on the *Finland* (Office of Medical History; U. S. Army Medical Department, history.amedd.army.mil/booksdocs/wwi/adminamerexp/chapter24.html)

I loved getting into my father's WWI chest and trying on his gas mask.

His "things" from World War I were in an army trunk in the attic, and I loved to put them on, smell the faint odor of gas in his gas mask, and look at the pictures of the war.

At the end of the war he stayed in France two years and set up a children's hospital in the village of Savenay. When he left, the village presented him with a bronze statue of a musketeer with an inscription of appreciation. The inscription reads:

> *Mairie Savenay*
> *Homage de la Ville de Savenay*
> *À M. Lieutenant-Colonel Estill*
> *Commandant de la Base-Hôpital № 8*
> *1917–1919*

On the base is inscribed "Émile Laporte," the sculptor.[4] In picking up the statue, the figure's sword struck me in the arm. That's as close as I came to spilling any blood in the liberation of France, because I was at Episcopal High School in 1944. I entered Episcopal High School in 1940 when I was just thirteen.

Later, when I was along with World War II veterans on a tour of Normandy American Cemetery and Memorial, I received a medal with the inscription "Struck on the occasion of the 50th Anniversary of the Liberation of the City of Caen in tribute to all those who took part in the battles is presented to you with the respect and compliments of Mr. Jean-Marie Girault Sénator Mayor of Caen."

---

4. Émile Henri Laporte (1858–1907), French sculptor who worked almost exclusively with bronze.

Like many war veterans, my father didn't talk much about his experiences. Yet he did tell of General John Joseph "Black Jack" Pershing making a surprise inspection of the Base Hospital and chewing him out for its appearance. They had just received a new shipment of casualties from the front, and Pershing was upset over the reception he received. My father didn't have much respect for him after that.

He also told of boarding a troop ship in New York and being sunk by a German submarine. They got safely off and back to New York and weeks later boarded another ship. As he was waiting in line he looked toward the end of the pier and saw a small black medicine bag sitting alone behind one of the posts. When he recovered it, it was his that had been with him on the ship that sank. No one ever knew how it had gotten there.

My father's experience on that troop ship was ironic because, despite his many trips abroad, he suffered from seasickness. On one trip he boarded his ship in New York and went right to his stateroom and got in bed. He was seasick all night, but when he woke up the next morning he said he felt better and went topside for some fresh air only to find the ship had not yet sailed because of mechanical problems and was only then pulling away from the dock!

My mother was born and raised in Baltimore, and while I never knew my grandfather Whitridge, she bore the name proudly in the midst of all the Kentucky Estills who "went back" to Captain James Estill, a contemporary of Daniel Boone, who died in battle with the Indians.

Mother told me that when I was off to Episcopal High in Alexandria, Virginia, and near Baltimore, I'd find that the Whitridges were every bit as fine a family as the Estills. She took a good deal of pleasure qualifying for the Colonial Dames on her own name and background.

I grew up being read to by her, and I would lie on the sofa with my head in her lap while we went through book after book. My father would be in his chair reading. I'm sure that a great influence on my later life was being formed.

Many memoirs I have read spend time going back into generations of their forebears. Except for the rather embarrassing connection with Pope Alexander VI, I have resisted that urge. I discovered this fact when I was on sabbatical at Oxford and did some research in the marvelous Bodleian Library. He was considered the worst pope and earned that title by his greed for lands and estates, his nepotism, mistresses and bastard children including my forbearer.

My relative Alfonso d'Este, Duke of Ferrara, married Pope Alexander's daughter, the infamous Lucrezia Borgia, who—it was rumored—had poisoned her first husband, Giovanni Sforza. Alfonso and his family d'Este ruled Ferrara. This bloodline melds later into the Huguenots of northern Italy and Provence, who ended up being persecuted by the Roman Catholics and forced to flee to New Jersey.

Still, when I think about Kentucky and its early settlers, I am convinced that I should mention Captain James Estill, for whom Estill County is named, and who appears in most histories under the heading of "Estill's defeat."

James was a contemporary and friend of the more famous frontiersman Daniel Boone, and as such was one of the early settlers in what was called the "Dark and Bloody Ground"[5] that was the hunting ground for numerous Native American tribes.

Captain Estill contributed to the bloody part of that title, as he fought the Native Americans, took their land away, and began the white man's relentless move westward. I believe the so-called revisionist history has its drawbacks, however. The early history of Kentucky shows the natives treated badly, their lands taken without a second thought, and their way of life changed forever. But back to Captain James.

In March 1780 he established Estill's Station about four miles southwest

---

5. Kentucky was known as the "Dark and Bloody Ground" when it was first settled because it was the site of numerous battles fought between the Native American tribes, including the Cherokee and Shawnee tribes. It was dubbed "a dark and bloody ground" by Cherokee Chief Dragging Canoe, at the time the Treaty off Sycamore Shoals was signed in 1775.

of what is now Richmond, Kentucky. The station was at the headwaters of Otter Creek. Two years later, in what was called "The Battle of Little Mountain," Captain James and seven of his force of twenty-five Pioneers were killed in hand-to-hand fighting with a band of twenty-five Wyandots. Estill's battle plan was derailed by a man named William Miller, who, instead of following a command to circle the battle and come in on the Indian's backside, cut and ran.

The Indians had raided the fort in the absence of most of its men and had killed a young girl and taken captive Monk, Estill's slave. They had not killed him because of his worth when they would trade him to the British. The British were encouraging the Indians in their resistance and enlisted them to aid in their ongoing wars.

One of the men with Estill, Adam Caperton, was shot in the head and ran, crazed, into the open toward the Indians. Estill ran after him to bring him back, but another bullet killed him. The rest of the battle gets some editing by historians, but it is clear that Estill engaged in a hand-to-hand fight with one of the Indians (some say it was the chief). Nonetheless a hand-to-hand battle ensued, and neither man had an edge until Estill's arm, wounded in a former battle, broke, and the Indian finished him off with a knife plunged into his heart. A shot from one of Estill's men killed the Indian, who fell over Estill's dead body. Legend has it that Monk, now freed from the Indians, carried his master's body back to the fort. That probably did not happen, though he did carry some of the wounded to safety. Records show that Estill's body along with several others were buried in makeshift ways several days later on the spot where they were killed.

James Estill meets the Wyandot.

Monk was freed in 1782 by Captain Estill's son, Wallace in gratitude for Monk's bravery at the Battle of Little Mountain, becoming the first freed slave in Kentucky. He became a Baptist minister and served in Shelbyville, Kentucky. During the course of his life he married three wives and sired, according to the record, thirty children, most of whom were educated through the equivalent of high school. He died in Madison County, Kentucky, in 1835.

Even though Estill's family freed Monk, again here the records conflict, some saying Monk refused his freedom and continued on with the family.

As a young boy I went to the Richmond Cemetery and, with other Estills, pulled the cover off the statue of Captain James. At that time I believe I was the last living male descendant of the famous fighter. If I am not mistaken, my son, Bobby, has that honor now.

So it is that my roots go deep in my old Kentucky home, now far away.

I wrote the following poem on one of the anniversaries:

THE 200TH ANNIVERSARY OF ESTILL'S DEFEAT

What last thoughts were yours ancestral forebear,
As your arm, weakened long before,
Gave way; and thus a
Savage knife sliced your young life in two?

Were you aware of who it was you fought?
Who it was who grappled there with you,
turning in violent thrashing, locked together
in the dusk?

Did not the dark and bloody ground seem alien,
All at once?
Did not you grasp the awful fact of your
intrusion there?

Monk, more at home in those dark woods
    than you,
Picked you up and bore you, white and
    dying to the Fort.
Hinkston Creek was red with blood that
    day in March.
Two miles below the Little Mountain,
What last thoughts were yours?

Rumor has it that you grappled with their chief,
    Chief upon Chief.

Would that the others could have stopped and watched.
Then only chiefs would die, and McMillan, Cook,
    South, Colefoot, McNeely, and Caperton
    would live.

Would that wars were fought that way.
With all our young ones looking on. And
    Miller never would have had to
    run away.

Estill's Defeat! Ah yes, it was defeat.
No blood is spilled without a loss.
Silent now the woods, long past the shouts;
    And farther still away the native son.

—Robert W. Estill,
Great-great-grandson of Captain James Estill,
who died March 22, 1782.

I mentioned earlier my love of books, but for the life of me I can't remember specific books that left a mark except those of Kipling and a lovely book I still have, titled *Grindstone Farm*.[6] I must have soaked up a love for books there in my mother's lap, because I still have that love.

West Second Street was one of the finest places to live in those days. Second Street, Third Street, Hampton Court, Gratz Park were prime addresses. Then one had to skip Fourth Street—that's where the Insane Asylum[7] was—and jump all the way to Fayette Park and Sixth Street. Ashland Avenue, on the other side of town, was developing, as were some homes around what was then known as the Ashland Golf Club.

We had friends on nearly every street and knew how to go through backyards, alleys, and rooftops to reach each other. Two friends who lived in Fayette Park, Winky and Packy Clark, were great bike riders and kept their bikes at the ready beside their front porch. One morning Winky (the older brother) came running out the door, across the porch, and leaped into the air over his bicycle only to find in a horrified split second that Packy had removed the seat! I lost track of the Clarks after leaving Lexington, and I have often wondered whether Winky ever had any children of his own.

Happily for my father, we were within walking distance of St. Joseph's Hospital, where he was chief of pediatrics, and his office on North Upper Street. He could walk from there, or take the bus to the Good Samaritan Hospital. He often walked home at the end of the day, and I would run to

---

6. Henry Bolles Lent, *Grindstone Farm* (New York: Macmillan, 1935).
7. Eastern State Hospital in Lexington, Kentucky, is the second-oldest psychiatric hospital in the United States.

meet him. Usually he would have "something" for me; I collected a grand
army of lead soldiers including Ethiopians and Italians during that war.[8]

He sometimes used the city bus to get to the Good Samaritan Hospital
to make his morning rounds. One morning two teenagers got on and sat
behind him. He overheard one of them ask the other, "Has you did your
Greek?" He loved to embellish on that and other stories, some of which
came from the medical journals and were for a limited number of people
in health care. When I came on the scene just as he had turned fifty, he
began to work me into his stories and jokes. It must have bored his patients
and their parents. A typical one went: "Bobby came home from the first
grade yesterday and said they had been given a spelling test. When I asked
how he had done, he replied, 'There were ten words and I missed eleven!'
'How did that happen?' I asked. He replied, 'I missed one word twice!'"

While we lived on Second Street, I went through the rigors of after-
school piano lessons. My first teacher was a Miss Duck, and after I convinced her that I was never going to succeed, she passed me on to (I
know it sounds as if I am making this up) a Miss Drake. I got as far as
a recital Miss Drake held at the end of the school year. My friend Bo
Rankin was also a student, and on the day of the recital, Miss Drake's
house was filled with mostly mothers, a few aunts, and one or two men.
I suppose they were fathers.

Bo's time on the program was just before mine. He went to the piano,
adjusted the seat, and then just sat there. Finally, we all heard Mrs. Rankin
say in a loud whisper, "My God! He's forgotten it!" Bo stepped down in
disgrace, and I ascended the stage, played poorly, ended with relief felt by
all present—including Miss Drake—and we all, including the Rankins,
had refreshments.

---

8. Italo-Ethiopian War (1935–1936), an armed conflict that resulted in Ethiopia's subjection
   to Italian rule. Often seen as one of the episodes that prepared the way for World War II,
   the war demonstrated the ineffectiveness of the League of Nations when league decisions
   were not supported by the great powers.

We'd go after supper to the Cincinnati Zoo and the Zoo Opera.

That experience, along with my brief career as a trumpet player, ended any thought of a music career. But I learned to love opera through our trips to the Zoo Opera in Cincinnati, and was a fan of Stan Kenton and his progressive jazz, but my "calling" in musical circles is as a listener.

Summer evenings remain in my mind to this day. The whole neighborhood would be out on porches, and the children playing kick the can. After dark we would walk around the block, stopping at an ice cream parlor where they featured "walk-away sundaes." These were the days before air conditioning—and we were allowed to stay up until the evening cooled and we went to bed on a screened-in sleeping porch. Like the three bears (multiplied), there was a bed for my parents, one for me, one for my grandmother, great aunt, brother, and sister. Dogs, children, and adults would walk around the block, calling out greetings to the porch sitters and *always* going clockwise for some reason that no one thought to question. The very small children would stay especially close to the adults as we walked along Broadway—a busy north/south link and the way downtown and out of town, depending on your direction.

In addition to inheriting a love of books, I grew up with a love of dogs. We had Scotties in those early days. Tam was the oldest, and she loved to join my mother and father on their Friday golf day. She stayed on a leash until they were out on the course but then would take all the short cuts with the caddies. As the club would occasionally change a tee on a hole, she would sit on the old spot and look at us as though we were losing our minds. She also liked being dragged by her leash on her back! That job often fell to me when I began to play with my parents.

Jock was our next Scottie, and he broke up my first love affair. Martha Van Hooser had long blond hair and visited my neighbor Marian Douglas regularly. I was getting along fine with her until Jock nipped her on the cheek and ended our affair. In later life, she became well-known as a dog breeder and shower—perhaps getting her start from Jock.

My brother—called Oscar in those days and later O.T. and even later, Taylor—was thirteen when he came to live at 471. He was thin and gangly and, even in those days, interested in snakes and bugs and scientific things. He and my father understandably had a rather difficult relationship. My great aunt Edith (we called her "Neo") always took Oscar's side of things, and I'm ashamed to admit I often got him into trouble with my father. Much later when I was in the navy at Great Lakes and he was teaching at Northwestern, we got to know each other in a new way and became good friends. He told me of one incident where we were all at the table, and I was in a high chair. I flipped a spoon full of soup and it hit my father. Taylor said, "Everyone at the table stopped talking and looked at Dr. Estill. We were waiting for him to explode and finally to discipline the little brat. Dr. Estill looked directly at me and said, 'Oscar! Leave the table!' You got off scot-free!"

It's a wonder Taylor would ever forgive me, but he did, and we spent happy times together in Evanston and later in Amherst. He died at a very young age (in his forties) of cirrhosis of the liver. He was a very bright scientist and had grants to work on cancer cells in tiny, almost invisible bugs called fruit flies. He also made a great gin out of laboratory alcohol—which probably contributed to his cirrhosis.

When Taylor was teaching at Amherst and Joyce and I were in

Cambridge, we visited him over the Thanksgiving weekend. Taylor was an excellent cook, and often his house was filled with faculty and students who were aware of his talents. For this Thanksgiving he had bought a live turkey and taken it to his lab and, with the help of his assistants, strung it up, killed it, and through various tubes and bottles, drained its fluids out and pumped a rich mixture of gravy and herbs into it. He bragged that he would not have to baste it. As the guests arrived, he served gin drinks made in his lab out of laboratory-strength alcohol and some flavors known only to him. It was powerful and delicious! After a proper cocktail hour, Taylor went to check on the turkey, only to find to his horror that he had failed to turn on the stove.

Needless to say, the cocktail hour stretched into several hours, and only then those of us left standing were able to negotiate our way to the table. The day after became a Thanksgiving Day of a sort for those of us who survived.

Taylor never married, though he had a longtime relationship with Susan Clay from Kentucky. Their professional lives kept them apart, though I gather they were fond of each other. Looking back, I believe Taylor was gay—though in the times I was with him, I never saw any overt homosexuality. He always had a lot of students around him, both male and female. Still, his longtime roommate, Will, was openly gay, and Taylor left him his things when he died. He was buried in the Hinton Lot in Paris, Kentucky.

Sara Revell was younger when my mother divorced and remarried and always seemed to have a good relationship with "Dr. Estill." She took the Estill name, which Taylor never did. I made her life miserable as any younger brother might do. To this day I have a scar on the little finger of my left hand where I went through a French door chasing, or being chased by, her.

As Sarah Revell became a teenager and from there on, she was very popular, often having a "late date" after an original date. I especially liked one of her most regular suitors, Joe Cogar. Joe seemed to like me, too. He always had something to show me or give me, and I looked forward to his visits and grieved when he and Revell broke up. His older brother, James Cogar, was to become famous for being one of the persons responsible for restoring Williamsburg, Virginia—and later, Shaker Town in Kentucky.[9]

In those days, the Kentucky River was the popular place in the summer, and the Cogars had a cottage there with a rope hanging from a huge tulip poplar. Joe and Sarah Revell were both excellent swimmers, and they would swing out over the river and at the last minute drop into the water.

Later on when we were at the university, the river was a popular place to take a date, especially if it included going to Johnnie Allman's, with its beer-cheese and thick steaks.[10] One night, we were driving back to Lexington in John Gaines's station wagon. I was driving and my date, Joyce, and John and I were in the front seat. The road up from the river is full of hairpin, curves and as we clipped along doing about fifty miles an hour, Joyce, sitting with her knees on the dashboard inadvertently hit the headlight switch, which in those days was on the dash. We were plunged into darkness as I jammed on the brakes. We came close to killing all of

---

9. James Lowry Cogar, first curator of Colonial Williamsburg and first president of Shaker Village of Pleasant Hill in Mercer County, Kentucky, graduated from the University of Kentucky in 1927 and obtained a master's degree from Harvard in 1929. He studied architecture at Yale and taught American history at the College of William and Mary in Williamsburg. From 1931 to 1948 he served as the first curator of Colonial Williamsburg. Cogar was recruited to lead the restoration of Pleasant Hill in 1962; he remained active with the Shaker Village, serving as director and president, until 1974. Cogar was nationally known as an important leader in the field of architectural restoration, historical furnishings, costume, and museum management.

10. Johnnie Allman was a native of Richmond, Kentucky, and always had a love for the Kentucky River. He had a variety of jobs in his younger days before he got into the restaurant business. He was a lifeguard at Fort Boonesborough, took over his father's grocery business for a while, and worked at Jack Turpin's funeral home and at Richmond's daily newspaper. For a ten-year period he served on the Richmond Police Department and the Kentucky State Police Force, worked his way up to the rank of captain, and was personal aide to two Kentucky governors.

After retiring from the Kentucky State Police Force, Johnnie Allman began his historic restaurant career. It all started in the late 1930s on the banks of the Kentucky River near Boonesborough where he opened his first restaurant, the Driftwood Inn. This was the restaurant where Johnnie Allman first served his cousin Joe Allman's now famous "Snappy Cheese."

us, including an heir to the Gaines dog food business and founder of the "World Series of Horse Racing," the Breeders' Cup.[11]

Our experience brought back a story my mother told about driving back from the river. She was several months pregnant with me, and she and my father were in their car while their friends Dr. and Mrs. Scott Breckinridge were in their car behind them. As they rounded one of the many curves, to their horror a mule and wagon was coming at them in the middle of the narrow road. They hit it head on. My mother was thrown from the car, and she and I rolled away into a ditch. My father rushed to her side while Dr. Breckinridge went to the aid of the wagon driver. The mule never knew what hit him and was dead. The tongue of the wagon had gone between the driver's and passenger's seat in my father's car. Dr. Breckinridge knelt at the side of the wagon driver and called out, "Julian, he has lost his leg below the knee!" By that time my mother was on her feet with only a few scratches. My father hurried to the side of the wagon driver and in a quick examination informed his medical colleague, "Scott, he only has one leg, the other was a peg-leg. Here's the peg!" The story, in a sense, had a happy ending, except for the mule.

A number of our friends had swimming pools, and Mrs. Haggin's was one of the most popular, though the water that came from Russell Cave was cold. She had an estate over the cave, and her farm, Mount Brilliant, was a Thoroughbred operation. The dressing rooms were in her boxwood garden, and the smell of a boxwood bush today brings back the memory of

---

11. The Breeders' Cup World Championships was created as a year-end championship for North American Thoroughbred racing, and also attracts top horses from other parts of the world, especially Europe. The idea for the Breeders' Cup was proposed at the 1982 awards luncheon for the Kentucky Derby Festival by pet food heir John R. Gaines (1928–2005), a leading Thoroughbred owner and breeder who wanted to clean up the sport's image (Amanda Duckworth, "Oh, Breeders' Cup," *ESPN.com*, October 30, 2013; therail.blogs. nytimes.com/2011/11/02/from-horsemans-vision-the-breeders-cup-was-born/?_r=0)

The story ended happily for everyone ...except the mule.

that garden. The elegant colonial house was a decorators' showplace. Alas, it is no more. The current owner demolished the 150-year-old mansion.

My father was the Haggins' doctor, and later the doctor for their children's children. Emma Haggin Molloy was a Catholic and had lots of children. They seemed to get sick or have accidents at off times, and so my father was always seeing one or another of the Molloys. When he retired, they recognized his service, and so in appreciation they gave him a mint julep cup with an inscription on the bottom: "From those damn Molloys."

We also swam at the Talberts on Eastin Road. The bathhouse there had two sides divided by a wall that was full of holes. Mr. Talbert would nail the tops from tin cans over the holes when he found them. One time I entered the boys' side just as several girls entered the girls' side. There were three of us, and I had found a hole Mr. Talbert had missed. "Whaddya see?" hissed one of my friends. "I can't tell," I

The Talbots had a swimming pool.

whispered back, and then I realized what it was. It was an eye looking at us from the girls' side!

I learned to swim in that pool when one of my cousins—Howard, I believe—pushed me in. It was a small pool, and we loved to play underwater games like Red Rover and could swim across and back underwater.

The Deepwood subdivision was under way, and when I was about nine or ten, we later moved near there into a smaller home in the suburbs right on the edge of the country as my father was beginning to retire from his practice. My mother had "the oldest house in Yorktown, Virginia" replicated on four acres on Eastin Road, and we moved into it when I was in junior high school.

Taylor and Sara Revell were gone, and my great aunt Edith died soon after the move. And while I was at Episcopal High School, my grandmother died. So it was just my parents until I came home from school for vacations to this suburban setting. The "in" club was the Lexington Country Club on the Paris Pike. It was there we swam, played tennis and golf, and when we were older, danced on Saturday night. The Paris Pike—all the roads were called "Pike" until the early 1940s—has most of the famous horse farms on it and led to Paris, Kentucky, where more horse farms were. It was in Bourbon County, which was dry!

When we moved to Robin Hill on Eastin Road, our crowd consisted of Betty Alden Talbert (whose family owned the pool), Pat Thompson, Charlotte Garr, Nancy Wilder, Murray Tilton, and me. Later, we conscripted Sam Strother, but until then I was the only boy. While we really never had what one would call "dates," we went around together—mostly in the neighborhood.

Robin Hill was situated on several acres in what might today be called a subdivision. In those days it was called "Dog Hill" by the Kentucky Sam Waltons, whose house was the center piece around which were built our house and two others. Instead of a roof to explore as on Second Street,

Robin Hill

I had a huge sycamore tree to climb, a creek to catch crawfish and small snakes, and a large vegetable garden, grape arbor, and flower garden. By that time we had a big male English springer spaniel named "Brandy," who was my constant companion.

We had a garage with an attic that became a fine clubhouse for the neighborhood. I painted a large sign on the garage wall saying, "Keep Out by Order of Bobby Estill." Years later when I returned to Lexington to be rector of Christ Church, the man who had bought Robin Hill wrote under my sign, "Rector of Christ Church"!

After we moved to Robin Hill, I decided I would take up the trumpet, so I saved my money and bought a used one at the local pawn shop for five dollars. I went to my room and for several days made mournful sounds—which sent Brandy under the bed—and gave myself a fat lip. After about the fourth day the doorbell rang, and when I answered

Lots of space for Brandy and me.

How much did you pay for it?

it, it was our neighbor from across Eastin Road, Reb Newsome. He said, "I hear you bought a trumpet." When I told him the price, he replied, "I'll give you ten for it!" Sold! And thus ended my career as a trumpet player. Harry James was safe.

As I write this in the 2000s, Betty Alden died in 2006. She was married to Sam Van Meter of Winchester. Pat Thompson married a Henry Clay High School football star; Jimmy Mahan was killed in a company plane crash (Ashland Oil); Nancy Wilder married and lives in Tennessee; Murray Tilton married John Barrow and lived in Lexington until her death; Charlotte Garr married Dick Schubert. Charlotte has died and so has he.

Sam Strother, who was much younger than most of us, had a somewhat wild time, and at one point was involved in a party in which a friend's wife was killed, Mary Mars Swineboard Cawein. Her husband, Madison Cawein, was suspected, but nothing ever came of it in the courts. Sam and Betty Strother divorced—and after Sam died, she married a much older man and moved to Dallas where we saw something of them from time to time when we were there. Their daughter and our son, Bobby, were at Texas Christian University together and dated for a while.

The country club pool was especially popular and had a high-dive platform. One of my friends, Bunny McKinley, was the best diver and did a great swan dive that all of us envied. Years later I would bury Bunny's daughter, who committed suicide, and even later bury Bunny himself.

Swimming parties were popular events. Herrington Lake was the largest body of water near us. It was created by Kentucky Utilities' damming of the Dix River, a tributary of the Kentucky River, in 1925 to generate hydroelectric power. It had treacherous tree stumps that often caught swimmers or pulled off outboard motors. Around the lake, several families had cottages where we enjoyed parties and outings. The Kentucky River also had its fans, and Camp Otonka was the very popular YWCA camp for girls. Sara Revell went there and later was a counselor.

Hamilton Grammar School

The earliest academic endeavor on my part ended in failure. It was politely suggested to my parents that I was not ready for kindergarten at the University Training School for teachers at the University of Kentucky. According to the reports, I had "gone number two in the playhouse" and then had "refused to come out." I left in disgrace.

I was ejected from kindergarten.

Hamilton Grammar School started on the campus of Hamilton College on Broadway near Fayette Park and that was where I went next and stayed up to junior high. They didn't have a playhouse, and I apparently did not have any more accidents. I only vaguely remember that school, but it soon melded into another house farther down Broadway near the dreaded Fourth Street with its Insane Asylum. There were only eight students in my

Hamilton Grammar School—four boys and four girls

class, four boys and four girls, and our only recreation was a yard in the back where we could run at recess. I took on the role of class clown and missed most of the recesses for punishment. My best friend was Junie Roberts. In our neighborhood my best friend was Marian Douglas, who lived two doors down. Sadly, her father was an alcoholic and her mother ran things, including her three daughters. They had a wonderful attic, papered in old comic strips—which fascinated me—I was drawing a lot and my parents let me use the backs of the National Geographic Maps for my artwork.

Years later, Harry Feamster, a fraternity brother and a candidate for a PhD, was doing a kind of residency at the asylum. In our unenlightened youth we thought that the people there were crazy, but later Harry added a different view of the patients. Each morning when he arrived, he had to pass through the dementia ward, where a number of patients were comatose or in various stages of dementia. Alzheimer's had not yet been identified.

There was a patient who always was sitting near the door in a wheelchair with her head down in what seemed to be a deep coma. Her name was Edna. Without much thought, when he passed by, Harry would pat Edna on the shoulder and say, "Good morning, Edna. How are you today?" and go on through the next door to his assigned ward.

About two years passed, and Harry was waiting for a bus in downtown Lexington. A nicely dressed woman came up to him and said, "Excuse me, Dr. Feamster, but I wanted to thank you for speaking to me all those mornings in the dementia ward. I'm Edna, and your greeting and your touch on the shoulder were all that gave me hope that I could conquer my depression and go back to living life. Thank you!" And she disappeared into the crowd on the street.

Harry never forgot that, and I haven't either. He had made the dreaded Fourth Street Insane Asylum a place of healing.

My best friend, Marion, had a series of girlfriends visit from time to time, and at one point two of them decided we would have a nudist colony. It was to be held in our garage. When the time came, we gathered. I stripped down, but the girls went down only to their underwear.

I insisted they "play fair," but the best I could achieve was to get them to lower the flaps in the back where I could peek at some skin.

The only other boy in the neighborhood was Billy Bronson, who was several years older and lived with his

When the time came ... I stripped down.

mother. On occasion he would come across the street and beat me up.

My Uncle Dan, who was, at the time, unmarried and had no children, decided that I needed to be able to protect myself even though he didn't know Billy Bronson. So he employed a retired boxer, Ben Blue, to give me lessons. Every Friday and Saturday night they had regular boxing matches at one of the parks in Lexington. They were very popular, and that's likely where Uncle Dan met Ben Blue. A friend of Uncle Dan's, Harry Scott, signed his son up, too, and every Saturday morning "little Harry," who was bigger than I but rather chubby and a slow mover, and I would go at it in a vacant stall on the Scotts' horse farm. The lesson usually ended when Harry would start to cry.

Ben Blue told Uncle Dan, wise man that he was, that he "wouldn't be responsible for Bobby's left hand; it was so lethal!" Uncle Dan immediately signed me up for another year of lessons.

Junie Roberts's father was manager of Miss Clara Peck's Winganeek Farm, a well-known saddle horse breeding

The lesson usually ended when Harry started to cry.

farm on the Richmond Road.[12] It was a glorious place for small boys. We could play in the creek that went through the farm, catching crawfish and snakes, swim in a large pond, and in the winter, ice skate on another. Junie and I fashioned a large tunnel network in the bales of hay and straw in the loft of the breeding barn. We could play hide-and-seek with each other and with other boys who came to spend the day.

One afternoon we watched fascinated as one of the stallions mounted a mare below us and our first lesson in sex education took place. We kept it a deep secret, but as I look back I think Mr. Roberts knew we were up there getting an eyeful.

The Roberts had a black driver and handyman named Robert. He became a fast friend and taught us a lot about what it was like to be black in Lexington, Kentucky, in the 1930s and 1940s. He had his own car with one of those iron bull terriers on the running board. He loved to ask unsus-

Mr. Roberts was a dapper little Englishman.

pecting people to pet his dog—which was wired to the battery and gave them a pretty good shock.

Junie's father, Mr. Roberts, was a dapper little Englishman who wore a stick-pin with a horseshoe on it and had a mustache and an accent. He was also active in the Lexington Junior League Horse Show every summer.

He was one of the top saddle-horse men in the United States and judged the horse show in Madison Square Garden each year. Mrs. Roberts was German, and her parents lived over the garage in an apartment. "Grossfather" kept the garden and did odd jobs around the place. He hardly spoke English.

12. Francis Arthur "Junie" Roberts grew up on Winganeek Farm in Lexington where his father, Arthur Roberts, a well-known trainer and judge of American Saddlebreds, was farm manager. In the oral history Roberts describes his childhood on the farm and tells stories about Miss Clara S. Peck, the owner of Winganeek. He discusses his father's career and his job on the farm, assisting his father with training and breeding horses.

As we got a little older, we began to spy on Junie's sister, Pearl, but never saw anything of interest. She dated John Ward and eventually married him. He was a very successful horseman and trainer, especially known for breaking yearlings. He broke the famous horse First Landing, among others. His son, John,[13] is a top trainer today, and won the Kentucky Derby with John Oxley's horse, Monarchos who won the Kentucky Derby in 2001. Oxley also owned Beautiful Pleasure, the 1999 American Champion Older Female, the winner of the Breeders' Cup Distaff.

In that Central Kentucky bluegrass environment, it's no wonder I have had a lifelong interest in and love for horses. Ed Madden, master of Hamburg Place, was an enthusiastic polo player and had started the Iroquois Polo Club on the Winchester Pike. It had a pool and tennis courts, but its main purpose was to provide space for polo. It was actually part of his Hamburg Place farm and across the pike from my uncle Rodes Estill's farm.

Mr. Madden's right front canine incisor was imbedded in a polo mallet and hung over the bar in the clubhouse. He promoted polo with boys my age by giving them a Shetland pony, and when they outgrew that, a polo pony. They then started to learn the game, and unless they valued their teeth more than the excitement of polo, they played for the Iroquois.

Clint Harbison, son of my godfather, played here and went on to play for Yale before going into the Naval Air Force and being lost at sea in World War II. "Bobo," as he was known in high school, had gone to Episcopal High in Alexandria, Virginia, and because of that and our family's closeness, I was to go there, too. But I'm getting ahead of the story.

A combination of Ed Madden's sudden death and World War II ended the Polo Club. One day Ed drove over to Hughes Lane, which was named

13. John T. Ward Jr. (born August 2, 1945, in Lexington, Kentucky) is an American racehorse trainer. He is a graduate of the University of Kentucky with a degree in agricultural economics, where he was a member of Delta Tau Delta fraternity. He is a third-generation horseman on both sides of his family. He took charge of the family farm at age twenty-five when his father became ill in 1970.

for my great-grandfather Jacob Hughes, and took his own life. Winnie, his wife, called my father, who was their children's doctor, and told him she was worried about Ed, so my father drove over to Hughes Lane from

One of them would give him a whack, and off we'd go!

our house (then on Eastin Road) and found him. Several years later Ed Madden's brother, J. E. Madden also committed suicide. He walked into Abercrombie's in New York City, asked to see a pistol, loaded it, and shot himself to death.

My pony, a light brown and white Shetland, was named Tony (Tony the Pony). He was as mean as a snake. I kept him at my uncle Rodes's place and, for the brief

times I was able to stay on his back, rode with my cousins Ann and Rodes.

On the rare occasions when Tony was going well, one of them would ride up and give him a whack and off we'd (I'd) go.

Later, we transferred Tony to my aunt Laura's farm in Woodford County and made a "buggy pony" out of him. We had a grand straw cart, and since nobody was on his back, he went well. I spent a good deal of the summer at Aunt Laura's Haltura farm, staying all summer one year during the polio epidemic.

Aunt Laura was a widow and had taken over running the 450-acre farm after Uncle Claude's death. He had been a gentleman farmer, and farms don't run well when the main man sits on the porch gazing out over his acreage. Aunt Laura was a hands-on farmer and soon had things back in order, earning the respect of every farmer up and down the Pisgah Pike.

Elva Montgomery had come out of the mountains and was Aunt Laura's right-hand "man." Elva lived with her until "Mrs. Williams"—as she called Aunt Laura—died. Elva and I were great friends, and we would hitch up Tony and drive into Versailles, about ten miles away, to shop. I helped her gather eggs, kill chickens and ducks, separate milk, and lots of other farm work that I'm sure she invented just for me.

Elva—we all pronounced it "El-vee"—was missing both her canine incisors and they weren't imbedded in any polo mallet. One of her existing front teeth was crowned in gold, and she was a big, loud country woman. I loved her. Elvie ruled the roost in a determined but respectful way. One day Aunt Laura had an elegant luncheon for some ladies in the Colonial Dames. When they were all seated at the table, and Elvie was serving the soup, Laura noticed that there were no napkins. "Elvie," she announced, "there are no napkins. Will you please put them on the table?" Elvie replied, "Mrs. Williams, *you* set the table!"

In fact, I loved Aunt Laura and I loved being at Haltura. In those days there was still a water pump outside the kitchen door, although the house had plumbing and running water. One special feature that would have brought on a fine today was that the toilets emptied out into a field away from the house.

My friend Buddy Buckner often came with me to Aunt Laura's. He and I would hurry to the pipe outlet and watch the blue toilet paper emerge— even more interesting to us than were the pigs and chickens.

There was a large ice-house next to the main house, too, and in the winter ice from the pond would be cut and stored in the icehouse, bedded down in straw.

The temptation to go down into the icehouse's dark interior was easily overcome when Aunt Laura told us a giant snake lived

There was a large ice-house next to the main house.

She assigned me the task of "checking on the sheep."

"down there." I had no doubts about the truth of that warning, though years later I began to wonder. Aunt Laura also told me that when sheep roll over on their backs, they can't roll back again and simply lie there and die. So she assigned me the task of "checking on the sheep," and from time to time would send me out of the house on that errand of mercy. I never found a sheep on its back. But it did get me out of the house, especially at cocktail time!

Buddy and I once "borrowed" a silver-handled buggy whip from an umbrella stand that stood next to Aunt Laura's wind-up telephone. We took it and Tony, hitched to the break cart, out for a spin in one of the largest fields, and when we returned, the whip was missing. I finally got up enough courage to say, "Aunt Laura, we have some bad news for you. We've lost your buggy whip." She replied instantly, "Well, I have some bad news for you, too. Go find it!"

Buddy ran into bad luck one night after we had gone to bed. We slept in a guest room next to Aunt Laura's with an enormous bed and an equally enormous—and ominous—wardrobe. We also got into bed on the far side of the wardrobe and imagined that all sorts of things lurked in it. This was long before we had read Lewis's *The Lion, the Witch, and the Wardrobe*. In the middle of the night I felt Buddy sit up in bed and then throw back the covers with a loud cough. I switched on the light, and the sheets were covered with bright red liquid. I yelled for Aunt Laura, and as she arrived in her nightgown, cried, "Buddy had his throat slit!" Fortunately, Aunt Laura had a level head. She hurried to the bed, saw Buddy was alive and looking sheepish, and identified the blood as the red raspberry ice cream we'd had for dessert.

The Estill family had a pattern of entertainment. Christmas Eve was at our house, New Year's Day was at Uncle Howard and Aunt Ann's, and Thanksgiving was at Aunt Katherine and Uncle Rodes's. At Easter, we went to Aunt Laura's. Except for Christmas Eve, all were lunch affairs—lots of bourbon flowed for a long time as the children found things to do. Then an enormous lunch followed with my father—as the senior Estill—carving. I don't think it had anything to do with his being a doctor. Nearly everyone smoked in those days, and after a huge lunch the men would go outdoors (our house was the only exception, since

I thought that was great!

the rest were all on farms). They lit up cigars and would go behind the garage or any other outbuilding and pee! I thought that was great, even though I wasn't included in either event.

With such a large family, most of the special days were spent as I have described. My parents also had close friends, and my father's closest friend was Dr. Scott Breckinridge. They had been together in New York, and my father encouraged Dr. Breckinridge to come set up his Ob/Gyn practice in Lexington—giving him his patients so that he could practice only pediatrics. I remember hearing him say, "I gave up obstetrics, as soon as I could afford to." Still, he was always very proud of those, as he put it, "with whom he had been when their mother delivered them." As I said in the beginning, it was Scott Breckinridge who delivered me.

Another doctor friend was Dr. Mithoeffer, an eye, ear, nose, and throat specialist in Cincinnati. He performed my tonsillectomy (and removed my adenoids) in Cincinnati. I remember going up for the operation the day before with Ann and Rodes. All three of us were scared stiff and spent a very restless night. The next morning as we were lying on our gurneys, waiting to go to surgery, it developed that both of them had achieved fevers in the night. They went home, and I was wheeled into surgery.

Dr. Mithoeffer did a fine job and as a reward gave me a million dollars in German money, which, with the rise of the Third Reich, was worthless. It gave me an early reason to despise Adolf Hitler.

Cincinnati was our big city. Lexington and Louisville were always a bit at odds. At one point in some debate, my father wrote a letter to the *Courier Journal*, saying that when "Lexingtonians want to go to a big city, we go to Cincinnati."

Later, he would have to admit that "the only good thing to come out of Louisville" was my wife Joyce! Nevertheless, he had an out-of-town membership in the Louisville Country Club and would go there for golf weekends and spend the night in the club rooms (no longer available). He played golf with his friend Dr. James Bruce and his cousin-in-law James Medcalfe.

When we visited Cincinnati, we would leave Lexington before sunrise, and by the time we were in Northern Kentucky, the streetlights would go off, and dawn would come in time for us to crest the Ohio River and the hills of Northern Kentucky and see the splendid city in the distance, sparkling in the early sun. I think we stayed at the Carew Tower.

Its magic included a trip to Pogue's,[14] the Women's Exchange and Best's for clothes, then lunch at a well-known restaurant, and afternoon baseball at Crosley Field with the Reds. After a brief supper, we'd go to the great Cincinnati Zoo and attend the Zoo Opera. Often arias were accompanied by sounds of lions roaring or elephants or monkeys calling to one another. I learned to love opera there, and it's a great shame that years later they moved the opera indoors. Only at the Bath of Caracalla in Italy did I ever hear again an opera in the out of doors—that one with a full moon over Caracalla and the baths.

As we were growing up, Dr. Ed Ray—another father of two sons, Teddy and Tommy—organized a gym class, headed by what in this day would be called a personal trainer: Larry Garland. We met in the gym at Castlewood Park but during football season at Dr. Ray's farm. I remember he marked off the field in stripes and had real goal posts.

My boxing lessons came in handy when Larry Garland had a "boxing day." I went into the ring against a boy named Wallace Horine. He was bigger than I, but I had always noticed that he had a rather large nose. Soon after we got in the ring, I was able to land a "Ben Blue left hook" on Wallace's nose. It spurted blood, and I won by default!

Years later at the University of Kentucky I boxed for Phi Delta Theta and had the same good luck with Mack Gay, whose nose with the help of my left hook obligingly popped open and bled.

---

14. During its heyday of the 1920s to the 1960s, Pogue's was well known by generations of Cincinnatians for their elaborate Christmas displays, including the Enchanted Forest in the Carew Tower arcade with Pogie and Patter, artificial deer wired with microphones into which children would whisper their Christmas wishes. In the store's fourth-floor auditorium, a miniature train wound through a holiday wonderland, convenient to the toys, books, and music departments.

Robin Hill

As noted earlier, when I was about eleven, my parents sold 471 West Second and built a reproduction of the oldest house in Yorktown, Virginia, on Eastin Road. We had about four acres and a wonderful creek that ran through our property, dividing it into an upper acreage, where the house was, and a lower acreage. My father set out an ambitious vegetable garden on the lower part, and on the upper end next to the house was a giant sycamore tree—which took the place of my roof hideaway on Second Street.

Several horses were pastured next to us on the Wilders' property, and the Waltons, Tiltons, and McVeys occupied the rest of the property—called appropriately Dog Hill.

My parents' bedroom was on the first floor, and on several occasions my overnight guest and I would shimmy down the back porch drain and ride our bikes into town to the late show at the Ben Ali Theatre, or to Joyland to listen—outside—to the big bands that came each summer. We never got caught.

Robin Hill was a great place to be at my age, with lots of space for Brandy, my springer spaniel, and me. As I mentioned earlier, the Talberts had a swimming pool that was open to the whole neighborhood.

My time at Robin Hill was limited, for in the fall of 1941, I was off to Episcopal High in Alexandria, Virginia, at the ripe old age of thirteen. My mother went with me on the C&O train. The C&O (Chesapeake

& Ohio) originated in Louisville and came into Lexington about 5 p.m., leaving promptly at 5:30. That is where the saying, "You can't have a drink until the train leaves the station," originated. There were always some Louisville boys on the train from Episcopal High School, and one or two from Lexington. I was the only one my first year.

Betty Alden, one of our crowd from Eastin Road, came to see us off, and my last glimpse of her was her running alongside the train, waving, and suddenly colliding with one of the posts. She certainly gave it her all.

My mother almost cried when she saw my Spartan living conditions.

I loved the train ride and the seeming miracle of waking up in the Northern Virginia country-side and later at the Alexandria Station. On that first trip I will always remember seeing a half dozen matching bags from a trunk on down with the initial, "MLC, III." That turned out to be one of my best friends, Mac Cates[15] from Spartanburg, South Carolina.

My "dorm room" consisted of a bed, a closet, and a window, squeezed between two partitions with a canvas curtain in the doorway. I think I also had a chair. When my mother saw my Spartan living accommodations, she almost cried! After she saw that I had settled in, then she was off to New York to see Revell and Taylor. At the time he was teaching at Columbia, and Revell was studying at NYU.

Episcopal High School modeled itself on the Eton-English boarding school: stark living and discipline. The honor system was central—written

15. Macfarlane L. Cates.

in each classroom and copied and signed at the
end of each paper and test.

Sports were strongly emphasized, and
there was a football team for each age and
weight. I was on the Cake Team—named
for the fact that after each season—win or
lose—Mrs. Hoxton, the headmaster's wife,
had a party that featured a cake. We played a
stiff schedule of four games and lost all four,
but got the cake anyway.

Starting left end, Cake Team.

One of the senior monitors, Ben Weems,
coached our team. We Rats (the name given to freshmen) thought the
senior monitors were gods, and I was overcome when Ben came to my
bunk the night before our first game to give me a pep talk and to tell me
how much he was counting on me. I think I cried. I remember being so
impressed with Charlie Sackett, another senior monitor, that I even tried
to copy the way he walked. That kind of hero worship and the male bond-
ing from living together and playing sports was, I believe, lost when the
school went coed. Yet the advantages far exceeded that, and the school has
prospered because of its integration.

In a setting like that, best friends soon develop. Mine were Billy Berkeley from Richmond, Sammy Hyde from New York, Mac Cates from South
Carolina, Henry Burnett from New York, and Donnie West from DC.

My only recollection of being homesick was when my mother stopped
off on her way back to Kentucky from New York, and we walked around
the campus together before her taxi arrived.

Living on the Holy Hill—so named because Virginia Theological Seminary was next door to EHS (we called it the "Hilly Hole")—we could see
the Washington Monument and feel the excitement of Washington itself.
We were allowed a free day, Mondays, to go into the district, and there were

occasional field trips as well. But all of that took on a different meaning with Pearl Harbor. The school, after the early shock, moved up the Christmas vacation time—to our delight!—and we were all sent home. There were serious concerns that the Japanese planned an attack on Washington next.

When we came back after Christmas, our woods were filled with antiaircraft installations, barrage balloons were flying over the city itself, and the trains were filled with military personnel. Our day off into the city was called off.

I remember at the football games, usually when the varsity played—but sometimes just one of the younger teams—a solitary figure would be seen sitting on a shooting cane near the far end zone away from the crowd. It was General George Marshall. Apparently, he had found a way to have some alone time in the midst of his wartime duties.

Years later I wish his Marshall Plan had been used after September 11, 2001, instead of the massive revenge motivated by George W. Bush.

My academic record at EHS was not very good, and it began to look like I was destined to be a six-year student. Mr. Hoxten, the headmaster, wrote my father that "Bobby is one of the best-liked boys in the school and

The woods were filled with anti-aircraft unites, barrage balloons dotted the sky.

is doing well in sports but not so well in his studies. Still, we have high hopes for him!" My highest grade was in Sacred Studies, taught by Mr. Hoxten.

My mother took me to New York over spring break. On Sunday we went to the massive Cathedral of St. John the Divine. We were ten minutes late, but the procession was still coming up the nave.

After the service, sitting on the steps waiting for a taxi back to our hotel, my mother waved her arms in a great circle and said, "If you would go into the ministry, all this could be yours!" I don't remember my

My last night at EHS.

response, but I did recall the offer as I arrived at my first assignment, little Saint Mary's, Middlesboro, in the heart of the Cumberland Mountains. Mother always thought big.

With the war and the prospect of being drafted before graduating, my parents pulled me out of EHS in the late spring of my third year and sent me to Mrs. Kavanaugh's high school in Lawrenceburg, Kentucky.[16] This move was one of my first real traumatic experiences.

I had to leave my close friends, a school I loved, special masters, the kitchen staff, and my fellow waiters. I was voted the high honor of "Best Waiter" and also the funniest!

In the taxi, driving down the long driveway and out the front gate, I burst

Voted Best Waiter.

---

16. Under the direction of "Mrs. K," Rhoda C. Kavanaugh, AB, founder and principal of the Kavanaugh High School for forty-one years, raised the school to be ranked among the nation's foremost preparatory schools for Annapolis and West Point.

into tears. The taxi driver said, "What's wrong, buddy?" and I replied, "I have to go to the navy." A lot of boys did. Sammy Hyde was killed in a helicopter crash in the Korean War, and several of the older boys died in World War II and places like Vietnam.

Kavanaugh was in an old house with about eight of us "living in." The food was terrible, and we were in study hall all day and after supper until ten. Each of us recited to Mrs. K on all our subjects. Several of her boys were prepared for West Point and Annapolis, and Mrs. K had never had one of her students fail. The rest of us were trying to graduate from high school.

My best friends and roommates were Jack Kannapel and Tom Wall, both from Louisville.

Monday nights we were marched, literally, downtown to the movies. Mrs. K owned the movie house. She sat in the back row so that she could keep an eye on us, but we learned to slip down under the seats and (sometimes!) join some of the local young ladies.

We were attached literally to the Kavanaugh High School building, and in the fall, students from Anderson County came and a regular high school operated. We attended that, but at night and in the afternoon, we returned to our study hall. Thankfully, I made the basketball team so was able to practice after school, and when the season began, to play at home and on the road two nights each week.

We played University High in Lexington, and I scored thirteen points against Buddy Buckner, one of my best friends. (Buddy was my friend who threw up that red raspberry ice cream at Aunt Laura's in the middle of the night, and I had

I made the varsity at Kavanaugh.

screamed to Aunt Laura that some intruder had cut his throat.) We also played Henry Clay, and I was not so lucky against Buddy Shouse and fouled out before the half.

We lost the district tournament, and the low point of the season was the discovery made by the *Courier-Journal* that one of our assistant coaches was caught betting against us under the stands before the game!

Mrs. K was coming into her last years when I went to be tutored. Still, she was equally at home with Latin, English, math, and every other subject and took us individually over our assignments. As far as I could tell, she only had one blue dress and, because she kept the house just above freezing, a shawl. The latter served as a handkerchief, dish rag, dust cloth, and heaven knows what else. In good weather she often stood out in the yard to relieve herself. She "slept" at the head of the stairs with a reading light that was always on. Her "correction," when you were reciting your work, was a slap in the face with a rolled-up magazine she kept handy.

Mrs. Kavanaugh.

While we had a woman, Neddy, who did most of the cooking on a stove heated from a woodpile enriched by Neddy's spit from the snuff she always had stuck in her cheek, Mrs. K cooked on Saturday nights and holidays. One night, those of us who were early at the table saw her drool into the salad

Mrs. K kept a firm hand on things.

Someone had the great idea to hide Mrs. K's wake-up bell.

... but she won in the end!

as she tossed it. We had, at that time, two brothers from Mexico, Oscar and Jamie Bermutez. Their father was governor of Juarez. They were hearty eaters and were always the last to come to the table. We all declined to have any salad when it was passed and watched with glee as the Bermutez brothers—and Mrs. K—ate it all. Of course, we could hardly wait to tell them of its ingredients after supper.

Mrs. K, a wealthy woman, charged us a fee equivalent to what we'd paid at EHS, and nearly starved us to death. She owned much of Lawrenceburg, including the meat store, and we had sausage at nearly every meal. To this day, I am still not fond of it.

On Saturday nights, one boy was designated to leave study hall and go into town and get hot dogs and hamburgers and drinks at the drugstore—which Mrs. K also owned. That probably kept us alive, and of course, we paid for it from our own pockets.

Jack Kannapel's family from Louisville visited one weekend and took us to Harrodsburg to see Fort Harrod.[17] His sister, Jane (who was in our

---

17. Fort Harrod was first established as a camp by James Harrod on June 16, 1774. Fort Harrod was built in 1777 on Old Fort Hill and named after James Harrod. The original camp on Landing Run Creek quickly became Harrodstown, the first pioneer settlement in Kentucky. The original site flooded, and the settlers constructed a new and larger fort

wedding later), took Jack and me into one of the small gun rooms and produced a small bottle of bourbon, which we chug-a-lugged right on the spot. I suspect Mr. and Mrs. Kannapel knew what was going on, but it was great.

I can't say I learned to study at Kavanaugh or EHS. That only came later after I got to college (partially)

Finally a high school diploma.

and seminary—where Dean Taylor taught me to study, write papers, and develop a hunger for the subjects that would shape my life and ministry. Graduation finally came May 29, 1945, and believe it or not, I won two awards: one for chemistry (!) and the other for Senior English.

I hardly had time to enjoy my freedom from school before I volunteered for service in the navy and was called up.

on Old Fort Hill. The community of Harrodstown grew into present-day Harrodsburg, the county seat of Mercer County. A 1927 reconstruction of Fort Harrod is located in Old Fort Harrod State Park near the Old Fort Hill location. The original spring still flows inside the stockade.

US Navy

The induction point for the US Navy was in Louisville, so I managed to stay with the Kannapels in order to catch the troop train for the Naval Station Great Lakes the next morning.[18]

Jack got me a date with Ginny Huber, and a bunch of us spent the evening at a place called Air Devils, drinking beer. I was sick in the night at the Kannapels and hardly able to eat a big scrambled-egg breakfast Jack's mother fixed for us. I had to ask her to stop the car on the way to the train and lost the scrambled eggs. She later wrote my mother to tell her I was safely off but understandably "upset" over going into the service. I don't think she suspected my indisposition was the result of the Falls City beers consumed the night before.

I boarded the train, taking along a paper cup just in case, sat next to a window, and closed my eyes. Someone moved into the seat next to me, extended his hand, and said, "I'm John Speed."

"Hello, I'm John Speed."

---

18. Naval Station Great Lakes (NAVSTA Great Lakes) is the home of the US Navy's only boot camp, located near North Chicago, in Lake County, Illinois.

That began a friendship that has lasted to this day. We spent all of navy boot camp together and then several weeks as ship's company—working in the kitchen before we both shipped out for overseas.

At the time my brother Taylor was teaching in the V-12, the Naval Training Program, at Northwestern. John Speed and I had several "college weekends" staying with him. My mother came to visit and took John

and me to a play in Chicago. On the way we bought a bottle of bourbon for my father because liquor was hard to get in wartime. After the play, with a sailor on each arm, coming down the steps from the balcony, the bottle got away and bounced down the steps under people's feet, bringing a pungent odor of bourbon to the scene. My mother said, "Keep walking," and the three of us stepped over the broken treasure and out into the cold and windy Chicago streets.

US Navy Boot camp
Great Lakes.

The navy gave us an "overseas leave" at Christmas, and I arrived home just in time to go to the Saturday dance at the Lexington Country Club, which was a fixture on everyone's calendar. The woman at the reception desk wouldn't let me in! Finally, I got a chance to send a note, and one of my friends vouched for me.

We shipped out upon our return to Great Lakes and loaded onto a troop train that took five days to get to San Francisco and the naval base on Treasure Island.

My mother, who grew up in Baltimore and often went to dances at the Naval Academy in Annapolis, wrote that an old beau, Pookie Orr (or a name like that), was, she thought, stationed at Treasure Island and that I should "look him up." As an S2/C,[19] I certainly wasn't about to look up an officer, but in the post office one morning, I looked him up on the Roster

---

19. Navy seaman, second class.

Off from Treasure Island, CA via "Victory Ship" to Shanghai.

of Permanent Residents, and lo and behold, he was commanding officer of the whole base and a three-star admiral to boot!

We had some leave in San Francisco, but every time I tried to go someplace, like the Top of the Mark Hotel, my dog tags gave me away as being underage for a place that sold liquor. I had just turned eighteen.

We sailed out of the bay and under the bridge in some of the roughest water anywhere, and it seemed the whole ship got seasick. We were bunked six-deep on cots (three thousand men on a Victory Ship), and you had to step on the lower cots to reach the top ones. We were confined to those cots, except when we went topside to line up for chow. That took most of the day, since the ship was so overloaded that you would line up for lunch right after breakfast and for dinner after lunch. That miserable trip took five weeks nonstop. We had hoped to put in in Hawaii but it didn't happen. Shanghai, China, was our destination.

You can smell China several days out at sea, and pieces of debris began appearing in the water about the same time. We entered the rather narrow Huangpu River, which gave us our first view of land as well as Chinese people working in the fields, riding bikes along dirt roads, and driving a very occasional truck or car.

When finally we docked, we were right in the center of the city across

USS Tausig DD746.

from the Bund[20] and next to a number of navy ships as well as Chinese junks, sampans, and what looked like floating homes.

We were quickly dispersed among the naval vessels in port, and my orders were to board an LST,[21] which I did. I found the crew celebrating the fact they had been ordered to sail for the United States and home! One of them said to me, "You are mighty lucky," just as an officer on the bridge called my name and told me to report to the gangplank. My orders had been mixed up (typical SNAFU). I was really assigned to a destroyer, the USS *Taussig* (DD746).

When I reached my new home, the duty officer said there are two jobs open: pharmacist-mate striker (assistant to the chief pharmacist mate) or deckhand. I chose the former with great relief—no chipping paint for me! The deckhand would mostly hang over the side, painting the hull, while another detail of deckhands hung over the other side, chipping paint.

---

20. The Bund is one of the most famous tourist destinations in Shanghai. The Huangpu River is lined with historical buildings that housed numerous banks and trading houses. By the 1940s, the Bund housed the headquarters of many of the major financial institutions operating in China.

21. Landing ship tank is the naval designation for vessels created during World War II to support amphibious operations by carrying vehicles, cargo, and landing troops directly onto an unimproved shore.

I got off a quick air-mail to my father for his advice in my new medical role, and he wrote back, "Just give them a PC [aspirin] and water."

Our medical staff consisted of a chief, a pharmacist mate first class, and me. The chief was a twenty-year veteran and an alcoholic who spent most of his time drinking the grain alcohol in our supply closet and staying in his bunk.

I discovered that our assignment was to sail with the 7th Fleet Carrier Division, sweeping mines, picking pilots out of the water, and carrying prisoners from Shanghai to the northern port of Tianjin. Our duty took us all over the Asiatic Pacific Theatre—the Philippines, Guam, Hong Kong, Saipan, Tinian, Iwo Jima, Northern China, and up and down the China Sea. We were the first surface craft into Manila after the war ended.

My friend John Speed was planning to go to Princeton after his navy duty, and while most of us read the sports sections of the newspaper or girlie magazines, John was reading books written in German and studying German grammar.

After we were separated when we got sea duty, John was on an LST. One morning a shipmate came to sick bay and said, "Some guy is calling for you from the bow of that LST that's moored next to us." It was John, and we had several liberties together in Shanghai.

Thanks to the USO we had dinner in Chinese homes.

They finally sailed. On one occasion when I was, as usual, hanging out in our ship's radio shack, we heard that John's LST had a man who had gone berserk in the night and had knifed several crew members in their sleep. We didn't get any more news for several days, but when the names of those who died were broadcast, I was relieved to see that John was not among them.

When I finally saw John again in Shanghai, he explained that he had a lower bunk and that one of the victims had screamed and woke up the rest of the crew, some of whom restrained the killer. The good news, in addition to John's survival, was that they had been ordered back to the United States and would be stationed in Norfolk for hearings and the trial of the killer.

Our one experience of being "shot at in anger" by the enemy—a Navy term—was on the way into Manila. Our captain was explaining Corregidor to us on the ship's loudspeaker and the death march and McArthur's cameo return when someone noticed little "pings" as something was hitting our hull. We discovered we were being fired upon by some of the Japanese who either did not know the war had ended or were going to fight on regardless. We went into full battle mode, shot up a good piece of Corregidor, and each got twenty points for being "shot at in anger."

The points added up to a total that allowed me to be eligible to go home.

Manila Bay was full of half-sunken ships and small craft, and the city itself was pretty much in ruins.

I took a local bus up into the Baggio Province to see the hospital and school that the great bishop Charles Henry Brent had started. Just a few minutes out of Manila, the jungle begins, and one sees small settlements tucked away in the woods with rather primitive facilities and people. The hospital building and what I could find in the way of school buildings were in bad repair and had borne the brunt of the war. Nonetheless, I was honored to be, for a time, in the footsteps of Charles Henry Brent, one of our finest bishops and now with a Holy Day in his name.[22]

At Hong Kong, our next port of call, we were disappointed to find

---

22. March 27. Charles Henry Brent was a missionary bishop. During the Spanish-American War (1898), arising from a dispute over Cuba and Puerto Rico, the United States also acquired Guam and the Philippines. In 1902 the Episcopal Church appointed Charles Brent (at that time serving as priest in charge of a slum parish in Boston) as missionary bishop of the Philippines. He arrived on the same ship with the American governor, William H. Taft, and carried with him the unofficial but very real prestige of the American establishment.

that the local authorities were unwilling for us to come ashore. In our intervals at sea, one of my duties was to give shots to the crew in preparation for landing in different places. The pre–Hong Kong dosage was for the Black Death (the plague)! That sounded like something out of another century and then proved to have been unnecessary since only our top officers went ashore. We anchored in the busy harbor and with the aid of binoculars could see "life on the shore." On one hillside outside the city limits, we could see people in whites, playing lawn tennis and sitting under umbrellas, sipping cool drinks. I would have been willing to risk the Black Death for one of those tall ones.

As I mentioned earlier, our duties took us to most of the well-known islands: Iwo Jima, Tinian, Saipan, Guam, and up and down the China Sea from Shanghai to Tinsen with Japanese prisoners aboard.

On one of those runs, we were caught in one of the worst typhoons in history. The seas were so enormous that our ships would rise into view with others in the fleet and then drop down into the bottom of the

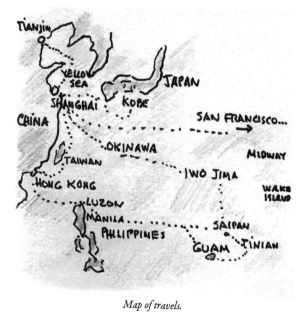

Map of travels.

swell out of sight. Several ships lost their radar antennas as we tossed and rolled. We later heard that some ships went down and that a number of lives were lost—though not in our fleet.

After that experience I had a whole new appreciation of Psalm 107:23–31:

> *Some went down to the sea in ships*
> *and plied their trade in deep waters.*
> *They beheld the works of the LORD*
> *and his wonders in the deep.*
> *Then he spoke, and a stormy wind arose,*
> *Which tossed high the waters of the sea.*
> *They mounted up to the heavens and fell back to the depths;*
> *their hearts melted because of their peril.*
> *They reeled and staggered like drunkards*
> *and were at their wits' end.*
> *Then they cried to the LORD in their trouble,*
> *and he delivered them from their distress.*
> *He stilled the storm to a whisper*
> *and quieted the waves of the sea.*
> *Then were they glad because of the calm,*
> *and he brought them to the harbor they were headed for.*

We never got any nearer to Japan than being in the China Sea and once being moored just outside the harbor of Kobe.

Aside from the typhoon, the only real danger came from the magnetic mines that filled the waters around Japan and in the China Sea. After the typhoon, even more of them than usual broke away from their moorings and floated out into open waters. When one was sighted (and we had both radar and lookouts at all times), we would go into battle mode and shoot it out of the water. Only once, to my knowledge, did one bump against our hull, and thanks be, it turned out to be a dud. My bunk was hung just under one of our torpedoes, and just over two of the depth charges used against submarines. Had we hit a mine, the *Taussig* would have lost its champion boxer, who would have been launched into space like a rocket.

On one of our visits we went inland to a Marine base at Tsingtao and played basketball. They also wanted to have a boxing tournament, and I broke the age-old navy rule (i.e., "Never volunteer for anything") and confessed that I had boxed in high school.

My opponent was a black Marine sergeant who I later discovered had been captain of the boxing team at Case University near Cleveland. Thankfully, we only went three rounds because he nearly beat me to a pulp. As I was lying back on the ropes in my corner, thanking God that the three rounds were over and that I had not been killed, the referee (also the sole judge for the fights) came over, raised my hand, and in a thick Alabama accent, yelled, "Di winnah!" My shipmates went wild, the Marines booed, and I apologized to the loser, who knew better than I how ugly racism can be. Even my old boxing teacher Ben Blue would have agreed that I was lucky not to have been knocked out in the first round.

In addition to covering for our chief, my duties in sick bay consisted of holding two daily open clinics with the pharmacist mate first class. Cough syrup was popular because of the alcohol content, and penicillin (just discovered[23]) was administered for gonorrhea (I became an expert in venereal diseases). We also handled regular inoculations and special ones, like the Black Death, broken bones (the chief came out of his bunk for those), and a variety of colds, allergies, diarrheas, upset stomachs, and the like. In my first experience "shooting people," I expressed to the chief that I hated to hurt people. His reply was typical: "Hell, man, it don't hurt you none."

---

23. The discovery of penicillin is attributed to Scottish scientist and Nobel laureate Alexander Fleming in 1928.

"Hell, man, it didn't hurt you none."

I took to it with such gusto that I shot over a dozen crew members using the same needle until the chief noticed a pile of fresh needles that had not been used.

Officers were not supposed to get gonorrhea, so when one of them came for a shot of penicillin, we listed it as the flu. We also issued "pro kits" before each shore leave, equipped with a condom, a tube of disinfectant ointment, and I believe a sulfur mixture to be taken orally. Sadly, many of the men came back and either passed out on the deck or before, and we had to administer the ointment ourselves whether they had sex or not. That was preventive medicine at its best, because an outbreak of the clap always came after we were back at sea, and we had to get up every three hours to administer penicillin. No one knows how many wives and sweethearts were infected when Johnny came marching home.

The staff on a destroyer is limited, so we did not have a doctor or a chaplain. There were no religious services, so on Easter I took my Prayer Book to a quiet place behind one of the gun mounts and had a sort-of Easter Service for myself. Finally, the good news came that those of us

The 4 PM sick call, lots of "colds"
(12% alcohol)

with enough points were being sent home for discharge. We put in at Guam, which was a gathering place, and left the *Taussig* forever. We were assigned to Quonset huts to wait for a ship back to the States. Twice we were marched down to a ship only to find it was full. One time we almost had our feet on the gangplank when a convoy of trucks pulled up and a whole bunch of nurses poured out and onto the ship in our place.

While we were waiting, we were assigned various duties. I was given the job of being the pharmacist with the military police team that had the night shift. There were still some Japanese holed up on Guam, and our patrol had the added duty of looking for them. Thankfully, we never found any.

Home!

It was hard to sleep in the Quonset huts because huge land crabs would drop out of the palm trees onto the roof or climb up the roof from the ground. It was the same sound as scratching a blackboard.

Finally, we made it aboard a Victory Ship and were on our way home after nearly six weeks on Guam. We got our discharges in San Francisco and, proudly displaying our "ruptured duck emblems," boarded trains for home. Except for remaining in the Naval Reserve, my navy days were over.

The University of Kentucky

fter a month or so of freedom, the task was a reorientation to civilian life. In the navy, the "F" word was big, and everything was "f—" up or "f—ing" this or that. My only slip up was asking my mother to pass the "f—ing butter." Fortunately she didn't understand what I'd said, but I had to be very careful for a while.

I enrolled in the University of Kentucky, and since I had played football at Episcopal High School, I thought I'd go out at UK. I showed up on the first day, registered, was issued equipment, and got my first warning that this wasn't EHS when in the locker room I was taking off my shirt and noticed several others removing their teeth!

They were taking their teeth out.

Paul "Bear" Bryant[24] had come to UK from Maryland, and Big Blue hopes were high. He had already put together a team, and they had been working out (I think

---

24. Bryant coached at Kentucky for eight seasons. Under Bryant, Kentucky made its first bowl appearance in the Great Lakes Bowl—played only once, on December 6, 1947, in Cleveland, Ohio, between the University of Kentucky and Villanova University. Kentucky won, 24-14. The 1950 Kentucky team concluded its season with a victory over Bud Wilkinson's number-one-ranked Oklahoma Sooners in the Sugar Bowl.

illegally) all summer. He announced that anyone who could stay on the squad would be able to dress for all the home games. Years later I heard from a neighbor of Bryant's that each morning during the season, the Bear would come out and go into the garage, start the car, get out, lean against the side of the garage, and throw up his breakfast.

Bryant was very successful at UK, taking them to the Sugar Bowl and having the best win/loss record of any modern-day UK coach. It was a great loss when he left for Texas A&M. But UK is a basketball school, and at that time Adolph Rupp and the Fantastic Five were national champs.[25]

The sad truth, though probably a blessing, is that I lasted a day and a half, threw up all night, and threw in the towel at noon the second day. The decision probably saved my teeth, and maybe my life!

I pledged Phi Delta Theta and was president of the Canterbury Club. At an opening dinner for Episcopal students held at Christ Church, Patricia Storey told me she was bringing two Kappa pledges from Louisville. We had a sold-out crowd, so when the three of them arrived, I took them to the Canary Cottage for supper. One of the pledges especially

caught my eye, and I called her room at Patterson Hall the next day to arrange a date. I wasn't sure who was who, so I asked the girl who answered the phone to put the one who had ordered the most food on the phone.

I especially liked the one with the curly hair who ate a lot!

It was Joyce Haynes, who

25. Rupp coached the University of Kentucky men's basketball team from 1930 to 1972. There he gained the nicknames, "Baron of the Bluegrass" and "The Man in the Brown Suit." Rupp's Wildcat teams won four NCAA championships (1948, 1949, 1951, 1958) and one National Invitation Tournament title in 1946, appeared in twenty NCAA tournaments, had six NCAA Final Four appearances, captured twenty-seven Southeastern Conference regular-season titles, and won thirteen Southeastern Conference tournaments.

from that moment on became and still is the love of my life, and at this writing is my wife of sixty-four years. (Thank God for the Canterbury Club and the big appetite!) I was a member of the Patterson Literary Society, where I won the annual speaking contest. Otherwise, I carried a rather heavy class load, including classical Greek.

The Inter-Fraternity Council had an active intramural program, and we played basketball against other fraternities and boxed. I got signed up again, won my first match by opening Mac Gay's nose and scored a TKO, survived an exhibition with Teddy Ray, and won, by default, the final match, getting a boxing glove with "K" on it for Joyce's charm bracelet. I retired from the ring undefeated!

Having a car, living at home, and belonging to the Idle Hour Country Club gave me some advantages the out-of-towners didn't have. Joyce and I were pinned on Valentine's Day in 1946.

My boyhood friend Billy Hays pledged Phi Delta but my best friend, Junie Roberts, was a Sigma Chi and had dropped out of school to get married. Wendell Hall became a close friend and dated Patricia Storey. Teddy Ray was around, and the rest of my male friends were brother Phis.

I made a decision to go into the ministry and changed my major to a topical one, which still included classical Greek but added New Testament Greek. Edwin Taylor, who was

Boxing.

Joyce and I were pinned on Valentine's Day.

I carried a heavy load of classical and New Testament Greek.

also going into the ministry, and I were the only two students in the Greek class.

Joyce and I were only in one class together—an art history class taught by a close friend of my sister, Revell. She was head of the Women's Athletic Association and taught modern dance, while her husband, Barrie, was working on his PhD as a clinical psychologist.

I made an A in the course, which helped keep my grade average up in the top 20 percent, required for admission to the seminary of my choice, the Episcopal Theological School in Cambridge, Massachusetts. I can't remember what Joyce's grade was.

I finished college in three years by going in the summer and taking a full load of classes each semester. The second summer I got a job as an orderly

Barrie Shaw, PhD; faculty member; R.W. Estill, BA

at St. Joseph's hospital. Don Harding, also a doctor's son, got the same job, and our shift was from 5 p.m. until 11:00 PM. We had a great time teasing the student nurses and staying out of trouble with the nuns. One of our tasks was taking amputated limbs from surgery to the morgue.

The Roman Catholics believed that the severed limbs should be buried in a Catholic cemetery. We had a gangrenous leg that had been removed, and we put it into a long florist box that was used for long-stemmed roses. We brought it down, put a ribbon on it, and gave it to one of the student nurses. She was thrilled until she opened the box and let out a scream that brought the nun on duty running to her station. We grabbed the box, jumped into the elevator, and headed for the morgue.

Another exciting moment came when one friend, Patricia Storey, came in for an appendectomy. I got the prep tray and went into her room. I assured her that I was a professional—actually we only prepped men—had done lots of women, and that we "needed to get on with it." Again, there was a blood-curdling scream, and I hurried out before the ever-present nun arrived to see what was wrong.

We had to take amputated limbs to the morgue.

Despite our jobs, I found that being an orderly was a great servant thing. We gave back rubs in the wards where people did not have private nurses, cleaned up people who were unable to bathe themselves, changed bed linens, and did hundreds of small things to make people comfortable in mostly uncomfortable situations. It was a great way to receive pastoral training, learn hospital etiquette, and experience crisis situations and death.

At Christ Church in Richmond, Kentucky, where I served during my last year at UK, I had an acolyte who could have lighted the candles with his breath!

My acolyte could have lighted them with his breath!

Episcopal Theological School

The Episcopal Theological School to which I went after graduating from UK was just beyond Radcliffe's campus on Brattle Street in Cambridge. We could see across the way the Quaker Meeting House and beyond that, on the Charles River, the Monastery of the Order of Saint John the Evangelist. Harvard Square was a short walk as was Harvard itself, and ETS was affiliated with Harvard and Andover Newton Seminary. All of that influenced my decision to choose ETS after having all my education to date in the South.

My class had three men with doctoral degrees—one in law and the other two with PhDs. Two others were Harvard grads, one from Yale, and others scattered around the country. Needless to say, the curve was pretty high and the quality of teaching superb. The school emphasized the academic side with the senior (third) year devoted to a yearlong tutorial covering all the basic studies and ending in a comprehensive exam in all the disciplines that one had to pass to receive a degree.

George L. Blackman, in his *Faith and Freedom*,[26] writes that Edward S. Drown of the class of 1887 taught at Episcopal Theological School from the years of his graduation virtually until he died in 1935. Although he retired in 1933 he continued to live across the street from the school and taught an elective course in 1935 on his favorite theologian, J. F. D.

---

26. George L. Blackman, *Faith and Freedom: A Study of Theological Education and the Episcopal Theological School* (New York: Seabury Press, 1967), 72.

Maurice.[27] Professor Drown wrote *The Creative Christ: A Study of the Incarnation in Terms of Modern Thought.*

Blackman writes, "It was [Edward S. Drown] who kept the memory of the early faculty ... fresh by recounting quaint anecdotes about them .... He was a symbol of the continuity in the school community." That role passed to his widow who lived just across the street from the school until her death. Mrs. Drown had been married to a former professor, A. V. G. Allen, before she became Mrs. Drown, and she first came to live at the school in 1907.

Mrs. Drown always was present during receptions for the new entering class. We were told to make a name tag with our last name at the top and our preferred name under it. When Mrs. Drown was introduced to the class, she went around the room reading the names aloud in a strong voice. "Estill, Bob; Clark, Jim; Taylor, Greer" ... and loudly, "Rising, Dick! 'Rising, Dick!' Oh, my!" That was the high point of the reception.

Mrs. Drown was famous for her teas. She invited only the students she thought might be interesting, or who had connections with the school or were the type who measured up to her ideals. I can't remember whether Dick Rising was an invitee or not. I made her list I think because I was from faraway Kentucky, accent and all. As George Blackman said in his book,

"Rising, Dick. Oh, my!"

27. John Frederick Denison Maurice, often known as F. D. Maurice (August 29, 1805–April 1, 1872), was an English theologian, religious author, and prominent Christian Socialist.

she did most of the talking, so I wasn't able to practice my southern charm. Still, for poor seminarians, her teas and cookies were most welcome.

As for Greer Taylor—Greer McClelland Taylor—when I think back on my classmate and friend I see him in his usual three-piece suit and tie, presiding over tea or sherry or both, with his family silver tea set—which he kept in the same drawer with his cat litter and food. When we visited Harvard Square on our way up Brattle Street to the school, Greer would sometimes pluck a mushroom off the outdoor stand and munch away on it as we walked. I didn't have the heart to warn him that mushrooms were grown in a liberal mix of fertilizer.

After graduation Greer was asked to be an assistant professor at our West Coast seminary, the Church Divinity School of the Pacific (CDSP). On a visit to San Francisco to attend a meeting I had a free day and called Greer, who invited me over to Berkeley. He had one class that day, which I attended. His brilliance as a lecturer and his knowledge of his subject were obvious, but he laced his talk with profanity and some off-color words that might even shock an undergraduate at the university.

Afterward I apologized to one of his students, and explained that he was probably showing off for me. The student laughed and said, "If anything, he toned down his lecture because you were here. Today was mild!"

Greer borrowed someone's Volkswagen Bug, and we drove back across the Golden Gate Bridge and up into the wine country to a winery he particularly liked. He opened a bottle of their wine, took a little grill out of the trunk and a steak, and we sat on the ground under a tree and drank wine and talked until the steak was ready. Paper plates and a lovely salad appeared, and we dined in splendor. Greer stayed in his three-piece suit throughout the banquet, and I was still in my clerical collar.

That was the last time I saw Greer. He had said from the very beginning of seminary that he wanted to be a bishop. He left CDSP to take a mission in Guadalajara, Mexico—thinking ahead about a possible appointment as a missionary bishop. He died soon after.

Years later when we were with some friends from Dallas for a golf outing in Guadalajara, I took a taxi and visited Greer's mission church. Sure enough, on one of the front pews was a bronze placard with his name and the dates of his life and death. He was one of the most interesting people I have ever known—generous and loving as a friend and gifted as a scholar and teacher. I trust they have good red wine in heaven.

At ETS we also had assigned fieldwork, where we served on weekends in a local church. I "auditioned" at St. Michael's on the Heights in Worcester, Massachusetts, and I got the job along with a middler, Milton Saville. We left Boston Saturday afternoon by bus, stayed in a parishioner's home, and worked with the Sunday school on Sunday morning. Sunday afternoon we made visits in the houses. And every place we visited we were served apple strudel, and my third apple strudel was enough.

St. Michael's on the Heights was a blue-collar parish with a workaholic rector, Bob Throop. He and his wife, Cynthia, had five children, and part of our job was babysitting. We usually had lunch with the Throops, but only after Bob had decelerated after the service by sitting alone in good weather on the garage roof and in bad weather in their bedroom.

More apple strudel!

I was in Worcester for two years and landed in my last year the job most wanted at Christ Church in Cambridge as assistant to Frederic Kellogg, the Episcopal chaplain at Harvard from 1940 until his death in 1958. I assisted in the weekly service, attended the equivalent of the Canterbury Club on Sunday nights, and called on students in their rooms one afternoon each week.

One afternoon after I had been there for several weeks, Fred asked me if I had ever wondered how I got the job that was considered the plum. As I thought of a modest answer, Fred went on to say, "I needed someone with a southern accent who hadn't gone to one of the big three or to one of the top prep schools. Harvard is expanding its enrollment, and I needed someone with your background."

Fred had gone to Groton and Harvard. Sadly, several years later Fred hanged himself in a closet at his home.

At ETS my best friends were Greer Taylor—who had been a lawyer in Boston, was older and one of the brightest people I have ever known (he had memorized the abbreviations for the eleventh edition of the *Encyclopedia Britannica*); Jim Clark, who had studied to be a newspaper writer; Jack Lesser; and later John Harper when he came into the junior class; and Ed Romig, who was a year ahead. Milton Saville also became a close friend.

The class work and the heavy load of reading were such that we didn't have much free time. I did get down to Wellesley to see my former tennis partner, Margaret Brooks Jewett, but dating was out of the question because Joyce and I were planning to be engaged at Christmas. I did make it to a few Harvard football games, and played squash at the law school courts and basketball in the little gym behind the school. We played some of the other seminaries in the area and had a pretty good team. The Baptists from Andover Newton were the dirtiest players we played.

They would come down with elbows flying and, when they connected, would say, "Oh, I'm so sorry, brother!"

They were the dirtiest team we played.

My cousin Al Shands was at Princeton. One day he called to say that he was coming for the Harvard game and asked to stay with me at the seminary. I told him I'd be glad to have him stay, but that after the game I had to leave for my fieldwork in Worcester. We arranged to meet at the half so I could give him the key.

Al smelled a little like bourbon when we met after his having driven up with some classmates. We chatted and I gave him the key and explained that I had a roommate who was sort of strange but that I would tell him that Al was coming. When I got back from Worcester on Sunday afternoon, my roommate, Arnold Hepworth, was angry. It seems Al came in about 3 a.m., had been drinking, threw up on the floor in our small living room, and kept Arnold awake most of the night. "Don't ever invite that man here again," was Arnold's Christian response. At the end of the

We were engaged at Christmas.

semester Arnold left school.

When I got home at Christmas, my cousin Mary Prewitt, Al's grandmother, had her usual family gathering, and when I arrived, she took me aside and said, "Bobby, I want you to know that if you never do anything else in your ministry, you have done a marvelous thing with your cousin Al. After his weekend with you at the seminary, he has decided to go into the ministry, too!"

Joyce and I were engaged at Christmas, and the months dragged by until that special day, June 17, when we were married at St. Mark's in Louisville by the rector, Bill Langley, and Lewie Pitt from the ETS faculty.

After the reception we left for Chicago on Eastern Airlines. When we finally got to our seats after a raucous good-bye from our groomsmen and bridesmaids who had come to the airport to see us off, the woman in the seat next to us said, "Life is strange, isn't it? The woman, who was sitting where you are, came to Louisville to bury her husband. His coffin was on this same plane." With that cheery note, Mr. and Mrs. Robert W. Estill headed off into married life.

Our honeymoon got off to a rocky start when we tried to check in at our hotel. We discovered that our groomsmen had cancelled our reservations. After finding lodging and spending our wedding night, we lunched at the Pump Room and caught the train for northern Michigan. Again, our dear friends had cancelled our train reservation, so we ended up in top bunks opposite each other. I tried to make the best of it by throwing odds and ends over the curtain into Joyce's bunk. Shortly, the curtains to my bunk were flung open and an irate porter said, "Young man, if you continue to bother that young lady across the aisle, I'll have you put off the train!" It did no good for me to try to persuade him she was my wife.

The reason for our northern Michigan honeymoon was that I

Joyce's father presents her.

The happy day for Mr. and Mrs. Robert W. Estill!

He would not believe she was my wife!

was required by the school to have a summer of what they called "clinical training." Usually that was in a hospital or mental facility, but since I had the pharmacist-mate training and had worked in a hospital as an orderly, they let me fulfill the requirement by setting up vacation Bible schools in the Diocese of Michigan.

My uncle Revel Whitridge had a cottage on Lake Leelanau, where I had been as a child, and he let us have it for the honeymoon before we went for the Diocese of Michigan's program.

We disembarked from the train in Lapeer, Michigan, and by taxi arrived at the lake and my uncle's cabin. His caretaker had not cut the grass or opened the cottage for the summer, and as the taxi departed, we waded through knee-high grass, took down the shutters that had closed the cottage for the winter, and opened the door. Our living room, though covered with dust, was alright, but we had a shock when we looked in the bedroom. Parked across the bed was my uncle's sailboat. In a fit of superhuman power and frustration, I grabbed the transom and pulled the damn thing out of the doors and into the yard. I would estimate that it weighed nearly a thousand pounds!

I remember having a deep sense of suddenly being responsible for another human being. Also, I guess because of being away at school and now away from Kentucky and home, I felt the old pangs of homesickness.

One night with the door open for the cool night air and the screen door locked, I was sure a bear was at the door. All I had to defend my new

Pulling the sailboat out of the cabin.

bride was a bow and arrow. I reached under the bed, took it, aimed at the screen, and let go an arrow. It went right through the screen, leaving a giant hole and no sign of a bear at all. In a minute the hole became a welcome mat for mosquitoes that swarmed in and headed for my bride and me.

The lovely ice-cold lake, the thousands of baby turtles that nibbled at your feet in the water, the sailboat, the quiet—the nearest house was a good half-mile away—and just being together redeemed the days, and when our taxi returned as he had promised, we were ready to go to work for the diocese.

An orientation meeting was held for all the summer workers at the Diocese of Michigan Conference Center. One other newlywed couple was there—the Timothy Pickerings—a dozen seminarians, and Bishop Emrich.[28] At the first dinner as we stood around a long table, the bishop said, "Will Mrs. Estill please say grace?" For the first time in her life, Joyce

28. Richard Stanley Merrill Emrich (1910–1997) was the seventh bishop of the Episcopal Diocese of Michigan. He was born in Mardin, Turkey, to missionary parents, and educated at Brown University and the Episcopal Theological School in Cambridge, Massachusetts. He was ordained to the diaconate in 1936 and to the priesthood in 1938, after which he served parishes in Connecticut and Massachusetts.

was speechless and she punched me on the arm, so I said it. The next morning at breakfast, the bishop said again, "Will Mrs. Estill please say grace?" Joyce made it this time, and later in the summer Bishop Emrich sent her a lay reader's license with a note that she was the first and only woman to have one in the diocese.

Our schedule sent us to Lapeer, Michigan, for the first vacation Bible school at Grace Episcopal Church[29] and then on to Royal Oak where we stayed with the Reverend Charles Jatho,[30] a nice little man who became a monster behind the wheel of his car. For an outing we went with the VBS across to Canada for a swim and picnic. I waded out into the lake and laid open the bottom of my foot on a shell. I survived a country doctor who sewed me up without cleaning the wound and without any anesthetic.

The final VBS was in the inner city of Detroit at St. Mary's. Johnny Walker had been a priest there in his first charge and later became a friend and bishop of Washington.[31] Our VBS was made up of children from the surrounding slums, and they took to our curriculum and even to our worship like they had been Episcopalians all their lives.

Our final day we had a parade with banners, crosses, children clad in cardboard armor—our theme of the VBS was "put on the armor of God", a small band of drums, bazookas, horns, and one pair of cymbals. Due to my injured foot (!) Joyce had to be in charge of the parade while I languished in the Review Stand with a few parents and the clergy from

---

29. gracechurchlapeer.weebly.com/.
30. The Reverend Charles Jatho was rector of St. John's Episcopal Church in Royal Oak, Michigan, from 1929 until 1960.
31. John Thomas Walker, sixth bishop of Washington, dean of Washington National Cathedral, and vice president of the House of Bishops of the Episcopal Church. Bishop Walker was born in Barnesville, Georgia, but the family moved to Chicago and then to Detroit, where he spent his youth. He was graduated in 1951 from Wayne State University in Detroit and that fall became the first black student at Virginia Theological Seminary. After graduation from seminary, Walker returned to Detroit and was ordained a deacon in 1954 and a priest a year later.

St. Mary's. She was getting an early initiation into becoming a clergy spouse.

Since our theme had to do with St. Paul's idea of putting on the armor of God, each student made a suit of armor out of cardboard—it was something to see little black knights wielding cardboard swords and running in and out of the alleys of inner city Detroit!

Inner-city Detroit was filled with VBS children clad in "The Armor of God."

We had a week or so back home in Kentucky, splitting our time between Louisville and Versailles, where my parents now lived. They had converted an old school house into a home, which was featured in the *Lexington Herald-Leader*.

Our Middle Year at Episcopal Theological School

Packed into an old Oldsmobile with all our things, we left Kentucky for Cambridge. The old car ran perfectly and made it all the way up to forty-five miles an hour on the open road! We only had one embarrassing moment, when a late-model Cadillac in front of us stalled in the Holland Tunnel. Immediately a long line formed, and the emergency-aid truck rushed in from the other end and got the car started. "George," the name we gave our car, took off at its usual starting speed while the Cadillac disappeared ahead of us. We chugged along, with each tunnel guard urging us on as though we had been the culprit.

The Episcopal Theological School.

In Boston I had arranged for us to live in the basement of a fancy five-story house on West Hill Place. At that time, married students had to find something off campus since only a few dorm rooms for married students were available. In return for our rent, we were weekend babysitters for two little boys. The boys were not very attractive and didn't think we were either. One of my jobs was to take them on a tour of FAO Schwarz, the oldest toy store in the United States, known for its high-end toys. I was to observe what they liked, and report back to their mother. She would then try to find the same thing at a cheaper store. The boys stuck pins in our pillows, poured ink in the bathtub, and the youngest turned on the faucet in the kitchen and flooded our basement apartment. His mother told Joyce to act as though nothing had happened and that she would pay for any damage and have the place cleaned up. We got even, in a sense, by scooping the top of the ice cream supplies in the freezer, which was in our basement apartment.

Dr. Newhouser, their father, was a doctor at what was then Peter Bent Brigham Hospital.[32] The basement was our living area, and our bedroom was on the third floor near the boys' rooms. My friend Stan Carmichael, also from Kentucky, and his new wife, Farley, rented the top-floor apartment. Each morning he and I headed out in the Boston traffic in George for Cambridge and ETS.

One of the high points of our West Hill residency was having Sam Shoemaker for supper.[33] He took it all in good humor and sat cross-legged on our one sofa to eat.

---

32. Brigham and Women's Hospital, Boston, Massachusetts.

33. Samuel Moor Shoemaker III, DD, STD (December 27, 1893–October 31, 1963) was a priest of the Episcopal Church. Considered one of the best preachers of his era, whose sermons were syndicated for distribution by tape and radio networks for decades, Shoemaker served as the rector of Calvary Episcopal Church in New York City, the US headquarters of the Oxford Group during the 1930s, and later at Calvary Episcopal Church in Pittsburgh, Pennsylvania ("Calvary Episcopal Church," *American Guild of Organists*, New York City Chapter).)Sam Shoemaker's interdenominational focus and the Oxford Group were significant influences for the founders of Alcoholics Anonymous. Bill Wilson attended Oxford Group meetings at Calvary Church, and Sam Shoemaker also helped start an Oxford Group chapter in Akron, Ohio (Mel B., *New Wine: The Spiritual Roots of the Twelve Step Miracle* [Minneapolis: Hazelden, 1991), 64–69], where Dr. Bob Smith became involved. Shoemaker's contributions and service to Alcoholics Anonymous had a worldwide effect. The philosophy that Shoemaker codified, in conjunction with Bill Wilson, is used in almost every country around the world to treat alcoholism. Similar programs are used to help relatives of alcoholics, as well as people suffering with other addictions, such as to narcotics. The Episcopal Church in the United States of America honors Shoemaker with a feast day on its liturgical calendar on January 31.

My mother had reminded me that Sam Shoemaker was a distant cousin through the Whitridges, so when he came to preach at Trinity in Boston, I went early and found him in the vestry room before the service. Typical of Sam, he had me on my knees in five minutes and accepting Jesus as my Lord and Savior—again! That began a friendship that included several visits by him to Cambridge, where I would line up people for him to see; a visit to Calvary in New York for one of his Faith Alive

Pea-Leg Whitridge.

Conferences; and, much later, his call to me to follow him as rector of Calvary Church in Pittsburgh. We even discovered that my mother was right when Sam unearthed a family tree with our mutual relative, Pea-Leg (!) Whitridge, on it.

Our West Hill hostess said to Joyce at one point, "Does your mother know you are living like this?" She was convinced that the Russians were going to bomb MIT and was amazed, as Christmas drew near, that we would be putting up some decorations and a little tree.

Fortunately, word came from ETS that a fourth-floor apartment would be available for the next semester and that we could move in during the holidays. The Carmichaels who had the upstairs apartment were not so lucky.

The fourth floor apartment was given to married couples, and the two bathrooms—sink, toilet, and shower—were designated "male" on the second floor and "female" on the third floor. To this day I can remember Polly Gifford from Ohio, in a blue bathrobe, passing me on the stairs on her way up as I was going down. The apartments consisted of a living room—the ones on the top floor with two dormer windows with window seats—and a bedroom looking out on the roof of the gym and across the alley and the houses that backed up to the seminary property. While we were there, Joyce got a temporary job at the Harvard Co-Op, we had a parking space for George, and we left our Boston landlords to wonder when MIT would be blown up.

One Saturday afternoon when Joyce was working at the co-op, she noticed a student looking around to find a clerk. He seemed quite jumpy and finally came over to her and said in a low voice, "I need to buy an athletic supporter." Joyce had a measuring tape around her neck, and as she turned to the case behind the counter where the athletic supporters were kept, she removed the tape measure and asked, "What size?" Before she could turn around again, the young man had fled.

Fortunately for us—and MIT—the blowup never happened and Joyce was offered an excellent job as a secretary-assistant to Dr. Charles Draper—one of the eminent scientists in the instrumental lab. One day as she was giving Dr. Draper a paper he had asked her to copy, she commented on the pile of comic books she had noticed on his reading table. He asked her, "Do you know who invented the first ejection seat in an airplane? It was Buck Rogers!"

She was only two subway stops from Harvard Square and was in a very interesting job in a fascinating place. She usually got home in time for Evening Prayer, and then we joined the rest of the school in the refectory for dinner. On weekends we were on our own and often we would go in together on lobster, which, in those days, was seventy cents a pound!

One of us would take the subway to Sculley Square, buy the lobster, cook it on one of the jerry-rigged hot plates that were in the hallways outside the apartments, and wash it down with beer. I still had to make the trip to Worcester each Saturday but would get back for the lobster feast most of the time. Joyce often went with me, but when she stayed she

Sunday night: lobster (70¢/lb), beer (75¢), hot plate pot (free)

would go to supper or lunch with those who were left on campus. This is how John Harper became such a friend and has remained one for life.

We stayed in Cambridge again for Christmas, and Joyce's parents came from Louisville to be with us. On Christmas Eve it snowed, and we'll never forget the midnight service at Christ Church. For Christmas they used real candles in the ceiling candelabra and had candles in the windows. Since the windows, typical of New England churches, were clear, we could see the snow falling and softly brushing against the trees.

Even though we were poor seminarians, we enjoyed many of the benefits of living in Cambridge and Boston. Broadway plays often previewed in Boston, and we saw Gertrude Lawrence and Yul Brynner in *The King and I*, and a number of plays we liked but never made it to Broadway.

Greer Taylor gave us tickets to the Boston Symphony on several occasions, and the great Koussevitzky was the conductor.[34] We benefited from an endless stream of speakers at Harvard and MIT, as well as local talent at the Brattle Street Theatre and, as the season rolled around, the Boston Red Sox. In those days we could take the subway directly to the famous

---

34. Serge Alexandrovich Koussevitzky (July 14, 1874–June 4, 1951) was a Russian-born conductor, composer, and double-bassist, known for his long tenure as music director of the Boston Symphony Orchestra from 1924 to 1949.

Fenway Park, pay one-dollar admission to the bleachers, buy a hot dog and beer for about two dollars, and spend the afternoon sitting in the sun watching some great baseball. Tickets were always available (we qualified for student tickets) for Harvard's football games, and the Charles River was alive with boat races and regattas.

Since many of our classmates were from New England, we visited in Gloucester, New Hampshire, the Cape, and the North Shore.

Each middler was assigned a prisoner either at a mental hospital or at the dreary old stone prison in Charlestown. Mine was there, and his current name was Emile St. Pierre (I found out he had several aliases). We were admitted to the prison visiting room and given permission to

sit next to our prisoner for an hour of talk. Emile was a talker. Swearing me to silence, he claimed to be part of the Brinks robbery—which was in the papers at the time. It was a good experience for me, but I'm not sure about Emile. He promised to visit when he got out—though he never did get out as far as I know. On the last visit after two years of bimonthly visits, the prisoners were expected to give the seminarians some kind of token they had made in the shop. Emile's gift was a wooden cross big enough for our Lord himself. I had to carry it back to school on the subway and endure the looks of those who thought I was some kind of religious nut.

At the end of the school year, I also bid a tearful good-bye to my friends at St. Michael's on the Heights in Worcester. No more apple strudels or bus rides. Especially during the fall at each of my visits to parishioners on Sunday afternoon, they would give me an apple strudel. After four, or sometimes five, of those within an afternoon, I was no longer a starving seminarian. Milton Saville, who had a more delicate constitution, always carried a supply of bicarbonate of soda, which he gulped on the way back to Cambridge on the bus.

Meanwhile, I had received a message from my bishop, William R. Moody, that he wanted me to be seminarian-in-charge of St. Mary's Church in Middlesboro, Kentucky, for the summer in the southeastern coalfield near Harlem and Hazard.[35]

---

35. The Right Reverend William R. Moody (1900–1986), a native of Columbus, Mississippi, received bachelor's and doctoral degrees from both Hampden-Sydney College and the Virginia Theological Seminary. He was ordained to the diaconate in June 1926 and to the priesthood in April 1927, and he spent 1927–1928 as priest in charge at St. Andrew's, Lawrenceville; Emmanuel, Callaville; and St. Mark's, Cochran, Virginia. Moody went on to serve as rector of parishes in Maryland and Washington, DC. He also spent a year as instructor of sacred duties at St. Alban's School for Boys in Washington. He was trustee of the Cathedral Foundation in Maryland, 1940–1945, and president of the trustees of the Episcopal Theological Seminary in Kentucky from 1945 until his death. Moody was consecrated bishop of Lexington in 1945, and served as its bishop until 1970.

Middlesboro, Kentucky

*O*ff to the mountains!

Joyce and I packed George, a picnic lunch, and most of our possessions and headed east. It was an all-day drive, and we arrived at Mrs. duPont's house (no kin to *the* duPonts) where we had an upstairs apartment with a sitting room, bedroom, and bath. She and her spinster daughter, Jean, lived together. Mrs. duPont's nickname was "Doo Dont," and everyone called her that. She made us feel right at home by having us downstairs for a great dinner, capped off with her famous banana cream pie.

An older man, Mr. Gloster, had been the senior warden and later, when I became rector, he and his wife had their fiftieth wedding anniversary. All their children and grandchildren came, and the crucifer was

Doo Dont's banana cream pie

Gary Gloster—then a teenager and later a priest in my diocese, and then elected suffragan bishop of the Diocese of North Carolina.[36] Bill Ralston was the Nehi Bottling owner and became a wonderful friend and warden. He wore suspenders and smoked a cigar. Mildred was the head of the altar guild and turned out to be a great friend and supporter as well. Their son, Bill Jr., was a student at Sewanee and planned to go into the ministry. He was a gifted musician and was a great help when we had a very successful vacation Bible school.

There was a particularly memorable event when I was talking about baptism at the VBS. I was using a doll to show what baptism was about when the head of the doll fell off and into the font.

Two of Bill's friends, the Rash sisters, who were Presbyterian, pitched in also, and the little church was filled with children making "the armor of God." That was the most successful thing that had been there in a long time. Also, the church services were well attended—perhaps to check out the new seminarian and his wife. When Bishop Moody told Bill Ralston he was sending me, Mr. Ralston later told me he said, "What's wrong with this one?" based on several bad experiences. We started a weeknight

---

36. James Gary Gloster, bishop suffragan of North Carolina, 1996–2007, began his ordained ministry in Indiana before moving to Cincinnati, Ohio, and then to Pulaski, Virginia. At the time of his election as bishop suffragan, Gloster was in his seventh year serving as the vicar of the Chapel of Christ the King in Charlotte. He also made good use of his well-established talents in clown ministry, most notably at his own consecration, when he invited the presiding bishop, the Right Reverend Edmond L. Browning, among others, to don clown noses.

Women's Bible / Prayer Group in the basement of the rectory, which served as a parish hall. One large Sunday school room was under the church.

I called on every member (there were about eighty on the roles), active and inactive, got the records back in order, read lay readers' sermons, presided at Morning Prayer on Sundays, and started an Inquirers' Class—

The doll's head falls into the baptismal font!

though the bishop was not scheduled for another year. This was a real honeymoon, and Joyce and I jumped at the invitation and Bishop Moody's approval to return in a year after graduation from seminary.

Senior Year at Episcopal Theological School

*U*sing the Harvard model, the senior year at ETS was a tutorial each week with reading and writing a paper for the next session. We had a chance to ask for our tutor, and I asked for Dean Charles Taylor. He became, and to this day remains, a role model and mentor.

Charles Lincoln Taylor Jr. graduated from ETS in 1924, joined the faculty as a teaching fellow, became an instructor in 1930, assistant professor in 1932, professor in 1937, and dean in 1944.[37] George Blackman writes in *Faith and Freedom: A Study of Theological Education and the Episcopal Theological School*, "He had a contagious enthusiasm for the Hebrew tongue, a forthright approach to biblical criticism, and a distrust of 'ceremony' amounting almost to physical discomfort and (like Fosbroke) a deeper serious moral emphasis." Two evenings a week, juniors would go to his house to hear him read aloud from his reconstruction of "The Memoirs of the Court of David (from I and II Samuel) and the Book of Jeremiah."

Dean Taylor offered electives on the Psalms and Jeremiah, and I was fortunate to take his elective on the Psalms, which made them come alive

---

37. The Reverend Charles Lincoln Taylor Jr., for thirty-one years on the faculty of Episcopal Theological (now Divinity) School as Professor of the Literature and Interpretation of the Old Testament, dean from 1944 to 1956, and former head of the American Association of Theological Schools, was a scholar of Latin, Greek, Hebrew, and Aramaic and an authority on the Old Testament. He is the author of *Let the Psalms Speak, Layman's Guide to Seventy Psalms,* and *Gleanings.*

for me and still remain in my mind as I read several of them each day. I fall short when it comes to Dean Taylor's hope and expectation that his students would memorize several psalms and several Collects of the Day from the Prayer Book.

For our first tutorial we were to have a general review of the year ahead and the subject to be covered. Dean Taylor, after catching up on what my summer had been, sat back in his chair and, fingering his Phi Beta Kappa key, said, "Let's warm up by naming the books of the Bible in order." I could feel the hair on my neck stand up, and I only made it to Deuteronomy before collapsing. Needless to say, the dean realized he had his work cut out for him.

Dean Taylor took me from this rather shaky start to getting my degree. He taught me how to study, how to write a good paper, and in a real sense, shaped my whole ministry. His house was on a corner of the close, and it was one of the marvels of the school that his study light was on almost at daybreak and far into the night. He never missed daily chapel each morning and evening, and if someone was missing or continued to miss, they were sure to hear from the dean even if it was a cheery, "I missed you in chapel this morning."

Among his other academic accomplishments—he was a noted Old Testament scholar who contributed the introduction and exegesis for Nahum, Habakkuk, and Zephaniah for the newly published *Interpreter's Bible* (1951–1957)—he had practically memorized the Psalms. When I was ordained a deacon, he came to Lexington and preached. He gave me a copy of the Revised Standard Version of the Bible with an inscription of Psalm 55:15 marked. Dean Taylor's inscription reads: "We took sweet counsel together and walked with the throng in the house of God," and he apologized for taking the verse out of context![38]

---

38. BCP, Coverdale translation, Ps. 55:15: "We took sweet counsel together, and walked in the house of God as friends." The KJV of the same verse is Ps. 55:14, "We took sweet counsel together, and walked unto the house of God in company." RSV of Ps. 55:14: "We used to hold sweet converse together; within God's house we walked in fellowship."

Starting with the Old Testament, I read books he suggested and wrote a paper each week and read it to him. He took the paper after I had finished and gave it back to me with his comments the next week. We went through the major subjects: Old Testament, New Testament, Church History, Theology, Ethics, Liturgics, and Homiletics. Those subjects would at the end of the senior year be on a comprehensive examination. Passing that exam was required for a degree.

My fieldwork for my senior year, which I have described earlier, was at Harvard with Chaplain Fred Kellogg—a favorable report at the end of the year was necessary, too, for graduation and the degree. Both Bob Throop, the workaholic rector at St. Michael's on the Heights, and Fred Kellogg from Harvard came through for me.

My ethics teacher, Joe Fletcher,[39] was one of the first liberation theologians, though that designation came much later. A group of us, under Joe's supervision, took the train into New York one weekend and then the subway out to Long Island's Garden City. We demonstrated against the bishop of Long Island, who had removed the Senior Dr. John Howard Melish from his parish and literally locked him out. I can't remember what Fr. Melish had done or not done, and I didn't meet Bishop Louttit[40] (though later his son, Henry,[41] was a friend and colleague in writing the 1979 Prayer Book and serving in the IV Province[42]).

39. When Joseph F. Fletcher (1905–1991) published his *Situation Ethics* in 1966, it was hailed by many as a much-needed reformation of morality, and to others it was an invitation to anarchy. Proposing an ethic of loving concern, Fletcher suggests that certain acts—such as lying, premarital sex, adultery, or even murder—might be morally right, depending on the circumstances. Hotly debated in the media, churches, and the classroom, Fletcher's provocative thesis remains a powerful force in contemporary discussions of morality.

40. The Right Reverend Henry I. Louttit, retired bishop of the former Diocese of South Florida from 1951 to 1969 and of the Diocese of Central Florida from 1969 to 1970. In the 1950s, Louttit spoke out forcefully against racial discrimination and segregation

41. Henry Irving Louttit Jr. (born June 13, 1938) served as the ninth bishop of the Episcopal Diocese of Georgia. He was the 901st bishop of the Episcopal Church in the United States of America (ECUSA).

42. Province IV of the Episcopal Church included the Dioceses of Alabama, Atlanta, Central

The Reverend William Howard Melish and his father, the late Dr. John Howard Melish, were at the center of a bitter struggle in the 1940s and 1950s that divided their parish. To put an end to the schism, Bishop James P. DeWolfe of the Diocese of Long Island closed the Holy Trinity Church in downtown Brooklyn in 1957 and ousted Mr. Melish, who had assumed the duties of rector when his father had been removed in 1949. Dr. Melish had angered some parishioners for supporting the activities of his son, then the assistant rector. The dispute focused on Mr. Melish's chairmanship of the National Council of American-Soviet Friendship, a target of Senator Joseph P. McCarthy's anticommunist campaign. The Rev. Melish was an advocate of both peaceful coexistence with the Soviet Union and civil rights.

Florida, Central Gulf Coast, East Carolina, East Tennessee, Florida, Georgia, Kentucky, Lexington, Louisiana, Mississippi, North Carolina, Southeast Florida, Southwest Florida, Tennessee, Upper South Carolina, West Tennessee, and Western North Carolina.

We had placards, marched around the church, went to supper in New York, and took the train back to Boston. My first demonstration!

Massey Shepherd was one of the giants in the field of early church history and liturgics and had written the *Oxford American Prayer Book Commentary,* a companion book to the 1928 *Book of Common Prayer*. He was, in those days, a rather formidable personage, and it was difficult to follow the ETS custom and call him "Shep." I followed him to Sewanee at the Summer Graduate School and got to know Shep and Gaby (his wife in his later life)[43] and her daughter by another marriage. Her former husband had died, and she lived on Lookout Mountain in Tennessee. We were on a first-name basis from then on.

Jim Clark, Trib, and their new daughter, Mandy, plus Gus, their black lab, joined Joyce and me—with our daughter Helen and our dog Pookie—at the summer school and rented the DeRosset House. We had the Shepherds over for a drink on the porch, and Gus, lying under Shep's chair, kept wafting bad air, which caused everyone secretly to think it was Shep. He liked cats.

Later, as I will record, I served on the Standing Liturgical Commission with Shep, and we wrote the 1979 *Book of Common Prayer*, which is the official BCP of the Episcopal Church to this day.

Gus was run over and killed, and Jim and I took him and buried him on a bluff overlooking the valley below, and in the far distance, Winchester, Tennessee. It was a sad day.

Bill Wolf, who had written one of the best books on the Atonement, was our theology teacher.[44] Charles Buck, a young protégée of our New Testament teacher, Sherman Johnson, and Frederick Dillistone,[45] an Englishman

43. Gabriella Taylor Connor, an artist and watercolorist; they had one daughter, Nancy Lloyd, who is married and has two children.

44. William J. Wolf, *No Cross, No Crown: A Study of the Atonement* (New York: Doubleday, 1956).

45. Frederick William Dillistone (1903–1993) was educated at Brighton College and Brasenose College, Oxford. Ordained in 1928 he began his ecclesiastical career with a curacy at St. Jude's Southsea. Later he was a tutor at Wycliffe Hall, Oxford, and then vicar of St.

*"So that's what the parish
ministry is going to be like."*

and another author of
theological works, filled the
rest of the teaching faculty.
And then there was Theo-
dore Parker Ferris, rector
of Trinity Church, Boston,
a renowned preacher, who
taught us homiletics.[46] Ted
Ferris would arrive for his
class in a limo with a uni-
formed driver.

It was all we could do to
keep our minds on his lectures for looking out the window and thinking, "So
this is what we're preparing for!" Robert H. Pfeiffer, who wrote the definitive
commentary on the Old Testament, was part-time with us and part-time at
Harvard Divinity School.[47] And, of course, there was Dean Taylor.

We had a dear old man, Mr. Lunt, who claimed kin to Alfred Lunt,
and taught us elocution.[48] He worked one on one in the chapel and would
stand behind you with his arm around your chest while you "elocuted."

Andrew's in the same city. From 1938 to 1945 he was professor of theology at Wycliffe Col-
lege, Toronto, and from then until 1952 held the same position at the Episcopal Divinity
School at Cambridge, Massachusetts. Moving back to England he was canon residentiary
and chancellor of Liverpool Cathedral from 1952 to 1956 and then its dean until 1963.
From 1964 until his retirement in 1970, he was fellow and chaplain of Oriel College,
Oxford. In 1968 he delivered the Bampton Lectures (Oxford) under the title, "Traditional
Symbols and the Contemporary World." An eminent author, he died at age ninety.

46. Theodore Parker Ferris (December 23, 1908–November 26, 1972) was ordained deacon
on June 11, 1933, and priest on May 27, 1934. From 1942 until his death, he was the four-
teenth rector of Trinity Church, Boston, Massachusetts. From 1943 until 1963, Ferris was
instructor in homiletics at the Episcopal Theological School, Cambridge, Massachusetts.

47. Robert H. Pfeiffer, *Introduction to the Old Testament* (New York: Harper and Bros., 1941).

48. Alfred Lunt (1892–1977) was an American stage director and actor, often identified for
a longtime professional partnership with his wife, actress Lynn Fontanne. Broadway's
Lunt-Fontanne Theatre was named for them.

He was teaching us to breathe diaphragmatically. The story has it that he was doing that one afternoon when two Cambridge dowagers came into the chapel to see the windows. Instead they saw Mr. Lunt embracing a student! They hastened back out to Brattle Street, and it may have been the first time (many would come later) that the school was accused of fostering gay relationships.

Harvard and surrounding schools like Radcliffe and MIT brought speakers and visiting scholars from around the world to Cambridge. Paul Tillich,[49] Karl Barth, Reinhold[50] and Richard Niebuhr,[51] and Albert Schweitzer[52] were among those we heard speak. The story is told that when Barth arrived at Logan Airport, the press rushed to meet the great theologian to be the first to get an interview. One intrepid reporter called out, "Professor Barth! Can you summarize your theology for us?" Barth, whose great opus covered volumes, thought for a minute, and then in his heavy accent, said, "Jesus loves me—this I know, for the Bible tells me so."

As mentioned earlier, the general exams came at the end of the senior year and covered nearly everything we had learned and discussed in our tutorials. I felt confident because of Dean Taylor's excellent

49. Paul Johannes Tillich (August 20, 1886–October 22, 1965) was a German American Christian existentialist philosopher and theologian who is widely regarded as one of the most influential theologians of the twentieth century.
50. Karl Paul Reinhold Niebuhr (June 21, 1892–June 1, 1971) was an American theologian, ethicist, public intellectual, commentator on politics and public affairs, and professor at Union Theological Seminary for more than thirty years. The brother of another prominent theological ethicist, H. Richard Niebuhr, he is also known for authoring the Serenity Prayer.
51. Helmut Richard Niebuhr (September 3, 1894–July 5, 1962) is considered one of the most important Christian theological ethicists in twentieth-century America, most known for his 1951 book *Christ and Culture* and his posthumously published book *The Responsible Self.* The younger brother of theologian Reinhold Niebuhr, Richard Niebuhr taught for several decades at the Yale Divinity School. Both brothers were, in their day, important figures in the neo-orthodox theological school within American Protestantism.
52. Albert Schweitzer (January 14, 1875–September 4, 1965) was a German—and later French—theologian, organist, philosopher, physician, and medical missionary in Africa, also known for his historical work on Jesus.

You can't tell the depth of a well by the length of its handle.

preparation—but the wait on the last day when the faculty met to sum up the grades and make their decision was nerve-racking. Each of us waited in our room for our tutor to come with the news. Dean Taylor was so excited—and, I think, pleased—that he called to me from the driveway in front of our entry to tell me I passed!

Joyce, who had taken time off from MIT to be with me on that important day, suddenly disappeared. I discovered later that she had already ordered my hood at the co-op and had jumped into George, parallel-parked in Harvard Square—no small accomplishment—and rushed the hood up the three flights to me. What a day and what a girl! Three of my classmates failed the generals and did not receive their degree.

We left ETS and Cambridge shortly after graduation. Bob and Cynthia Throop came from Worcester, and I had telegrams from home. Before departing, snuggled into our parked car was the newest Estill family member, a tiny Welsh terrier we named Pookie. Dr. Dillistone peered into the front seat as we were leaving and asked, "What's that?"

Ordination to the Diaconate

Middlesboro Redux

After a short time at home with parents in Louisville and Versailles, the day of ordination to the diaconate arrived. I had asked Dean Taylor to be the preacher, and he graciously accepted. Edwin Taylor, who had graduated from Virginia Theological Seminary, was also to be ordained. We had grown up at Christ Church together, but Bishop Moody set the ordination at the Church of the Good Shepherd in Lexington.

The oral examination required by the diocese and the national church I passed with ease, and thanks to ETS it was a breeze. Only once was I a bit unsure when Bishop Moody asked me what I knew about the book of Revelation. I said, "About all I know, I learned from reading *your* book." He seemed pleased and took off on a revision of some of it that took so long that we had to break for lunch. We never got back to Revelation, and I sailed through other questions.

Dean Taylor and I had a day together before the ordination, and since my parents had moved to Versailles, I thought he might like to see the Kentucky River. We drove to Clifton, and he exhibited his amazing knowledge of trains as we passed over what I would have considered a remote, unused, rusty track, and he remarked that it was a freight line used by the L&N Railroad and still in use! As we sat on the floating dock after a swim in the river, he computed the flow of the river! He preached a grand sermon, which for me was the high point of the ordination service.

The service on June 27, 1952, lasted so long that my uncle Bob Estill skipped out after the sermon, went to the Idle Hour for a drink, and came back for the final part of the service.

The Church of the Good Shepherd has a plaque in the narthex that reads, "This church is dedicated to the Glory of God by the lovers of the horse." Grateful horse lovers had donated money to build the church after the rector, a Mr. Settle, had gone before the legislature and testified that there was nothing in the Bible that prohibited pari-mutuel betting.

The Church of the Good Shepherd began in October 1888 as a mission chapel sponsored by Christ Church, and mission continued for seventeen years at its South Broadway location. In 1906 the chapel was taken down and moved to a new location on Maxwell Street to accommodate increased membership and attendance. But, on the night of January 1, 1918, disaster struck when a fire destroyed the chapel and most of its records. With the proceeds from the sale of the lot, the insurance and fire settlement, and donations from many local people, a new lot was purchased on the corner of Main Street and Bell Court, the church's current location.

The story of the modern Church of the Good Shepherd is the story of a man and his dream. The man, the Reverend Thomas Lever Settle, was a native of England who had come to Lexington in the post–World War I era when work was being resumed on the construction of the parish house. Mr. Settle found John Rump, another Englishman, who agreed to go ahead with the building, donating his services.

The Bishop Burton Parish House, as it was called, was dedicated on February 1, 1921, and at the request of the congregation, Christ Church Cathedral recognized Good Shepherd as an independent congregation. Mr. Settle, however, had a bigger dream of a beautiful stone church, and eventually he found a way to realize this dream. In 1923 there was much agitation throughout the Bluegrass over a bill introduced in the Kentucky legislature to abolish pari-mutuel betting. At one of the mass meetings, Mr. Settle spoke staunchly against the proposal, arguing that pari-mutuel betting was a fairer way of gambling than the bookmaking that would surely follow. He reasoned that enactment of the proposal would drive the horse industry out of Kentucky. Mr. Settle was asked to repeat his eloquent and logical speech before the Kentucky legislature. He did so, and the measure was defeated by one vote.

Over the five-year period that followed, commencing in July 1924, the horsemen raised nearly two hundred thousand dollars to build a church in demonstration of their gratitude to Mr. Settle. Contributions came from all over the country—from Roman Catholic, Jewish, Protestant, and Muslim horsemen, from owners and breeders and exercise boys.

On a plaque in the narthex of the church are these words:

> *To the glory of God this Church is given*
> *To Him by the lovers of the horse from all*
> *Over the country as a token of appreciation*
> *Of their Father's goodness to His children—man*

The bishop of the time, Bishop Burton, laid the cornerstone on August 20, 1925, and a year later the church building, complete with pews, was turned over absolutely free of debt. However, Mr. Settle was still not satisfied. Unknown to the congregation, he went deeply in debt, a debt the church would also inherit, when he ordered the intricate rood screen and the wood carving by Anton Lang of Leonardo da Vinci's *Last Supper* and other works. He also ordered the elaborate stained-glass windows crafted of two-hundred-year-old German glass, as well as a pipe organ costing ten thousand dollars. When Mr. Settle departed Lexington in 1930, he left Good Shepherd with a large debt that took over twenty years to liquidate.[53]

My grandfather had provided most of the stone for the exterior, thereby clearing a lot of stone from his fields and avoiding a cash donation

---

53. www.goodshepherdlex.org/about-us/history.html.

as well. He and all the Estills at that time in Kentucky were members of the Christian Church (Campbellites), later known as the Disciples of Christ.

After, as Rudyard Kipling would have it, "The tumult and the shouting dies; The Captains and the Kings depart,"[54] we headed for our first parish: St. Mary's, Middlesboro, Kentucky.

This time we were in the rectory, a one-story frame house with two bedrooms, a large living room opening into a dining room, a study with a separate door off the front porch, and a kitchen. It was built on the slope of the hill just below the church. The basement served as another parish hall and meeting room. There was a garage beneath the kitchen, which actually served as a storage area. A large attic served as an overflow bedroom and catch-all.

When I met with Bishop Moody to talk about St. Mary's in Middlesboro, I asked him what his hopes were and what he would expect from me. His reply surprised me at first, but I later saw the wisdom in his advice.

He said, "Get yourself voted 'Outstanding Young Man' by the Junior Chamber of Commerce!"

In that community when I made my pastoral visits, my new clerical collar wasn't well received by some of the patients. The old mountain men kept their overalls on even in bed, and often turned away toward the wall when I would stick my head in their room.

Visiting parishioners in the nursing home.

There was one nursing home in town, situated in a house that had been converted for that purpose. We did have one elderly woman from St. Mary's there, and I called on her and found she

---

54. Rudyard Kipling, "Recessional," 1897.

had not had communion for years. On my next visit I took the reserve sacrament, lighted a candle, and read as much of the service as a deacon was allowed. I gave her the host, turned to get the cup of wine, and when I turned back to her, she had picked the host out of her mouth and had it

I gave her the host.

between her fingers, looking at it. As I reached for it, she shot it out onto the floor on the other side of the bed!

There were four beds in that room, each with an occupant and each tied to the bed with a catheter and a bottle hanging below. I got down on the floor among the beds, ate several dust balls, and finally found the host and consumed it. So much for my first private communion!

Following Bishop Moody's advice, I became involved with the local Red Cross as well as Planned Parenthood. I joined the local ministerial association and did my turn on the local radio station's "Morning Devotions." It was a five-minute spot the station was required to give as a public service. Since "Morning Devotion" took place "live" every morning, except Sunday, most of the clergy tried to get out of the duty. It began at 7:00 a.m.! I took my regular turn and eventually ended up with it as a regular duty each morning. I hoped it would reach *some*body and help raise the presence of the Episcopal Church and St. Mary's.

After nearly three years, I lost the job by saying one morning, "God didn't write the Bible. Men did." That was not what the majority of listeners believed or wanted to hear, and I found out there was a larger listening public that I had thought. From there on, the more evangelical clergy were alerted to take their turn.

Commercials preceded and followed the program. The one just before

I went on advertised toilet paper, and the one afterward, Purina Hog Chow with Eddy Arnold singing. My final blessing was followed by a Delsi Toilet Paper ad! I didn't join a service club, since Rotary was the best in town, and they already had their Protestant minister slot filled. Bill Gray, the Presbyterian minister, and I became good friends, and it was refreshing to have someone to share things with and talk a little theology.

Nelson and David Harris and his wife, Imelda, became good friends, and David and I built a cabin boat on a hull we bought, and launched it on Norris Lake, one of the TVA lakes across the line in Tennessee. It gave us a getaway.

Middlesborough (spelled that way officially) had been settled by English people. All the streets had English names, and St. Mary's was one of the older churches in town.[55] The town claimed the oldest golf course in America, and Babe Didrickson Zaharias, who played a celebrity round, said she believed that it was the oldest golf course in America because of the condition of the tees. I got to know a number of men by playing golf and belonging to the club. At the Saturday night dinner dance, there was no sign of liquor (Bell County was dry), yet most people seemed to be pretty well oiled. We discovered they had brown bags either under their tables or in their cars because "the preacher and his wife were here"! When we served drinks before dinner at our first rectory party, the ice, so to speak, was broken.

---

55. In 1889, a mission to be known as St. Mary's was formed in Middlesboro. The Town & Lands Company gave the lot on Edgewood Road, where the church is presently located, to the congregation for building purposes, with the church to be built thereon, costing approximately two thousand dollars. On August 3, 1890, Rev. Sneed instituted St. Mary's Mission and nearly one hundred adult communicants were enrolled. Formal dedication of the church took place on February 11, 1891. The church building is listed on the Kentucky and National Registers of Historic Places and is considered one of the finest examples of carpenter Gothic architecture in America. The handsome structure, with its beautiful stained-glass windows and imposing steeple, is one of the most photographed churches in the country ("St. Mary's Episcopal Church (Middlesboro, KY.), *Ronald Morgan Postcard Collection*. Kentucky Historical Society).

One could buy liquor by calling a local taxi that ran a bootleg business. If you asked to be picked up at 10:00 a.m., that meant a fifth of bourbon, 11 a.m. was gin, and so on.

In addition to bootlegging, Bell County was known as "Bloody Bell County" because of all the disputes and sometimes fatal shootings around the coal mines. During the 1930s a former senior warden at St. Mary's, a mine owner, was killed, and his heart cut out and thrown up on the porch of his widow. His brother, who had driven him to the mine, survived by rolling under the car as it was fired upon. There were no "good guys" in all of this, for the owners were as brutal and unbending as the miners. Due to superstition, neither women nor clergy were allowed in the mines— which was fine with me!

We also fit in with a group of young couples who, except for the Harrises, belonged to other churches.

One of my assignments with the Red Cross was to go with a social worker up one of the hollows and bring out the children of an abusive woman whose husband, such as he was, was long gone. They lived in a shack with no running water or electricity, and the youngest was on a dirty blanket on the springs of what must have been a bed. I remember helping the social worker cut off a filthy diaper full of what looked to be half-digested bean soup. As we left with the children, the woman, who had stood by without saying anything, called out, "I know you have a child, preacher, and I'm coming to git her!" She never kept her threat, but I went through some anxious days and nights without telling Joyce.

Ordination to the Priesthood

Six months after our ordination to the diaconate, Edwin Taylor and I were ordained to the priesthood in Christ Church, Lexington, by Bishop Moody. Ed had the choice this time and asked the Reverend Lawrence Baxter, then rector of St. John's Versailles, to be the preacher. It was a fine service and capped off for me by my baptism and confirmation at Christ Church.

For the first time in recent history, St. Mary's had its own priest, and we celebrated my first communion on the Sunday after the ordination.

In those days, there was always a final prayer after the closing hymn, and I had heard someone chant it and asked our little choir to be ready to sing the "Amen" after my chant. They faithfully performed that act that was new to them, and as I was coming from the church door to the vesting area, I heard Mildred Ralston answering someone's complaint by saying, "It's some damn thing he learned in seminary!"

The next big event in our lives, and in the life of St. Mary's, was the birth of Helen Haynes Estill on October 10, 1953. As mentioned earlier, the hospital was over Perry & Pope's Drug Store on Main Street. I waited outside the

Ordination to the priesthood.

delivery room for Dr. Bowles to bring her into the world, and at one point a nurse came through the doors with a huge bundle in her arms. My first thought was that we'd had triplets—on a salary of three thousand dollars. It turned out to be dirty laundry. I was close enough to hear most of what was going on in the delivery room, and at one point I heard Joyce say, "Nothing is coming out!" In due time, Helen came into the world and into my arms.

Joyce's mother, who was from Louisville, was, without saying so, horrified at the hospital facility. I went to Louisville and drove her down. We were near Halloween, and the mountain way of celebrating it began early and included the usual decorations. They also put bales of straw in the road and sometimes lit them. That for her was a bit unsettling, and on top of that she had never been in the coalfields and its mountains. I think she thought I'd taken her daughter to a foreign country. Joyce's father soon joined us and then my mother—along with her big springer, Bunkie.

It was on a prior trip shortly after we had returned to St. Mary's that my parents visited us. My father had reached over into the backseat to rearrange Bunkie and felt a sharp pain in his lower back. It turned out to be multiple myeloma, and he died a month later at St. Joseph's Hospital, Lexington, on what was to be, a year later, our daughter Helen's birthday.

I was there with him at the end. He was buried in the Estill lot in the Lexington Cemetery by Addison Hosea, the rector of what had become their parish church, St. John's Versailles. Years later Addison was elected bishop of Lexington in an election in which I was also nominated and finished third. "A prophet is not without honor, except in his own country."

My father, who died in 1953, never saw his first granddaughter. My mother's death followed his two years later. She was in Florida visiting my sister.

When my mother was hospitalized, my sister, Revell, called, and I flew down and was there with my mother for several days. She was diagnosed as having an aneurysm in an artery at the base of her brain. She was a heavy smoker. After a few days Mother was feeling better, and I needed to get back to St. Mary's for Sunday services. When I got to the Atlanta airport, Revell had left a message telling me my mother had died, so I turned around and headed back to Florida. "Though my father and my mother forsake me, the Lord will sustain me" (Psalm 27:14).

We arranged to have her body buried next to my father's, and Bunkie and I (yes, Joyce had taken Bunkie to Florida) set out in her car for Kentucky. It's a long drive, and there were no interstates in those days. We drove all night and arrived at a diner outside Jacksonville as the sun was coming up. The man in the diner admired Bunkie, and I decided on the spot to tell him I was taking him back to Kentucky and would be giving him away. Would he like to have him? He was thrilled, didn't charge me for breakfast, and took Bunkie on his leash for a walk as I drove away.

I made it for twenty miles, burst into tears, turned around, and drove back twenty miles to the diner. I told Bunkie's now owner that my sister had raised Cain with me on the phone, and said she had promised Bunkie to some cousins in Kentucky. Bunkie forgave me instantly, flopped into the backseat (he weighed over a hundred pounds), and off we went. At least I got Bunkie and me a free breakfast.

Helen was the first infant to be baptized at St. Mary's in a long time. The last baptism, done by my predecessor, John Piper, had been a whole family from "up the hollow"—the Ray Longs. They had several children and John did them all. Afterward, Mrs. Long said, "Rev. [sic] Piper, did you baptize that little boy there?" pointing to one of the children. "I sure did," John replied. To which Mrs. Long said, "Well, you'd better unbaptize him. He's a neighbor's child who just came along to watch!"

John was a man of action but he couldn't, or perhaps didn't want to, keep records. I spent a lot of time and energy running down names he had listed as "communicants." Some had died, and some, like the Longs and this little twice-baptized neighbor, had simply disappeared. With Middlesboro being right on the Cumberland Gap, there were names on the rolls of people living in Tennessee and Virginia and even one family listed in North Carolina.

Our time in Middlesboro was a honeymoon time for us and, I believe, for the church. They had had so many years of ups and downs, with more downs than ups. Now, with a full-time rector, things were going well. Joyce's second pregnancy was upon us and then came the first real tragedy in our lives—the baby came early and was too feeble to make it. I baptized him in the delivery area, Robert Julian Estill II, and after a few hours, he died. Dr. Bowles did all he could and performed a Cesarean, but Julian lived only a short time. The hospital was ill equipped for a premature birth. The local funeral home provided a small casket, and I made the arrangements with the Lexington Cemetery, which had a lot right next to the Estill lot, and on the next day I drove to Lexington and buried him. Several family and friends who knew of his death were there at the graveside. Looking back, had we been in a hospital with more sophisticated equipment Julian may have lived. Our little congregation was lovely and upheld us in their prayers, gifts of food, and visits. Joyce's mother came to take care of Joyce and Helen—and me.

Time passed, and things were going well in the parish. I was elected "Outstanding Young Man" by the Jaycees, just as Bishop Moody had ordered.

When Bishop Moody made his visitation, we had Sunday lunch in the rectory. Mr. and Mrs. Gloster (he being the senior warden) and Bishop Moody sat at the table, and Joyce brought in a chicken she had baked for me to carve. On the first slice, I knew we were in trouble, for it felt like a rubber chicken. I hacked away again, and the whole bird slid off the plate and right into Mrs. Gloster's lap! The meal was redeemed at the end with one of Doo Dont's banana cream pies.

Word had come via the clergy grapevine that I was being considered by Christ Church in Lexington, the largest Episcopal church in the state

The chicken shot off into Mrs. Gloster's lap!

and my home parish. Jim Kennedy[56] had moved on after a remarkable ministry that had turned the parish into what it was, from being rather down at the heels under a long pastorate by Christopher Sparling. Sparling's daughter Audrey had taught me in Sunday school. Jim Kennedy had presented me for ordination both for the diaconate and priesthood.

I filed the news into my daily prayers and couldn't help but imagine what it would be like and what I could (and could not!) accomplish. As always, there was a strong urge to stay put and continue to build up St. Mary's.

Bishop Moody called to tell me that he had recommended me and that he hoped I would accept if called. I shared that with Bill Ralston, who had become senior warden, and we decided not to tell the vestry unless Christ Church issued a call.

It wasn't long in coming. Mr. Harbison, my godfather who was junior

---

56. The Reverend James W. Kennedy was a native of Denison, Texas, and a graduate of Seabury-Western Theological Seminary and the School of Theology, University of the South. He was ordained deacon in 1932 and priest in 1933. Fr. Kennedy served as curate at St. Paul's, Kenwood, Illinois, 1932; assistant at St. John's, West Hartford, Connecticut, 1932–1933; rector of St. Cyprian's, Lufkin, Texas, 1933–1935; priest in charge of Trinity, Dickinson, Texas, 1936–1937; priest in charge of St. George's, Texas City, Texas, 1936–1937; rector of Epiphany, Atlanta, Georgia, 1937–1939; rector of All Saints', Richmond, Virginia, 1939–1945; rector of Christ Church, Lexington, Kentucky, 1945–1955; rector of Ascension, New York, 1955–1964; and director and editor of Forward Movement Publications, Cincinnati, Ohio, 1964–1978.

warden, called to say that he and Ed McDonald, senior warden, would like to drive to Middlesboro to talk with me. When they arrived, typical of lawyers, they presented me with a written call to come as rector of Christ Church.

There had been some time since Jim Kennedy left, and while Bishop Moody had served as sort of interim, they hoped I could come as soon as possible. I told them I had prayed about the possibility of a call, had talked with the bishop and my senior warden, and of course with Joyce. The end result was that I was pleased to accept their call and could begin on the first Sunday in Lent, 1955.

By the time I shared the call with the vestry and my decision to accept, the whole congregation seemed to know. On our last Sunday I did fine until, while administering communion, I saw a tear come down Doo Dont's cheek. So the rest of the service I shared in the tears, and for the next week made a special effort to bring about closure and to say my good-byes and my thanks to our wonderful little flock and to the Middlesboro community.

Christ Church in Lexington, 1955–1964

We were thrilled to be going home. The rectory, bought during Jim Kennedy's tenure, was on the south side of town near the University. By our standards, based on St. Mary's, it was huge. A large bedroom and full bath on the first floor and a master and two smaller ones bedrooms and a bath on the second. A large living room opened onto a side porch and a dining room and TV room, plus breakfast room and kitchen. A two-car garage had a finished attic-like room above it, and there was a deep backyard as well.

Christ Church had added to its appeal with a lovely chapel, renovated parish house, and a garden. Still, the church itself was much as it had been when I was growing up. The box pews had the same doors on them, the font was where it was when I was baptized, and the pulpit still had what we in the boys' choir called a "preacher squasher"—a sounding board that gave the jack-in-the-pulpit flower its name. The church even had the same smell I remembered.

In an article about the call of the Reverend Mr. Estill as rector of Christ Church, the reporter writes, "The Rev. Mr. Estill, who is 28 years old, is the first rector of Christ Church to be born and reared in the parish. He was baptized there by Bishop Lewis Burton, the first Bishop of Lexington, confirmed there by Bishop Henry Pryor Almon Abbott, the second bishop, and ordained there by the Rt. Rev. William R. Moody,

When I was in the boys' choir and later served as an
acolyte, Christ Church had installed real bells in the bell
tower. They were operated from the organ console, and a
wonderful and dedicated old lady came each afternoon just
before six o'clock and rang them. She did the same thing
on Sundays and special days. One of her biggest challenges
was Good Friday. At the close of the three-hour service,
she tolled the bell thirty-three times for each year of our
Lord's life on earth. Since we were in the choir at that time,
we were able to see her at the organ bench. She brought
thirty-three matches and laid them out on the console.
Since we counted each toll we discovered that she would
move a match each time she struck a bell. Sadly, once she
had a pile on one side she would get confused and move
from left to right and then right to left. We used to place
bets on how old Jesus would be each year. I remember Ray
Murphy won one year by guessing forty-five!

the present bishop," and "was a choir boy and an acolyte at the church as
a youth."

When I was a child, children couldn't receive communion until they
were confirmed. So when our parents would go up to take communion,
we would crawl under the box pews and see if we could make it to the
back and return before being caught. Otherwise, I would go through my
mother's pocketbook, which she would leave in the pew.

I still remember where people sat: always in the same general area and
most often in the same pew, though pew rent was a thing of the past. We
sat about eight rows from the front in the middle section. There was the
Fayette Park area in the left rear, and the Harbisons sat near our pew but

on the side nearer to the pulpit. When I came back as rector, those same seatings were in effect.

Christ Church listed over a thousand members, and I inherited an assistant, Bill Tyte, who was a nice, quiet man and almost completely deaf. I would ask him to do something or call on someone and find that he didn't hear me. Nonetheless, he was a good pastor and well-liked. Henry Burton (no kin to Bishop Burton, the first bishop of Lexington, who baptized me) was a recent graduate of "Bishop Moody's seminary" (ETS Kentucky), which he had resurrected from an old effort that had died years ago.[57]

Another assistant, Erwin Little, who was in his late fifties, was also a graduate of ETS Kentucky and was especially gifted as a hospital visitor. Since I was twenty-eight at the time, on one Sunday when the graduating nurses from the Good Samaritan Hospital came to the eleven o'clock service, I preached a kind of baccalaureate sermon. Afterward at the door, a parent of one of the nurses said to me, "Please tell Mr. Estill that we thought it was wonderful of him to let you preach! You're so much closer to their age and speak their language!" I bowed and said, "He's a wonderful person."

I went to work putting together a team of clergy, and Ward Jackson, two years ahead of me at ETS in Cambridge, and his spouse, Pat—both Christian Education experts—came along with Marty and Elaine Knutson, also on the staff of a national Christian group life movement. Elaine was a psychiatrist as well. I started an adult class on Sundays between services, and with coffee and donuts, it became very popular, with over a hundred in attendance each week.

---

57. Episcopal Theological Seminary in Kentucky, formerly a diocesan seminary, was founded in 1834 at Lexington by Bishop Benjamin Bosworth Smith to educate clergy for the western frontier. The school was granted a charter on February 24, 1834. It went into a quick decline because of financial troubles in 1837 and controversy between the diocese and Bishop Smith. After 1840, for a short time, it had a nominal existence as a department of Shelby College in Shelbyville, Kentucky. Bishop William Robert Moody reopened the seminary in September 1951 with four students. In its last years it trained students for the diaconate. The final graduation service for the remaining diaconal students was on June 9, 1990.

A number of younger men and women came and sat together each Sunday. They dubbed their group "The Unreachables"—but they were far from that. The main leadership group in the church was made up of the sons and daughters of lifelong members and were one generation ahead of my own: Sam Walton, Garland Barr, Hendree Milward, Angus McDonald, Hope Wiedeman, Len Cox, Logan Shearer—who became one of my closest friends—Nathan Elliot, Rufus Lisle, and Emmet Milward, to name a few. Soon, a younger crowd came along as well. Joe Graves Sr. had been very active, and his son, Joe, came on board, too, and became one of my best friends and supporters.

Among the women there were very strong leaders as well: Retta Wright, Liz McDonald, as well as the spouses of the above-named men. Cousin Margaret Johnston was one of the pillars, along with Mrs. George Hunt, Dr. Carolyn Scott, Mrs. Florence Cantrell, and a host of others. Mrs. Hunt remembered me as "that little boy who always ran through my yard on Second Street." Martha Storey, whose husband, Barckley, became junior warden, and whose daughter Patricia was (and is) a lifelong friend, once handed me a piece of the bulletin on which she had written after

"You said 'heart rende*ring'!"*

my sermon, "heart rending." I had felt Mrs. Storey did not completely approve of a young rector the age of her daughter. So when I saw her a week or so later at a party, I headed over and started to say, "I've lived off your nice comment after my sermon," when she interrupted me and said, "I hope you don't mind my note. *You* said, "heart *render*ing! It's heart *RENDING!*"

While at Christ Church I was invited to serve Bishop Moody

as his chaplain at the opening services at the Lambeth Conference, the convention of bishops of the worldwide Anglican Communion. It was presided over by the archbishop of Canterbury, the Rt. Rev. Geoffrey Fisher.[58] The conference met at Lambeth Palace in London to deliberate on five major topics, such as the Bible, church unity, international conflicts, and for this particular conference, the place of the family in contemporary society.[59]

For those attending the conference, the social schedule was full—a Royal Church Music Festival, a reception by the Lord Mayor of London, and, of course, the Queen's Garden Party at Buckingham Palace. While we were away, Joyce's mother and father looked after Bobby, who was just one and a half, and Helen, who was four. After a short tour of the continent, we returned home at the end of July on the RMS *Queen Elizabeth*.

Christ Church was a busy place, and unlike Middlesboro, I didn't have much time for extra activities! I did become active in the Ministerial Association and the Kentucky Council of Churches—of which I later served as president. And, because race relations were at a low ebb, I helped organize, along with Joe Graves Jr., a local committee on human rights. We took on the task of integrating movie theaters, which in Lexington were under the Schines family management.

In the midst of all of that, one day while in my office I had a call from Frankfort. An aide to Governor Bert Combs,[60] whom I did not know, was on the phone and said, "The governor would like to talk to you in his office. When can you come to Frankfort?"

---

58. Geoffrey Worth-Fisher, Baron Fisher of Lambeth GCVO, PC, DD (May 5, 1887–September 15, 1972) was archbishop of Canterbury from 1945 to 1961.

59. 1958: IX Lambeth Conference, London. I was chaplain for Bishop Moody.

60. Bertram "Bert" Thomas Combs (August 13, 1911–December 4, 1991) was a jurist and politician from Kentucky. After serving on the Kentucky Court of Appeals, he was elected the fiftieth governor of Kentucky in 1959 on his second run for the office. Following his gubernatorial term, he was appointed to the Sixth Circuit Court of Appeals by President Lyndon B. Johnson, serving from 1967 to 1970.

I came right away and was ushered into the governor's office, where I found Edward F. "Sonny" Prichard,[61] an old friend and recently an attendee at Christ Church and a dollar-a-year adviser to the governor.

In Lexington, Edward Prichard was one of my most interesting friends. Our mothers were close friends, and mine often said she had helped raise "Sonny." Fortunately, when he went off to Princeton, he became known as "Prich." In his biography by Michael Ignatieff,[62] Isaiah Berlin called Prich "one of the brightest young New Dealers" and "a jovial and preternaturally quick young lawyer from Kentucky...former clerk for Felix Frankfurter, and a member of the White House staff." Later in the biography Berlin quoted Arthur Schlesinger Jr., who said that "Prich was a corpulent figure who joked when he was conscripted that they had reached the bottom of the barrel and were now coming for the barrel."

Katharine Graham, on a weekend at her country home, shared with me that Prich hit the bottom of the barrel himself. He had turned down several jobs in Washington, including assistant attorney general for civil rights and head of the Americans for Democratic Action (ADA) and moved back to Kentucky to start a law firm. During the Kentucky Senate race in 1948 between Virgil Chapman[63] and liberal John Sherman Cooper,[64] Katherine Graham in her autobiography wrote, "Someone

---

61. Bourbon County native Edward F. Prichard Jr. (1915–1984) was considered a friend and adviser to many politicians throughout his life and dubbed "the philosopher" by Governor Bert Combs.

62. Michael Ignatieff, *Isaiah Berlin: A Life* (New York: Henry Holt & Co., 1998).

63. Virgil Munday Chapman (March 15, 1895–March 8, 1951), a Democrat, represented Kentucky in the US House of Representatives and in the US Senate. In 1948 Chapman defeated incumbent John Sherman Cooper for a seat in the US Senate. An automobile accident in Washington, DC, killed Chapman on March 8, 1951. He was buried in the Paris Cemetery. Later in life, Chapman was said to have suffered from alcoholism. In Robert Caro's Pulitzer Prize–winning book *Master of the Senate*, Chapman is chronicled as a senator who was routinely inebriated at work in the US Senate.

64. John Sherman Cooper (August 23, 1901–February 21, 1991) was a politician, jurist, and diplomat from Kentucky. He served three nonconsecutive, partial terms in the US Senate before being elected to two full terms in 1960 and 1966. He also served as US ambassador

came to him and asked him to sign some ballots with faked names. He did."[65] Prich had been best man at her wedding to Phil Graham. Prich and his law partner Al Funk were indicted, and Prich was given a two-year sentence. He served five months and was pardoned by President Truman just before Christmas in 1951. Kay wrote that "the pardon was largely at the behest of John Sherman Cooper, who had won the election."

Prich often dropped by my office for a chat and at a later date shared his hotel room with me at a General Convention. I had been elected first alternate from the Diocese of Lexington and later admitted that I had prayed so hard to go that one of the deputies had a heart attack and I took his place! This was at the last minute, and all the rooms were taken in the convention hotel. Prich, who was a lay deputy, graciously offered a twin bed in his room, and we were roommates for the two-week convention. After each session Prich would pick up several books from the book display and take them to bed and spread them out over his rather corpulent stomach. Almost as fast as he could turn the page, he would devour each one. Finally, one night I reached over to the bedside table and grabbed the book he had just finished. I said, "Now tell me what's in this book! I think you're faking your speed reading." He screwed up his face as he often did and repeated almost word for word the last page he had read.

A year or so later, I believe it was Prich who suggested my name to Governor Bert Combs to head the new Kentucky Human Rights Commission.

Sadly Prich died in 1984 after being diabetic and becoming blind. What a waste of talent and ability! His wife, Lucy Eliott, stuck with him to the very end.

Governor Combs began my interview by saying he wanted me to head up the newly formed Kentucky Commission on Human Rights. He went on to say that he knew of my family's background and long history in Kentucky. Throughout he called me "Reverend Estes"!

to India from 1955 to 1956 and US ambassador to East Germany from 1974 to 1976.
65. Katharine Graham, *Personal History* (New York: A. A. Knopf, 1998).

I told him I would be most interested, but that I felt I needed to clear it with my vestry and would get right back to him. In due time I had the blessing of the vestry as well. That started a long period of organization, the hiring of an executive director—Galen Martin, one of the best and most-respected professionals in the field[66]—and getting a representative group appointed as members. I kept the road hot between Frankfort and Lexington.

Before long we had organized, appointed the membership, set up advisory committees across the state, had several meetings, and formed legislation for the governor to approve and send to the legislature.

In 1966 Kentucky became the first state in the South to pass public accommodations legislation. Earlier, in 1964, Martin Luther King Jr. had come to lead a march on the capitol in Frankfort in support of this legislation, but the Kentucky General Assembly was not ready in 1964.

When we moved to Louisville I became friends with the Reverend A. D. Williams King, MLK's brother and a Baptist minister.[67] He invited me to dinner with his famous brother and was instrumental in getting MLK to return in 1966 for the signing of Kentucky's public accommodations legislation. By then, Ned Breathitt was governor and had reappointed me to head the commission.[68] Ned and I had been at UK at the same time,

---

66. Galen Martin (1927–2006) was a civil rights activist and human rights official in Kentucky. He served as executive director of the Kentucky Commission on Human Rights from 1963 to 1989 and was instrumental in the drafting and passage of a state civil rights law in 1966. In 1972 Martin was a lawyer for plaintiffs who sued the Louisville and Jefferson County school systems to force desegregation. He also helped draft the desegregation plan that resulted from the lawsuit. In addition, he served as executive director of the Fair Housing Council in Louisville.

67. Alfred Daniel Williams King (July 30, 1930–July 21, 1969), known as A. D. King, was the younger brother of Martin Luther King Jr., the leader of the American civil rights movement. A. D. King was also a civil rights activist and a Baptist minister. On July 21, 1969, nine days before his 39th birthday, he was found dead in the swimming pool at his home. Cause of death was listed as accidental drowning.

68. Gov. Edward "Ned" Breathitt (1924–2003) was governor of Kentucky from 1963 to 1967. A Democrat elected with the support of civil rights leaders, he built on the record of his predecessor and mentor, Governor Bert T. Combs, who that year signed an executive

and both Joyce and I knew his wife, Fran, who was also in school with us. I felt honored to be among those with MLK as we watched the governor sign the legislation.

At Christ Church we had a large staff, with full-time clergy and a director of Christian Education, a choirmaster/organist, several secretaries, and a receptionist. When we had a vacancy, I made the hiring decision, and at that time I thought we should take the lead and hire a black secretary, which I did. It wasn't long before the flack began. A former vestry member came to my office to express his negative feelings and left me with the distinct feeling that "either she goes, or you go!" She proved to be a very fine secretary and stayed until she left of her own accord. I didn't leave either!

Christ Church still had many of the older members I had known as a child and who were friends of my parents. My mother had been active in the women's groups and my father had served on the vestry.

Christ Church had been the diocesan cathedral until Jim Kennedy came and felt it would do better as a parish (and less under the bishop's control!). Christopher Sparling was the dean while I was growing up and became less and less able as he grew older. On one Sunday he got up at the announcement time and stated that he had gotten a call to another church and asked the congregation to keep him in their prayers.

According to my father, who felt Christ Church needed a change, two weeks later Dean Sparling got up again and said, "Your prayers have been

order forbidding racial discrimination by state-licensed businesses. At the Southern Governors' Conference in 1964 he voted against Alabama governor George Wallace's proposed constitutional amendment to give state and local authorities sole jurisdiction over public schools. The amendment would have prevented implementation of the *Brown v. Board of Education* (1954) decision. Breathitt's opposition helped scuttle the amendment. His crowning achievement was the passage of the 1966 Kentucky Civil Rights Act, which banned discrimination on the basis of race, national origin, color, and religion in public accommodations and employment. When Breathitt signed the bill into law, Kentucky became the first southern state to pass an integration statute.

answered. I'm going to stay here!" My father insisted that the prayers had been in the other direction.

As I have said earlier, Clinton M. Harbison was my godfather (and became even closer) during my time at Christ Church. We asked Mrs. Harbison, who had been a close friend of my mother, to be godmother for Bobby.

Lots of the older members were really characters.

Paul Justice was well along in years, and his two outings each week were on Sunday for services at Christ Church and Monday for Rotary Club. One Sunday, while I was in the pulpit, I looked out and saw Mr. Justice in the act of getting out a cigar.

I suddenly realized that he was mixed up and thought I was the speaker and that we were at the Rotary meeting. My uncle Bob Estill, who had returned to live in Lexington and sat in the Fayette Park section of the church, saw what was going on, too.

I could hear Uncle Bob's raspy voice say, "God damn," as he got up and was hurrying toward Mr. Justice's pew. Too late. Mr. Justice had gone through all the preliminaries one goes through with a cigar (I'm not sure where he spit the end he had bitten off) and had lit up. The little cloud of smoke hung over his pew like incense until Uncle Bob finally reached him, after uttering another audible, "God damn!"

Lighting up in church.

In the congregation we also had the great-great-grandson of Henry Clay, Henry Bullock. I'm not sure what his condition was, but he had autistic "gifts," an occasional seizure, and a full-time man who drove him around. They sat in the balcony, and I learned right away to watch out when I asked rhetorical questions from the pulpit. Henry would shout the answers! His occasional fits would take place with much thumping and bumping in the balcony. He had the amazing ability to remember birthdays, and his driver would bring him to the door of our house to deliver birthday greetings. He lived for a while at Ashland, the Henry Clay estate, but his fits scared people and they moved him to an apartment in town.

Two of the happiest times of our life at Christ Church in Lexington were the births of Robert Whitridge Estill Jr. and Elizabeth Rodes Estill, each at the Good Samaritan Hospital. The rectory was now full. John Keyes was our attending physician, but Caroline Scott, who attributed her call to medicine to my father, grabbed Bobby and paraded him around the nursing stations, saying, "This is Dr. Julian Estill's grandson, and I'm going to be his pediatrician!" Caroline was a character in her own right and had some strange medical opinions. It wasn't long before Joyce wished for a change, and then Caroline announced her retirement. Joyce and I quickly said our thank-yous and good-byes and put all three children in the capable hands of Jody Trapp. Caroline, it turned out, didn't retire after all, and the word was that it had been a loyalty check. I think even our children were relieved to start drinking cow's milk instead of goat's milk. Caroline had announced that cow's milk was 80 percent water and 20 percent allergies!

Mr Justice thought he was at Rotary.

Joe Graves and I decided to get into the horse world by joining the historic Iroquois Hunt Club.[69] We took some brush-up lessons from Kob Ryan, an Irish horseman who taught us the finer points of jumping. He had a strong Irish voice, and looking back I think the horses obeyed his voice rather than our riding skills. During the lessons he would often call out, "Get off your buttocks, Mr. Estill, get off your buttocks," as I galloped the tired old horse around and around the ring.

I bought a hunter I named Lucifer, and Howard Tilson taught him to jump while Kob Ryan taught me. An old friend Fonnie (Lafon) Ingels joined us, and we spent many happy Saturdays and some Wednesdays in the hunt country, riding behind the colorful master Fauntleroy Pursley and his wife, Charlotte, who was field master. Lucifer didn't see why he should not be right up in front with the master (though, as foxhunters know, that's a terrible breach of manners). In fact, he and I were supposed to stay behind Mrs. Pursley. After several passes, Mrs. Pursley cried out, "Loose horse!" I was humiliated and ended up solving the problem and controlling Lucifer by going to a twisted wire snaffle bit.

Foxhunters look forward to being recognized as members of the hunt when they receive their buttons and colors. Betty Hagin, writing for the *Lexington Herald* in her column "Saddlelites," reported that the Iroquois Hunt Club awarded buttons and colors to those who knew the proper manners in the field, at all times, and who had a complete knowledge of the rules for organized hunting. During the annual meeting at Grimes Mill at the end of the hunt season in 1956, I and seventeen other hunters were awarded our robin's-egg-blue hunt colors and the coveted buttons for our vests.

One of the great moments of the Iroquois was the day Mrs. Pursley turned over her duties for a few minutes in order to respond to a call of

---

69. The IHC was founded in 1880 by General Roger D. Williams. In 1929 the Iroquois Hunt was recognized by the Master of Foxhounds Association of America.

nature. She chose a secluded place near a creek and had just dropped her jodhpurs when the fox, hounds, and hunt suddenly changed course and came charging by her in full cry. Mr. Pursley, leading the chase, is said to have doffed his hat and said, "Good afternoon, Charlotte!"

The Iroquois Hunt Club occupied an old mill in the hunt country toward Athens, Kentucky. There were a lot of black people who served as waiters at that club, and, of course, the cooks were black. And what we found out later is that when the club members and their guests were there at cocktail parties and drinking—of course, they'd talk about various issues— well, the black waiters, of course, were serving those drinks. And they heard and also realized that they knew who the bigots were and who the good guys were, from their point of view. And that word kind of got back in the black community, so there was a little intelligence network there. When I was called to go to Louisville, a small group held a party for Joyce and me for dinner at the Hunt Club; I guess maybe there were ten people at this table. There were a lot of other people there at this club just having their own dinners. So it wasn't a high-profile party. As the meal was concluded, our waiter said, "We have a present for Mr. Estill." He was talking to me, and I said, "Well, that's fine." The waiter said, "We have something we want to bring him." The cooks came out with a big cake. All the waiters and cooks stood around our table and they said, "Thank you, Mr. Estill."

Another episode came with the Annual Hunt Club Horse Show. Joe Graves and I entered this tandem jumping competition and schooled our horses over the course in advance. The first jump was to be done in tandem with one rider going over first and the other following. The next obstacle was a split-rail fence, and the pair was to accomplish that side by side.

Our team was announced. We headed toward the first jump in tandem, and then I took the lead and the jump. Lucifer performed well, and as I landed, the only thing that followed us over the jump was Joe's hat. His horse had stopped at the jump and Joe—hatless—was hanging on to his horse's neck. Needless to say, we were disqualified and disgraced.

The next thing to clear the jump ... was Joe's hat!

A year or so later, I was disqualified and disgraced all by myself at the prestigious Junior League Horse Show under lights, when Lucifer not only refused the first jump but chose to jump sideways into the crowd of well-wishers. Neither Joe nor I ever had any mishaps in the hunt field, with the exception, as I related above, of Lucifer passing the field master.

Hart Hagin Graves's mother, Betty Hagin, wrote for the *Lexington Herald* and was the one who reported the death of Lucifer. I was with him when he died on Saturday, November 29.

In Lucifer's obituary, Betty Hagin recalled the two years that I hunted with him. He respected me as his master, but while in the pasture he was in charge. Hagin wrote that when it was time to be caught he would lead the other horses away from the gate. He was the most difficult to catch, only agreeing to it when he was ready. The morning he passed away, he was ready to leave the pasture right away and he became sick quickly. We were unable to go on our last hunt that day.

Tom Satterwhite was a regular member of the hunt and was always perfectly turned out both in his own attire and in his tack. One day, on a run, Tom's horse dropped dead under him with a heart attack. One of the rules, unless someone is hurt, is to keep going—and the hunt did that as Tom got up unhurt but shaken. We were way out in the hunt country.

Tom unsaddled his dead horse and walked through the field until he came to a road. Finally, a pickup truck with two farmers in it came by and stopped, no doubt surprised to see a man in a pink coat, top hat, and boots, carrying a saddle and bridle. They gave Tom a lift (he in the back of the truck), and Tom gave way to some tears over his poor horse. Then he stopped crying. It is reported he said to himself, "Dammit to hell, why am I crying? It could have been *me* with the heart attack, not my horse!"

Bishop Moody did the honors when it came to the yearly Blessing of the Hounds at the beginning of the hunting season. I was not sure how I felt about that kind of thing, but got Lucifer ready (we had to braid manes) and had a couple of potent bull shots (bouillon on the rocks with a shot of vodka). As I got Lucifer into position for the blessing, I saw out of the corner of my eye a big gray mare, and thinking it was Mrs. Pursley's, I brought Lucifer up behind the mare. She turned out to be from the visiting Cincinnati Hunt and kicked me almost knocking me down. I saw the kick coming and turned just in time to receive the full blow in my ribs in the back. I've always thought I proved myself that day because I hunted for nearly four hours, danced the night away at the Hunt Ball, preached and taught the adult class on Sunday, and could not raise up in bed Monday morning! I'm not sure whether it was the blessing or the bull shots that got me through.

Meanwhile, at Christ Church, we had started a fund drive to build a much-needed office and church school building. Again, it was the leadership of the young vestry members that made the difference. We went over the top and were ready to start the building well in advance of our original date. The Church of the Redeemer in Baltimore had an excellent new building that complemented their old traditional church and parish house. The great Harvard School of Design architect Pietro Belluschi[70]

70. Pietro Belluschi (August 18, 1899–February 14, 1994) was an Italian-born American architect, a leader of the Modern movement in architecture, and responsible for the design of over one thousand buildings. Born in Italy, Belluschi's architectural career began as a draftsman in a Portland, Oregon, firm.

had done the work, and I called him to ask if he could do ours. He declined because of a heavy load of teaching but recommended the local (Baltimore) Alex Cochran, an architect who had worked closely with him.[71] We had a great experience with him, and our building was soon a reality. Caroline Scott, whom I've mentioned earlier, complimented it by calling it "Bobby's Bowling Alley"! That convinced me; if Caroline didn't like it, it must be perfect.

During this time I had a call from Sam Shoemaker, telling me he was retiring as rector of Calvary Church in Pittsburgh and wanted to recommend me to the vestry (this was before the days of search committees and the search process). I didn't see how I could leave Christ Church in the midst of the new building that was under way and the wrap-up of the financial part of the fund drive. Still, Sam had been a great force in my life, and he insisted that we "at least come up to Pittsburgh for a visit." I told my wardens of the call and of my reluctance, but that Joyce and I had agreed to visit on July 14, 1961.

The visit went well. A most attractive, young, dynamic group of vestry persons and their spouses took us on a tour of the church and hosted a lovely reception and dinner at the Pittsburgh Golf Club (where there is no golf course). We had lunch with Bishop Austin Pardue—one of my "hero" bishops[72]—and met and prayed with Sam, who rose from his prayers, saying, "Bob, old boy, I'm convinced God wants you here!"

We saw the large Victorian rectory and noted to ourselves that our breakfront wouldn't fit any of the walls. After returning to Lexington we

---

71. Alexander Cochran of Baltimore (1913–1990) was described as an "architectural missionary." Born to a wealthy local family, Cochran had trained under Walter Gropius at Harvard, becoming a devout disciple of Bauhaus philosophy. Besides being devoted to modernism, Cochran was a highly romantic, deeply religious humanist who desired to keep the best of the past while adapting to modern needs. He transformed his city, pointing the way to its later renaissance in the 1960s.

72. Austin Pardue (August 9, 1899–April 28, 1981) was the fourth bishop of the Episcopal Diocese of Pittsburgh. He served as diocesan bishop from 1944 to 1968.

had a formal call from the vestry. After a lot of prayer and thought, I called their senior warden and declined. A day or so later, I got an anonymous letter with a five-thousand-dollar check and a note: "Anonymous gift in honor of your having refused the call to Pittsburgh in order to continue the remodeling of Christ Church that you started. In thanks for you saying 'no' to Pittsburgh and 'yes' to us!"

While at Christ Church I was nominated to be suffragan bishop in Tennessee and led after the first ballots. At a lunch break, it was reported to me later, Bill Ralston Jr. went around and told the delegates that I was "a radical sonofabitch" who had integrated Christ Church (I wish), raised racial tensions all across Kentucky, and would do so in Tennessee. Bill was the son of my senior warden at St. Mary's in Middlesboro. When Bill was ordained to the diaconate, I preached at his service. Needless to say, I finished a distant second in the final vote.

My philosophy, right or wrong, was that if someone in the church wanted me to consider a call, I would honor it and test whether the Holy Spirit was calling me or not. That led to other nominations for bishop in Atlanta, West Virginia, Pittsburgh, and Southern Virginia and later in both Lexington and the Diocese of Kentucky. Meanwhile we were seeing some progress in civil rights in Kentucky.

Governor Combs was one of Kentucky's finest governors in my opinion, and he backed us on the Kentucky Human Rights Commission and helped with legislation. One Saturday night in Lexington, shortly after he had appointed me chair of the Human Rights Commission, Joyce and I were at the Idle Hour Country Club on the dance floor. The woman at the desk came out on the floor and said, "Governor Combs is on the phone and says it's urgent!"

"Reverend Estes," the governor said, "this is Bert Combs, the governor. I'm here in Louisville outside the Brown Hotel, and the demonstrators are raising hell!"

I said, "As you know, I'm in Lexington and—"

He interrupted me to say, "I know that, but you're head of my Human Rights Commission, and we need to do something to stop this before it gets violent."

So I said, "Alright, Governor, I'll see what I can do," and we hung up. I made a call to Galen Martin, our executive director, who was at his home in Frankfort. At his suggestion, I called Frank Stanley, a member of the Human Rights Commission, living in Louisville, the editor of the only black-owned newspaper in the state.

The demonstration ended—whether because of my efforts or not—and I assumed the governor was satisfied. By the time this was finished, the dance had ended and the Idle Hour was about to close for the night.

Last Days at Christ Church in Lexington and Beginnings at the Cathedral in Louisville, 1963–1969

One of the wastes in the church, I found, was that of ex-wardens, whose terms had run out and who often were lost to leadership positions, despite their experience and expertise. I started what we called the "X-Rated Wardens," made up of former junior and senior wardens. They met monthly, a week after the vestry, and had the vestry minutes, financial reports, and anything else for their information and interest. I continued that in the other parishes I served.

Looking back on my own experience in the boys' choir at Christ Church, the vestry and I restored the choir of men and boys, which had been dropped in the Kennedy years. We kept the senior choir and added a girls' choir as well. Our great Holtkamp organ (which Jim Kennedy had purchased) made our music superb, and a lot of people were drawn to church because of it.[73] Our Christmas Eve service was always packed and was a Lexington tradition across denominational lines. The annual Christmas Dinner Dance at the Lexington Country Club even had a

---

73. The Holtkamp was voiced by workers from the Aeolian-Skinner company. As the story goes, "Holtkamp walked into the church after the completion of the organ and stated: If there has to be one of my [Holtkamp] organs that sounds like that, at least it's in an English cathedral."

long intermission so that people could come to church. Many came in evening dress, and there was a noticeable odor of bourbon in the nave.

John Jacob Niles, who had become a good friend and faithful attendant, anchored the broadcast of the service, and I heard him (he was a well-known folksinger and musician) say, "God rest ye merry this Christmas Eve, this is Johnny Niles, coming to you from Christ Church and bringing you a glorious Christmas gift in this service."

Bob Quaide was our organist/choirmaster;[74] we hired him after I had been there a couple of years. Our search committee was made up of the heads of the Music Department at UK and Transylvania as well as John Jacob Niles and two vestry members. When Bob auditioned, he played two magnificent pieces from Bach and Buxtehude, and then an incredible piece that shook the church; he used every key on the organ as well as the foot pedals and left our committee and me spellbound. When we asked him what *that* was, he said he was improvising! We discovered he had come in second nationally in the American Guild of Organists (AGO) competition for improvisation. The final test the AGO gave was to print a few bars of music and let the organist take it from there.

We had issues at Christ Church, just as every church does. Renovations of the old parish house and building of a new office and Sunday school, which change the appearance; the civil rights issues—especially since I was often in the news as chairman of the Kentucky Human Rights Commission; the various changes in the liturgy, both locally and from the national church; and the usual problems, pastorally and with committees, altar guilds, and vestries, to say nothing of a large staff of clergy and laypeople, all kept the pots boiling.

Hunt Williams (later my suffragan bishop)[75] tells of his mother, who

---

74. Robert Quaide was organist from 1961 to 1967. In 1962 he started the boys' choir.
75. Huntington Williams Jr. (October 27, 1925–January 28, 2013) graduated from Harvard in 1949 and Virginia Theological Seminary in 1952. After his ordination, he served parishes in Maryland and New York before coming to North Carolina to serve as the rector of St.

was an active and lifelong member of the Church of the Redeemer in Baltimore. My friend Bennett Sims,[76] later bishop of Atlanta, was her rector.

She resisted the building of a new church, the changes in the Prayer Book, and the ordination of women—but was always at church and active in its activities. When she died, Hunt found her well-worn 1928 Prayer Book beside her bed. In it she had written: "Neither life nor death, nor angels, nor principalities, nor height, nor depth, nor Bennett Sims, nor any other thing, can separate me from the Love of God in Christ Jesus, our Lord." Bennett was the rector who had championed all those changes!

I'm sure some of the old members of Christ Church Lexington had me in a similar position in their prayers. Then there were the really ugly calls in the night about civil rights with threats along with vulgar and profane warnings. "Blessed are you when men say all sorts of things about you."

I was pleased to see an upswing in attendance on the part of the college students at UK and Transylvania. We encouraged fraternities and sororities to come to services as a group and always recognized them at announcement time. A large number of students came for pastoral counseling, and at one point I had a girl, Paula, who would spend her hour telling me how much in love she was with a fellow student named David Shirley. Another male student John Akers often came and talked about how he was in love with Paula. Then David himself showed up and wanted to talk about the possibility of entering a monastery after graduation! Much later I asked for and they gave permission for me to tell this story.

Timothy's, Winston-Salem, in 1956. Williams had been the rector of St. Peter's, Charlotte, for twenty-seven years when he was called to be bishop suffragan of the diocese, 1990–1996.

76. Bennett Jones Sims (August 9, 1920–July 17, 2006) was the sixth bishop of the Episcopal Diocese of Atlanta, consecrated in 1972. During his episcopacy, he was in strong opposition to the rising divorce rate, and spoke about his preference for the integrity of marriage vows. Among the issues receiving his support and leadership were racial integration of the public schools, revision of the Episcopal Prayer Book, the ordination of women, and ultimately, the acceptance of homosexuals in the church.

God apparently sorted things out because Paula and David were married after graduation and had five children. So much for celibacy and monasticism. Paula's other admirer, John Akers, went to seminary, married a lovely young woman, and came as my assistant to Dallas, and later followed my call to come to Greensboro as an assistant at Holy Trinity.[77] I later presided and preached the homily at his funeral. Ten men went into the ordained ministry from Christ Church while I was there.

UK's football coach Blanton Collier and his family were members of Christ Church. One of my assistants, Ward Jackson, was an ardent fan, and Blanton made it possible for him to attend practice when he wanted to—which, it seemed to me, was often! UK's football fortunes have never been high, except for Bear Bryant's years, and poor Blanton didn't fare well either—he would often call and ask me to drop by after another loss.

One weekend I was out of town and UK lost. Blanton, whose voice broke when he talked naturally, and especially after a loss, called Ward Jackson. Jackson, who had envied me for having the pastoral duty, thought it was me playing a joke on him. So when Blanton called and said, "Rev. [sic] Jackson, this is Blanton Collier," Jackson said, "Oh, hell, Estill, get off the phone!" Ward said there was a moment of silence and then the voice, trembling more than usual, said, "Rev. Jackson?"

One party we attended revolved around a bunch of lobsters that you could order by mail. Included as a bonus was a peck of clams—which I love. Not many at the party shared my love of clams, so I ate a lot of them.

Jump ahead to Lent, and I was the preacher, of all places, at Christ

---

77. John Shelley Akers III (November 11, 1932–April 17, 2014) served in the army, attended Transylvania University, then graduated from the University of Louisville. He was called to the ministry and graduated from the Episcopal Theological Seminary in Lexington, Kentucky. Fr. Akers served as vicar of St. Phillips in Harrodsburg, Kentucky; as assistant to the rector at the Church of the Good Shepherd in Lexington, Kentucky; as rector of St. Peter's in Paris, Kentucky; and at St. Michael and All Angels in Dallas, Texas, where he was on staff as well as chaplain of the school. In 1984 he continued his ministry in Holy Trinity Episcopal Church in Greensboro, North Carolina.

Church, Raleigh, North Carolina! Joyce and I had never been to Raleigh, and we were wined and dined each day. I had, what I thought to be, the flu—but you can't be a no-show at a week of Lenten preaching. So, after each event I'd go back to the hotel and lie down. One evening we went to Tarboro and I preached at Calvary Church where Moran Weston,[78] a black priest and friend in New York, had grown up. His mother was in the congregation, and Jack Spong,[79] rector of Calvary and priest in charge of the black church, was the host.

We had a call at midweek that my aunt Laura Williams had died, so Joyce went back to Lexington, and I stayed to complete my responsibilities. On Friday, still feeling punk, I got on Piedmont Air and flew home. Joyce met the plane and took me right to our doctor, Dick French. I had infectious hepatitis!

I was put to bed in our downstairs bedroom which had a white lace canopy to match my yellow skin. No one could come near me, and poor Joyce had to slide a tray of food in the door. Once a day a nurse would come by to take some blood and give me a shot. It wasn't long before I was feeling better, but I was in isolation for six weeks. I ended up reading all of Winston Churchill's memoirs, talking on the phone and to my loved ones who could come to the door but no farther. I had to write thank-you notes to all my hostesses and hosts in Raleigh, and after thanking them, I added, "I have infectious hepatitis and my doctor suggests you have a

---

78. Milton Moran Weston II (September 10, 1910-May 18, 2002) studied at St. Augustine's Junior College in Raleigh, North Carolina. He was the church's business manager and contributed to the founding of the church's credit union. He was the sixth rector of St. Philip's church.

79. John Shelby "Jack" Spong (b. June 16, 1931) is a retired American bishop of the Episcopal Church. From 1979 to 2000 he was b (based in Newark, New Jersey). Spong served as rector of St. Joseph's Church in Durham, North Carolina, from 1955 to 1957; rector of Calvary Parish, Tarboro, North Carolina, from 1957 to 1965; rector of St. John's Church in Lynchburg, Virginia, from 1965 to 1969; and rector of St. Paul's Church in Richmond, Virginia, from 1969 to 1976. He has held visiting positions and given lectures at major American theological institutions, most prominently at Harvard Divinity School.

gamma globulin shot!" Fortunately, no one remembered that incident when years later I was elected bishop of North Carolina.

Three cheers for clams!

I had become active in what we called the National Church and City organization and often met in Washington. Paul Moore, then dean of the cathedral in Indianapolis;[80] Frank Sayre, dean of Washington Cathedral;[81] and a number of clergy and laypersons were trying to bring the church and its concerns back from suburbia to the city. Later when I was dean of the cathedral in Louisville, the annual Deans' Conference was held in Chicago. Our host for the week was Mayor Daley—the infamous "ruler" of Chicago. We went with him each morning to tour "his" city and then had discussions with him and his staff afterward. The Deans' Conference was the best church conference I ever attended. We went to San Francisco and visited the people at Berkeley who were into space exploration and had played an important role in the making of the atomic bomb; went to

---

80. Paul Moore Jr. (November 15, 1919–May 1, 2003) was a bishop of the Episcopal Church and former US Marine Corps officer. He served as the thirteenth bishop of New York from 1972 to 1989. In 1957 he was named dean of Christ Church Cathedral in Indianapolis, Indiana. Moore introduced the conservative midwestern capital to social activism through his work in the inner city. Moore served in Indianapolis until he was elected suffragan bishop of Washington, DC, in 1964. During his time in Washington he became nationally known as an advocate of civil rights and an opponent of the Vietnam War. He knew Martin Luther King Jr. and marched with him in Selma and elsewhere. In 1970 he was elected as coadjutor and successor to Bishop Horace Donegan in New York City. He was installed as b of the Diocese of New York in 1972 and held that position until 1989. During his lifetime, he was perhaps the best known Episcopal cleric in the United States, and among the best-known of Christian clergy in any denomination.

81. Francis B. Sayre Jr. (January 17, 1915–October 3, 2008) was dean of the National Cathedral in Washington, DC, for twenty-seven years. He was the first grandchild of President Woodrow Wilson. He was a vocal opponent of segregation, poverty, McCarthyism, and the Vietnam War. In March 1965 he joined Martin Luther King Jr. on the voting rights march from Selma to Montgomery, Alabama. Sayre was unafraid to denounce Senator Joseph McCarthy, Republican from Wisconsin, during the heyday of the latter's influence in the 1950s. In 1954 Sayre called McCarthy a "pretended patriot," adding, "There is a devilish indecision about any society that will permit an impostor like McCarthy to caper out front while the main army stands idly by."

England and spent a week at Coventry Cathedral; spent a full week with Daniel Patrick Moynihan, the gifted senator from New York; visited the cathedrals in Missouri, Kansas, and Washington; and followed up on the goals of the "National Church and City" organization.

Several books were published at this time showing renewed interest in the urban ministry and remain excellent resources even today. Gibson Winter's book *The Suburban Captivity of the Churches*[82] and Paul Moore's *The Church Reclaims the City*[83] are typical. Bishop Bayne[84] wrote, "The mission of the Church is something more than putting more roofs over more Anglicans in more suburbs."

The controversial bishop of California, James Pike,[85] called to say he had recommended me for the largest church in his diocese—St. Paul's Episcopal Church, Oakland. At his request, I flew out alone since Joyce had to stay with one of the children who was sick. Darby Betts,[86] canon

---

82. Gibson Winter, *The Suburban Captivity of the Churches: An Analysis of Protestant Responsibility in the Expanding Metropolis* (Garden City, NY: Doubleday and Co., 1961)..

83. Paul Moore, *The Church Reclaims the City* (New York: Seabury Press, 1965).

84. Stephen Fielding Bayne Jr. (May 11, 1908–January 18, 1974) was born in New York City, and he received his BA from Amherst College in 1929 and his STB from General Theological Seminary in 1933. Ordained deacon on May 22, 1932, and priest on June 11, 1933, Bayne served as rector of Trinity Church, St. Louis, Missouri, 1934–1939, and rector of St. John's Church, Northampton, Massachusetts, 1939–1942. On June 11, 1947, he was consecrated bishop of Olympia and served in that position until he resigned on December 31, 1959. From 1960 until 1964 Bayne was the first executive officer of the Anglican Communion, and from 1964 until 1968 he was the director of the Overseas Department of the Episcopal Church. In 1970 he returned to General Seminary as professor of Christian mission. In 1972–1973 he was dean of General Seminary. One of the best known of his thirty-three major writings is *Christian Living* (1957), a volume in the first Church's Teaching Series.

85. Bishop James Albert Pike was an extremely controversial figure because he believed in the ordination of women, racial desegregation, and the acceptance of LGBT people within the church. He served as the fifth bishop of California until 1966 when he began working with the Center for the Study of Democratic Institutions.

86. The Venerable Darby Wood Betts, eighty-six, priest of the Diocese of California, died August 14, 1998. Fr. Betts was an authority on church architecture and founder of the Episcopal Homes Foundation and of the Diocese of California's Episcopal Charities Appeal.

to the ordinary bishop Pike, met the plane and took me to a motel where
Bishop Pike was having a meeting with some of his clergy. The famous
Bishop met me at the pool, clad in a rather brief bathing suit, and holding
a pitcher of martinis!

Later I visited the vestry; toured the church and Oakland; preached at
St. Clements, Berkeley; and flew home. Bishop Pike had written in *Look*
magazine, "There is in the air in California a pioneer spirit, a willingness to
take chances and not worry about making mistakes or saving face, a much
greater readiness to say not 'We've never done this before,' but 'Let's go!'"
One of the perks at St. Paul's was a Japanese gardener for the rectory:

After a lot of prayer and talking with Joyce and my wardens, I wrote
Oakland and Bishop Pike and declined their call.

When my half-brother Taylor died in Los Angeles on November 28,
1962, I was unable to attend the memorial service by the faculty at UCLA
where he was teaching, but I did preside at his internment in Paris, Kentucky, in the Hinton lot.

A native of St. Louis, Missouri, he graduated from Washington and Lee University and
Virginia Theological Seminary. Ordained deacon and priest in 1938, he served as curate
at Ascension, St. Louis, Missouri, 1938–1940; rector of St. Paul's, Kingsport, Tennessee,
1940–1942; rector of Whittle and Piedmont Parish, The Plains, Virginia, 1942–1943;
rector of St. Clements's, Alexandria, Virginia, 1943–1950; canon of the Cathedral of St.
John the Divine, New York, 1952–1955; dean of the Cathedral of St. John, Providence,
Rhode Island, 1955–1960; and canon to the ordinary, Diocese of California, 1960–1961.
From 1962 until his retirement in 1986, Fr. Betts was involved in nonparochial ministries.

Charles G. Marmion, bishop of Kentucky (1954–1974), cooperated more than any church head with our Kentucky Human Rights Commission. He asked me at one of the meetings to come speak at the cathedral (I had done so when Norvell Wicker was dean[87]) and then he asked if I would consider coming to Louisville and the cathedral. Dean Wicker had died in the pulpit!

On November 22, 1963, I was at work in my office in Lexington when word came that President Kennedy had been shot—and then the awful news that he was dead. There was a moment of silence on the radio, then the National Anthem. I hurried over to the church, and we opened the main doors and almost at once the church began to fill. I went to the organ bench and tolled the bells. Dan Chandler[88] came and sat with me on the bench in tears. Our morning services on Sunday were packed, and in the afternoon I drove to Louisville to be the speaker at their Diocesan Youth Conference at the Church of the Redeemer. I scrapped my speech and talked about our national tragedy. On Monday I gave the invocation at the memorial service at the University of Kentucky and heard an excellent address by President John Oswald,[89] who with his family attended Christ Church.

On December 7, 1963, I met with the search committee from Louisville, and they issued a formal call for me to become dean of Christ Church Cathedral. Bishop Marmion[90] included a letter urging me to

87. Norvell E. Wicker Jr. was dean of Christ Church Cathedral from 1944 to 1963.
88. Youngest son of Albert Benjamin "Happy" Chandler Sr. (July 14, 1898–June 15, 1991), a politician from Kentucky who represented the state in the US Senate and served as its forty-fourth and forty-ninth governor.
89. John Wieland Oswald (1917–1995) was the thirteenth president of the University of Kentucky, from 1963 to 1968.
90. Charles Gresham Marmion (August 19, 1905–December 7, 2007), the fifth bishop of Kentucky, was consecrated bishop of Kentucky in 1954 and served the diocese for twenty years. He provided leadership during an intense period of civil rights activity in the diocese and was strongly committed to the church taking a firm stand on issues of moral and human values. Bishop Marmion supported the ecumenical impulses associated with Vatican II and contributed to the national liturgical revision efforts of the Episcopal Church. He earned a business degree from the University of Texas and graduated from

accept. After talks with Bishop Moody, my wardens, and of course, Joyce, I accepted the call on St. Thomas Day, December 21, usually the shortest day of the year, yet this day usually commenced the Christmas preparation of cleaning and baking!

Philippians 3:13–14 had been on my mind while I was praying about the call, "Forgetting what lies behind and straining forward to what lies ahead, I press on toward the goal for the prize of the heavenly call of God in Christ Jesus."

We stayed at Christ Church until the annual parish meeting. Many nice things were said, and they gave us a lovely silver bowl and tray. Bishop Moody was there, and in his remarks he told them that "Bob did not love them *less*, but that he loved the Lord *more* in leaving."

The cathedral chapter, pushed by Booker Robinson and John Davenport, had sold the old deanery in the Iroquois Park area and that gave us a chance to pick our home. We bought a lovely house near the river and Upper River Road on Brittany Valley Road. A horse farm was just across the road beyond some houses. We had a mock-orange hedge in the front yard and a nice backyard for Bobby and me to play football. It is suburbia, but I thought that Joyce and the children deserved to be there while I spent most of my time in the city and, because of being chair of the Human Rights Commission, traveling.

We had the cathedral chapter out for drinks and dinner and to "see the new deanery." One of the members, who I suspected was a John Bircher, was looking in my library and came across Aleksandr Solzhenitsyn's great work, *The Gulag Archipelago*, in which Joe Graves had inscribed, "To Bob Estill, who taught me all that I know about communism." To his dying day, that chapter member never believed the "Joe Graves explanation."

Virginia Theological Seminary. Before his election to the episcopate, he was rector of St. John's Church, Columbus; Christ Church, Eagle Lake; St. George's, Port Arthur; and Incarnation, Dallas—all in Texas.

Five months later, I wrote in my journal that those first months at the Cathedral had been especially hard. Not only was I a big change from Dean Wicker, whose death in the pulpit made him an instant saint, but my chairmanship of the Kentucky Human Rights Commission that required a lot of travel and kept me in the newspaper headlines—and our emphasis on making the cathedral a

"You knew Solzhenitsyn?"

true cathedral dedicated to urban ministry—all added up to alarm many of the old guard who wanted the cathedral to be a small parish family and wanted me to be the country parson.

On the positive side, we rejuvenated St. George's Mission deep in the West End, and organized the clergy of the urban parishes into what we called the Urban Mission Council. Bishop Marmion was 100 percent behind us, and a strong core of laypeople stood up against those who resisted everything that was going on. I realized—a retreat at Kanuga with Bishop Stephen Bayne helped greatly—that I had been too concerned with myself, almost feeling I was God's gift to the cathedral, and when things had not gone to my liking, I'd taken it as a personal insult. How un-Christ-like and how unrealistic!

George Herbert's poem[91] is so apt:

> *Who would have thought my shriveled heart*
> *Could have recovered greenness? It was gone*

---

91. George Herbert, "The Flower," from *The Temple* (1633). See Appendix II for the complete poem.

And now in age I bud again,
After so many deaths I live and write;
I once more smell the dew and rain,
And relish versing. O my only light,
It cannot be
That I am he
On whom thy tempests fell all night.

I embarked on a visitation program to try to find some of the missing persons on our communicant list. It became clear that we were closer to six hundred members than the eleven hundred listed in the journal.

One of my more interesting visits was to a woman who was home-bound and a lifetime member of the cathedral. She greeted me somewhat coolly and announced, "Dean Estill, there have been two men in my life, my husband and Dean Wicker, and there isn't room for anyone else." I took that piece of news with mixed emotions, but just then a big yellow male cat came into the room and went right to me and jumped onto my lap. "Why, I believe Sunny likes you!" she said, incredulously. Almost as her words were out of her mouth, Sunny (who had been looking over my hand) took a big bite out of the fatty part below my thumb. To the glory of God, I put my bleeding hand in my pocket, gave Sunny a last pat on the head, and beat a hasty retreat.

Several months later, this same lady became ill, and I made a number of visits, taking her communion and kneeling beside her bed. Sunny always got me. He would dart out from beneath the bed or from behind the curtains and sink his teeth or scratch with his claws. Still, she would rave about how much he liked me. And I think she began to add me to her roster of those she included in her "room."

Finally, one day I had had enough. I let Sunny get into my lap, and as he was selecting a place on my hand to bite, I reached behind him where his very generous male symbols hung, and as he bit me, I squeezed him there! Sunny let out a whoop and shot off my lap, did a turn around the room without touching the floor, and disappeared into the bathroom. He never came near me again.

In a year or so, Sunny's owner died, and after her funeral, Henry Heyborn, her attorney and a friend of mine called and said, "Guess what? She has left Sunny to you in her will!" I replied, "Henry, I hated that cat—and the cat didn't like me!"

Henry, after controlling his laughter, said, "I'm just teasing you. I took Sunny down to the SPCA this morning and had him put to sleep."

I hated that cat, and he didn't like me!

May he (if he made it into heaven) and his owner rest in peace.

The grind at the cathedral made our upcoming trip to England for the Deans' Conference even more welcome. After landing (in separate planes for the children's protection), we joined the Robinsons, dean of St. Paul's Cathedral in Buffalo, for the train ride to Coventry.[92] We had to change trains in Oxford and had enough time for a quick look-through before hurrying back to the train station.

When the train arrived we realized that our mountain of baggage was on the other side of the tracks. After a frenzied dash with a porter, we were on our way again through the lovely green countryside.

Each couple was assigned to a host, and ours was a delightful couple

---

92. The Right Reverend Harold Barrett Robinson was dean of St. Paul's Cathedral of the Diocese of Western New York until he was elected bishop coadjutor in October 1967 at the diocesan General Convention. He was consecrated bishop coadjutor on February 24, 1968. Bishop Robinson became Western New York's eighth bishop when the Right Reverend Lauriston Livingston Scaife retired on June 1, 1970.

named John and Jessie Keyser. They lived in the nearby village of Stoneleigh. On the last Sunday after a glorious liturgy in the cathedral, I preached at Evensong in the little Church of St. Mary the Virgin in Stoneleigh. Lord and Lady Leigh entertained us at tea afterward in their great manor house. It had been so cold in the church that the tea was most welcome.

As I may have said earlier, the Deans' Conference was an excellent one and always well-attended by the deans in the United States, Canada, and parts of the Anglican Communion. Of course, a number of deans from England joined us at Coventry.[93]

We were fortunate in being at Coventry when Willy Brandt spoke at the opening of the JFK House—a youth hostel—on April 24, 1965. Our hosts, who had lived through World War II, were not convinced that he should be the speaker. But I think they were of a different mind after his address.

No German can ignore the fact that his country is linked with the destruction of Coventry... the word "Coventry" symbolizes the results of hatred and ruthless warfare. And yet, miraculously, Coventry has become also the symbol for the promise of a better world.... A new spirit has spread from Coventry. It is a spirit that strengthens confidence in the better qualities of the human being, and in the chances for a life of freedom and happiness. The world needs this kind of Spirit. Today, we know that it would be technically possible to solve the material problems of the world, of the nations, of the human race. Science and technology make reasonable solutions possible—*but the problem is to mobilize the spiritual power for the solutions of our difficulties.*

93. From the Archives of the Episcopal Church, April 7, 1965: "Deans to Meet in Coventry. More than 50 deans of American Cathedrals, along with several of their counterparts from Commonwealth countries, were to explore how the church of today can prepare for tomorrow at a Deans' Conference to be held at Coventry Cathedral April 20–27. Special events include the dedication of John Kennedy House, the new Cathedral Youth Hostel."

In his opening remarks, he reminded them that his cathedral in Dresden was also bombed into rubble.

On November 14, 1940, Coventry was firebombed by the Luftwaffe. No other English cathedral received such a bombing.

Behind the ruined altar of the old cathedral are the words, "Father, Forgive."

In the nave of the rebuilt Cathedral, engraved on the floor as one enters, are the words, "To the glory of God, this Cathedral Burnt." This was the theme of the entire rebuilding and the dynamic programs that flowed from its new life. Graham Sutherland[94] had executed an enormous tapestry in green for the west end, depicting a Christ with the world between his knees, and the architects had designed the new stained-glass windows on each side of the nave so that you see them as you return from receiving communion. The east end, looking out into the ruins of the old cathedral, was clear glass. Crosses made from the nails that had held the roof of the old cathedral were sold around the world, bringing the message of reconciliation and new life. The cross on the altar is made out of the same nails.

Speaking of new life, each morning during our sessions in the cathedral, at eleven, "elevensies" were served in the undercroft (gin, sherry, and scotch—neat!). We also toured local industries, housing estates, the Cotswolds, and Stratford-upon-Avon, where we had an evening of Shakespeare.

After Coventry, we toured Cambridge, Scotland, and Ireland, heading home on May 11, missing the Kentucky Derby.

Bishop Marmion, his canon Herb Donovan, and I attended a "group experience" in Bethel, Maine, for bishops, deans, and canons to the ordinary. On the free weekend, the three of us drove to the coast and spent

94. Graham Vivian Sutherland, OM (August 24, 1903–February 17, 1980) was an English artist, notable for glass, fabrics, prints, and portraits. His work is much inspired by landscape and religion, and he designed the tapestry for the rebuilt Coventry Cathedral. He was an official war artist in World War II.

one afternoon with one of the great old liberals, Bishop Will Scarlet,[95] retired from Missouri. He returned to Castine, Maine, and his house literally hangs out over the ocean. Bill Creighton, bishop of Washington, DC, was there at Bethel with his team and would later be "my bishop" when I went to St. Alban's.[96] Our team benefited greatly from the Bethel experience, and that became a help in the things we were trying to do together at our cathedral.

Gresh Marmion was one of the most conscientious people I have ever known. His lifestyle was simple, and he was, to a fault, fair to everyone to the extent that he would take a phone call from one of his clergy who

Brass lobster.

fought him on every issue while I would be trying to talk about cathedral business. His only expletive was "Gol durn." When we were in Maine, he and Herb and I were feasting on lobster one night and Gresh said, "Gol durn, Bob, is there anything you like better than lobster?" I thought for a second and said, "Yes, sex." I'm not sure whether he laughed or not, but later when I turned forty, Joyce gave me a brass lobster and a note, "Now, lobster is number one!" I did manage to laugh.

Shortly after moving to Louisville, my friend Hendree Milward invited me to be his partner at the annual Idle Hour Country Club Member-Guest Golf Tournament. We accepted with pleasure and arrived at the

95. The Right Reverend William Scarlett (1883–1973) was born in Columbus, Ohio, graduated from Harvard University in 1905, and attended the Episcopal Theological School in Cambridge, Massachusetts, receiving his degree four years later. In 1911 he was called to become dean of Trinity Cathedral in Phoenix, Arizona, a position he held for eleven years. Scarlett began his service as dean of Christ Cathedral in St. Louis in 1922 until his election as bishop coadjutor of Missouri eight years later and bishop in 1933. As bishop of Missouri and a tireless crusader for social reform, Scarlett committed the resources of the diocese to helping those left jobless and homeless by the Great Depression.

96. The Right Reverend William Forman Creighton (1909–1987) was the fifth bishop of the Diocese of Washington in the Episcopal Church in the United States of America.

Milwards' Thursday morning prior to playing a practice round. They had a Bloody Mary party for the group that would be playing, and it was good to see old friends, talk golf, and catch up on Lexington news.

I was talking with someone on my left at the table, and Joyce was talking with Hendree and Jane. I overheard Hendree say, "After Mother died, I moved her breakfront here into our dining room." I let that go on by, but then he said, "Our children took a lot of her furniture." And with that, I stopped the conversation and said, "Hendree, I'm so sorry to hear of your mother's death. Even though we're only seventy-five miles away we're out of touch. Your mother was one of my mother's best friends and was a loyal and active parishioner while I was rector. I certainly would have called you and would have come to her funeral."

Hendree looked confused and then, with the whole table now giving their attention, he said, "Bob, you buried her!"

Indeed, I had buried her while I was still rector, and I remembered Hendree's gratitude at the time. There was a brief silence at the table and then Hendree saved the day by laughing. I thought the weekend was ruined, but Hendree saved it—and me.

One final note:

It turned out Hendree was not feeling up to par and had asked Angus McDonald to take his place as my partner. Whether it was the relief from my embarrassment, or just plain luck, Angus and I finished tied with another twosome for first place.

On the first extra hole, a long par-4, my second shot made the green and rolled about ten feet from the hole. Angus and our opponents were off the green and had fairly easy chips and putts (I was still closer to the hole) and one opponent dropped his putt in for a par.

Almost all of the participants and the rather large gallery had followed us to the final hole. Most of them had drinks in their hands and were loud and boisterous. It was also getting dark. They surrounded the green while Angus and I studied my putt. Finally, I was over the ball and just as I began

A beam landed right on me.

my final routine, the sun broke through the haze and a beam landed right on me.

A murmur went up from the crowd, and I took a deep breath and holed the winning putt. A cheer went up, and I think several people were converted on the spot!

I tried to give the silver julep cup to Hendree, but he would not take it. In fact, for years afterward, when I saw him, he would say, "Bob, you buried her!" I chose to think he meant the putt.

The cathedral became the home for Louisville's Actors' Theatre for their rehearsals and for the Louisville Bach Society. Both performed in the cathedral from time to time, and on one Sunday, I had the Actors' Theatre perform the last act of Arthur Miller's powerful play *The Crucible* in place of the sermon. The Carriage House Players, another group of actors, did *Hamlet* in the cathedral at 8:00 p.m. on a weekday with a big crowd filling the nave. As always, I received some flak from some of the soreheads, but the performance of *The Crucible* even was noted by *LIFE* magazine. I was asked to be on the Planned Parenthood board (where several of the women on the board were pregnant!), which put me in touch with some of the younger doers, and I continued as chair of the Kentucky Human Rights Commission and as a board member of Actors' Theatre. We got in the Louisville Country Club, where my father had been an out-of-town member, and that also broadened my contacts with Louisville's leaders.

The Louisville County Club was for whites only, and there came a time when the federal government considered denying liquor licenses to segregated clubs. I played golf with a regular foursome made up of friends of long standing, one of whom was a prominent lawyer and a graduate of the University of Virginia.

As we were waiting to tee off one Saturday morning, we were discussing the federal government situation, and I said, "Why don't you let me recruit some black families who would be good additions to our club, and then we wouldn't lose our liquor license?" The UVA graduate thought for a second and replied, "I wouldn't be opposed to that. What I don't want in our club are any God-damned Roman Catholics!"

The integration never occurred while I was in Louisville, but now the Louisville Country Club has a large number of very fine Roman Catholics, and I believe they have integrated and still have a liquor license.

Barry Bingham Jr. asked me to be on a weekly radio program, *The Moral Side of the News*, on WHAS.[97] John Claypool,[98] then a Baptist and pastor of the huge Crescent Hill Baptist Church; a Roman Catholic; and a rabbi filled out the panel. We met at the station each Tuesday for lunch and looked at the paper to decide on an issue. Sometimes the "issue" would run for several sessions. The program was deadly dull; you had to be caught in your car to hear it. We taped it on Tuesday, and I think it came on Wednesdays at 10 p.m. The good side was that the four of us became good friends, especially John Claypool and I.

John was one of the few clergy actually involved in civil rights issues, and during the time we were together, his daughter became gravely ill and died. Later, John wrote a book describing those days, his divorce, and his coming into the Episcopal ministry, for which he gave me credit

---

97. *The Moral Side of the News* is one of the longest running public affairs programs in American broadcast history. Its first broadcast was May 14, 1952, on 840 WHAS and WHAS-TV. Each week, a panel of clergy from diverse faiths discuss current affairs and give their unique moral perspectives.

98. John Rowan Claypool began his career as a Southern Baptist pastor and theologian, but left the Baptist faith and was ordained an Episcopal priest in 1986. He served at St. Luke's in Birmingham, Alabama.

for helping him decide to change.[99] As I remember it, I had said to him once during the stressful days that I wish he could (as I did) go home for a drink at the end of the day. In his book, he wrote that my availability to the sacrament made a great difference and what he wished for was that Holy Communion that I had on a regular basis!

In a book of remembrances about John,[100] the Reverend Daniel Paul Matthews,[101] former rector of Trinity Church in New York and now retired, wrote,

> Bob Estill knew John Claypool well when they were both serving parishes in Louisville. They had joined a small group of clergy from various denominations who met regularly. In one of those meetings John was talking about himself and shared some of his struggles. Bob Estill, then Dean of the Episcopal Cathedral, interrupted him and said, "John, it seems to me like you are trying to earn your own salvation; you are never going to earn it and besides, haven't you heard what grace is all about?" With that statement Claypool left the meeting and began to ponder in his heart what his friend had said. It began to change the way he thought about himself, his ministry and his preaching.

Dan concludes, "I always have wondered what effect that brief confrontation had not only on John's soul at the time but on his eventual move from the Southern Baptist tradition to that of the Episcopal Church. Estill and Claypool were great friends and remained so for their entire lives."

---

99. *Mending the Heart* (Cambridge, Massachusetts: Cowley Press, 1999).

100. *Life Is Gift: Remembrances of John Rowan Claypool IV*, ed. Carolyn Sloss Ratlift (Birmingham, Alabama: St. Luke's Episcopal Church, 2015).

101. The Reverend Dr. Daniel Paul Matthews, rector emeritus of historic Trinity Church, Wall Street, was born in Chicago. During grammar school years, he moved to Western North Carolina. He spent the first twenty years of his ministry as a priest in parishes in Tennessee.

John had gone through the Continuing Education Program at VTS when Bennett Sims was director and was trained at the Episcopal Theological Seminary of the Southwest in Austin, Texas, in 1985, so he was no stranger to the Episcopal Church. After his ordination, he was in great demand as a preacher and ended up as rector of St. Luke's Episcopal Church in Birmingham, Alabama. Sadly, his ministry was cut short by cancer, and he died much too soon at seventy-four.

One night we were talking about racial issues, and I said, in the context of the whole topic, that Happy Chandler, when he was commissioner of Major League Baseball, wrongly claimed that he was responsible for recruiting Jackie Robinson as the first black player. The program was hardly off the air before my phone rang and it was Happy Chandler, saying, "Bobby, how could you have said that about me? I *was* the one who did that." Governor Chandler had alternated calling me "Bobby" (my father was doctor to the Chandler children) and since ordination, "Father Estill." I was amazed that he would have been up, let alone listening to *The Moral Side of the News*! I can't remember the outcome of our conversation, but I do remember that Emmet Milward; William Courtney, president of First National Bank; and one or two others met regularly with Governor Chandler in Lexington at the Idle Hour Country Club and called all the shots with regard to the issues. Fred Wachs, editor of the *Lexington Herald Leader*—and later my cousin Alex Campbell and his business mentor, Bill (W. T.) Young, also joined the group.

While in Washington at the annual Church and City Conference, I roomed with Jack Woodard, who described a program of church-sponsored housing for the poor. He put me in touch with Roger Schafer, a Baltimore architect who had helped me in Lexington with our new building, and who advises and helps churches plan for such.

We set up a committee of the chapter with Bishop Marmion's full support, filled out stacks of paper, and had the strong leadership of the Baltimore architect who had helped us in Lexington with our new building. It got down to the final signing, only to have the chapter (in a narrow vote) turn the whole thing down! It was the lowest point of my tenure as dean. The project, almost 100 percent financed by a government grant, would have put a high-rise for low-income people right behind the cathedral on our parking lot.

On a happier note, Bill and Lee Brettmann had come aboard our clergy staff, and Herb and Mary Donovan had joined the bishop's staff. Parke Street and Ann, whom I had inherited from Dean Wicker's day, left to go to Washington, DC. Parke had been an excellent colleague and had supported all that we were trying to do.

Bill Brettmann (who was to become a close friend and whom I brought to North Carolina when I became bishop) got right to work, and we started the Louisville Episcopal Action Program (LEAP) based on Psalm 18:30: "With you I will break down an enclosure, with the help of my God I will leap any wall."

We leaped over the walls of the cathedral and established a storefront outpost for street people and the inner-city people living nearby. When I first came to Louisville, our cathedral garden had a gate with the words, "Enter into His Gates with Joy." Underneath was a big lock and chain with the words, "Keep Out"!

Herb Donovan became and remains a close friend as well, and was very supportive in his role as canon to the ordinary.

At lunch one day I bemoaned the fact that my two o'clock appointment was an elderly member of the cathedral who made almost weekly appointments to talk about the cathedral garden (which committee he headed). It was not much of a garden, although now that we had unlocked the gate—"Enter into His Gates with Joy!"—it had become a good place for many street people to pee.

My visitor was very deaf, and he would talk on and on for the full hour as I tried, sometimes unsuccessfully, to stay awake.

During this visit, suddenly, a voice "from above" said, "Fall on your knees, this is God speaking!" That woke me up, though. Thanks be to

God, my visitor's deafness kept him from hearing the message—although the voice came through loud and clear. We went on with our meeting, and after he left, I discovered that Herb Donovan (whose office was on the floor above mine) had dropped a speaker down through my window and was "the voice of God."

"Fall on your knees! This is GOD!"

When we stopped laughing, we agreed that this had been over the top and that it wouldn't happen again.

It apparently didn't faze my cathedral gardener, who made an appointment for the following week as he left the office.

We now had an excellent team with a supportive bishop and a core of lay leadership behind what we were trying to do.

My role as chair of the Kentucky Human Rights Commission put me in the public eye, and the results of that caused controversy among the old guard at the cathedral and the racists who read the papers, watched on TV, and heard our pronouncements from meetings and sometimes from the pulpit.

One lapsed parishioner at the cathedral began sending me clippings from a right-wing newspaper in Nashville, along with comments—sometimes lewd—of his own. I would get at least one a day, both at home and at the office. I tried to call on him, only to find he would not open the door (I saw him inside), and for a while I tried to answer his letters. His wife was a lovely person and was active at the cathedral and apologetic regarding his actions. I finally began returning his missives unopened, which caused him to go to postcards. Sometimes he would paste racist pictures or cartoons to the cards.

Joyce finally got tired of this and also pointed out that it was upsetting the children when they saw the hate mail at home. She called the Postal Service and registered a complaint. The upshot was that a postal official called on the man, told him he was violating the law, and that he must cease and desist. The man called Joyce and said he was discontinuing the mail but that there may be one or two already posted. That ended his harassment, and I gave three cheers for Joyce. She had saved a shoebox full of his postcards and showed it to the postal authority.

We also got quite a few phone calls, mostly anonymous and often taunting. One, in the middle of the night, said, "Don't start your car in the morning, you n— lover." I embellished on that by saying in talks about civil rights that the next morning while shaving, I called to Joyce and said, "Honey, will you start the car so it'll be warm when I take the children to school?"

On January 27, 1966, I joined Governor Breathitt and other members of the Kentucky Human Rights Commission for TV coverage of the governor signing the state's public accommodations legislation. It was covered by the national press as well as our Kentucky papers and TV stations and was, symbolically, the culmination of my years as chairman of the commission. This legislation was also the first of its kind in any southern state. Dr. Martin Luther King Jr. was there for the signing.

In June 1966 I was Kentucky's representative at a national conference called by President Lyndon Johnson, the White House Conference on Civil Rights.

The White House Conference on Civil Rights was held June 1 and 2, 1966. The aim of the conference was built on the momentum of the Civil Rights Act of 1964 and the Voting Rights Act of 1965 in addressing discrimination against African Americans. The four areas of discussion were housing, economic security, education, and the administration of justice.

President Lyndon Johnson had promised this conference in his commencement address at Howard University the year before. Like that address, the conference was named "To Fulfill These Rights." The title was a play on "To Secure These Rights," a report issued by President Truman's civil rights commission in 1947. There were over twenty-four hundred participants, representing all the major civil rights groups except the Student Nonviolent Coordinating Committee (SNCC), which boycotted the conference. Out of the conference came a hundred-page report that called for "legislation to ban racial discrimination in housing and the administration of criminal justice, and...suggested increased federal spending to improve the quality of housing and education."

It was mostly talk, but the president came to the banquet and gave a very good address. He did more than any president to influence Congress to consider civil rights legislation. He was well received by those in attendance.

On the way home I met and had lunch with Amory Houghton, who came through Louisville. We ate at Stanford Field, and he wanted to know if I'd be interested in being rector of his parish in upper New York State. I think I discouraged him, though I said that my feeling was that if a call came, I would consider it along with the call to stay put. Houghton ran the Steuben Glass Company.

I was asked to preach the Baccalaureate Sermon at the University of Kentucky (my alma mater) on May 8 and had a good visit with my friends and former parishioners, Jack and Rose Oswald, he being the president of UK.

Helen went to camp in North Carolina (Brevard) and while there her cabin mate pierced her ears for her. We had told her she could only have it done by a doctor! This was her first time away from home, and she took to it very well. Meanwhile, Elizabeth celebrated her summer vacation by having a hernia operation at the Norton. She seemed to be one accident-prone child. So far, she'd had a bean stuck up her nose, eaten a disinfectant bar out of the diaper bin (with stomach pumped and an emergency ride to the hospital via a police car), and battled a bout with dehydration after a bad cold—that time in the Baptist Hospital while we were in Lexington. She always came through with flying colors.

Bobby, on the other hand, was into all sports and seemed to fare well with a minimal amount of scrapes and bruises. I tried to have time with the family by taking a day off each week and by arranging the summer by leading conferences at Kanuga; Camp Gailor Maxon in Monteagle, Tennessee; and at Sewanee. The whole family (and dog!) went, and we had fun going and coming with overnights on the road.

It happened one time when we were driving home over the mountains from Kanuga's Family Conference. At the conference, those of us on the staff were aware that one of the clergy and one of the wives of another clergy were getting pretty thick. We were packed into our old station wagon, it was raining, and the mountains were covered in a light fog. Suddenly, out of the silence, Bobby said, "I saw Mr. ——kissing Mrs. ——! I almost drove into the ditch, but hastened to say, "Well, everyone was hugging and kissing and saying good-bye." But Bobby was insistent. "No! I saw him lying on her over on the trail across the lake!" A year or so later, we heard that Mrs. —— had divorced her husband, but the affair with Mr. ——at Kanuga had not gone any further. In fact, that Mr. —— went back to his wife and five children.

Tom Smythe had called me to say he had put my name in for suffragan bishop of North Carolina at the diocesan convention in 1967. As usual, I said I would consider it if elected, although the word was that they were already going to elect the one whom Tom Fraser favored. The word too was that Tom Fraser would be very difficult to work with.[102] Tom Smythe called back to give me that information, and sure enough, Moultrie Moore was elected at the diocesan convention on February 1, 1967.[103]

I began my fourth year at the cathedral on that date.

---

102. Thomas Augustus Fraser (1915–1989), bishop coadjutor of North Carolina, 1960–1965; bishop of North Carolina, 1965–1983.

103. William Moultrie Moore (1916–1998), bishop suffragan of North Carolina, 1967–1975; bishop of Easton, Maryland, 1975–1983.

The year 1967 was important for me in that my duties with the state Human Rights Commission ended, but I had been appointed by John Hines,[104] the presiding bishop of the Episcopal Church, to the very important Standing Liturgical Commission. Their task was to present a "new" Prayer Book to the church as soon as possible. (It takes two successive General Conventions to adopt a new Prayer Book.) I believe Boone Porter, whose mother still lived in Louisville, nominated me.[105] He came to the cathedral when he was home and was always interested in the liturgical life and the changes we were making.

Being a member of the Standing Liturgical Commission would be a big and important job, but the chapter and Bishop Marmion approved, and I was off to Dallas for my first meeting.

I was appointed to the Kentucky Advisory Committee to the US Commission on Civil Rights and made chairman. The regional director was weak, and a lot of government red tape made much of the work ineffective. With these new credentials, several of us met with Governor Louie Nunn in hopes of his support for a state open housing law. He gave us a good bit of time but was cool toward sponsoring any civil rights legislation. I missed Bert Combs!

---

104. John Elbridge Hines (1910–1997) was a bishop in the Episcopal Church in the United States. When he was elected the twenty-second presiding bishop in 1965, at the age of fifty-four, he was the youngest person to hold that office, which he held until 1974.

105. Harry Boone Porter Jr. (January 10, 1923–June 5, 1999) was a priest and editor of *The Living Church* magazine. An alumnus of St. Paul's School (Concord, New Hampshire), he received his bachelor's degree from Yale University in 1947 and his STB from the Berkeley Divinity School in 1950. Porter was made deacon on April 12, 1950, and ordained to the priesthood on April 16, 1952. From 1950 until 1952, Porter was a fellow and tutor at the General Theological Seminary of the Episcopal Church, from which in 1952 he received an STM He earned his DPhil from Oxford University in 1954. He taught ecclesiastical history at Nashotah House, 1954–1960, and he was professor of liturgics at General Seminary from 1960 until 1970. He became editor of *The Living Church* magazine in 1977, retiring in 1990. In addition to many other responsibilities in the Episcopal Church, Porter served on the Standing Liturgical Commission from 1961 to 1976, and the General Board of Examining Chaplains from 1970 to 1982.

One of the benedictions in the Episcopal service that offers more inclusive language, is, I think especially fine. I use it whenever I can. "May the blessing of the God of Abraham and Sarah and of Jesus Christ, born of our sister Mary, and the Holy Spirit, who broods over creation as a mother over her children, be with you always.

On March 27, 1968, Joyce and I were in Washington, where I preached at St. John's Church, Lafayette Square. After the service, John Harper—an old friend from ETS days—and Barbie took us to lunch at the Cosmopolitan Club, where, among others, we saw Scotty Reston.[106]

Reston was one of my heroes, and I felt as though I should go over to his table (I did not) and thank him for all the sermon quotes I have gotten from his writings over the years. That very day, I had quoted him in my sermon as saying the political system is where a great deal of the hunger that young people have is being fed today. He wrote about the importance of honest discussion and the need to trust one another. He questioned whether political leaders were willing to risk everything, even defeat, so that we may begin to build that trust. Reston concluded by saying that it is already happening.

Sadly, in less than a month, on April 4, 1968, Dr. Martin Luther King Jr. was shot and killed in Memphis.

One of our friends and a civil rights advocate (and a member of the cathedral), Lukey Ward was there in that motel at the time.[107] The two

---

106. James Barrett Reston (1909–1995), nicknamed "Scotty," was an American journalist whose career spanned the mid-1930s to the early 1990s. He was associated for many years with the *New York Times*.

107. Lucretia "Lukey" Ward was a well-off white woman, who fought for equality in her hometown, Louisville, Kentucky, and in the rest of the South. She cofounded the Allied Organization for Civil Rights and the Louisville chapter of the Southern Christian

most mentioned marches that she was a part of were the march on Frankfort on March 4, 1964, in which Martin Luther King Jr. and J. Robinson were in attendance, as well as the march from Selma to Montgomery in March 1965. I also had been with Dr. King several times on various occasions and had marched with him in Frankfort in support of our legislation. His brother, A. D. Williams King, was a minister of the large Zion Baptist Church in Louisville and a friend and colleague. On one of Dr. King's visits I was invited to have dinner with him and a small group of Louisville people. His assassination represented a waste of talent and leadership for social justice and was far from Scotty Reston's hope for peaceful solutions to our problems.

A memorial service for MLK was held on the steps of the Jefferson County Courthouse, and I was one of only two white persons invited to speak. I tried to say that white racism killed Dr. King and that we white persons must take most of the blame when nonviolence fails. Riots were already breaking out in Washington, Detroit, and other cities.

For some time I had become convinced that Robert Kennedy would be the kind of president we needed. I volunteered to work for him in Indiana, which was having an early primary, and as often as I could, I would drive across the bridge, take off my collar, put on a tie and a Kennedy pin, and go from house to house, asking for support. They asked me to be responsible for that precinct, and I recruited Joan Bingham to work with me. She, the daughter-in-law of Barry Bingham,[108] was for

Leadership Conference.

108. George Barry Bingham Sr. (February 10, 1906–August 15, 1988) was the patriarch of a family that dominated local media in Louisville for several decades in the twentieth century. Bingham's family owned a cluster of influential media properties: the *Courier-Journal* and the *Louisville Times* newspapers, plus WHAS Radio and WHAS Television. The papers had been purchased by his father, Colonel Robert Worth Bingham, using proceeds from an inheritance left by his second wife, Mary Lily Kenan Flagler, herself the widow of railroad magnate Henry Flagler.

Adlai Stevenson II.[109] In addition to the house-to-house calls, we spoke at coffee klatsches and to anyone else who would listen. Joan had not made house calls, so I made one with her to demonstrate the routine. I rang a bell, a woman came to the door, and I gave my pitch and asked for her support. Joan seemed impressed, but as I finished, the woman said, "I live in Louisville, and I'm here to clean the house!" There went one vote.

Derby weekend gave us a chance to meet a lot of interesting people. Joan brought several members of Ted Kennedy's staff to the Derby, and I was able to have a long talk with Hugh Haynie,[110] the *Courier-Journal* cartoonist, who was very much for RFK. Hugh had sent me a copy of his marvelous cartoon after MLK's death with an inscription on it.

Tom Johnston, Joe Graves's cousin, had gone to work as a volunteer for RFK when he ran for senator of New York. He did such a good job that RFK asked him to be on his staff, and Tom came to New Albany with RFK on one of his whistle-stops. Tom took me to see and meet RFK, who was very gracious, thanked me for working for him, and asked, "How's it going?" All I could do was stammer, "Better!" I later had a chance to be with him at Barry Bingham's. RFK had been in the Kentucky mountains exploring poverty and meeting with the mountain people, many of whom were coal miners.

---

109. Adlai Ewing Stevenson II (February 5, 1900–July 14, 1965) served as the thirty-first governor of Illinois and received the Democratic Party's nomination for president in 1952 even though he had not campaigned in the primaries. Stevenson was defeated in a landslide by Republican Dwight D. Eisenhower in the 1952 presidential election. In 1956 he was again the Democratic presidential nominee against Eisenhower, but was defeated in an even bigger landslide. He sought the Democratic presidential nomination for a third time in the election of 1960, but was defeated by Senator John F. Kennedy of Massachusetts. After his election, President Kennedy appointed Stevenson as the US ambassador to the United Nations. He served from 1961 to 1965, dying on July 14, 1965, in London after suffering a heart attack.

110. Hugh Smith Haynie (February 6, 1927–November 30, 1999) was an American political cartoonist. In 1958 Barry Bingham Sr. hired Haynie to serve as a political cartoonist for the *Louisville Courier-Journal*, a position he held until his retirement in 1996, after which he was retained as an emeritus. His cartooning style was clean lined, heavily inked, and somewhat reminiscent of Al Capp. Haynie regularly penned his wife's name, Lois, into his drawings.

For Kennedy, February 14, 1968, started with a drive to Whitesburg and an early morning speech on the Letcher County Courthouse steps, followed by a formal hearing at the Fleming-Neon High School gym, visits with families in Hemphill and Haymond, and a speech at the Fiscal Court and Library in Prestonsburg—and ended with Kennedy being flown off in the governor's plane to attend a dinner in his honor at the home of the Binghams in Louisville, then owners and publishers of the influential *Courier-Journal*.

Joe Graves and I were among about ten guests, plus the Binghams, Tom Johnston, and RFK. As we dived into thick filet mignons, RFK told us in graphic detail about his visit. If I had not been for him before, that evening was overwhelming, and it gave all of us a renewed enthusiasm for his candidacy. We actually won our precinct, and RFK won Indiana on May 7, 1968.

A lot of able people were working for RFK, and this was the first time I had met Yann Weymouth,[III] Bonnie Bergeron, and for that matter, RFK. After the Indiana election, Tom Johnston promised to send me a picture of the senator and also gave me a Kennedy PT Boat tie pin, which I wore with pride. Later, as over a thousand poor people passed through Louisville on the way to Washington for a great demonstration, I also met Muhammad Ali, a Louisville native, who spoke to the crowd at the Kentucky Exposition Center.

Part of the strange worlds I live in came with an invitation to be the speaker at the Diocesan Women's Conference of the Diocese of Georgia—at Sea Island, Georgia. Joyce and I flew in and were soon asleep at the King and Prince Hotel with the warm ocean breaking outside our window.

Back in Louisville I was watching TV when a riot was announced in

---

III. After graduating from Harvard University in 1963 and MIT in 1966, Yann Weymouth served early in his career as chief of design for I. M. Pei on the National Gallery of Art East Wing, Washington, DC, and as the chief of design for I. M. Pei on the Grand Louvre Project, Paris, France.

the West End.[112] I hurried to make some calls and spent the night manning phones at the downtown YMCA, dispelling rumors and helping people respond to needs.

On June 4, 1968, I had stayed up late to watch RFK win the California primary. It was around midnight on the day of California's Democratic presidential primary when Senator Robert Kennedy and his supporters learned that he had won. Celebrating his victory at LA's Ambassador Hotel, RFK concluded his last speech with these words: "Now it's on to Chicago, and let's win there." While the crowd was still celebrating and chanting his name, people learned that RFK had been shot. Joy turned to confusion as people at the podium asked for a doctor. He died twenty-three hours later on June 5.

The bottom seemed to have dropped out of everything—again. We held a memorial service in the cathedral with some of the Clergy for

---

112. In Louisville on May 27, 1968, a group of four hundred people, mostly African Americans, gathered at Twenty-Eighth and Greenwood Streets, in the Parkland neighborhood. The crowd was protesting the possible reinstatement of a white officer who had been suspended for beating a black man some weeks earlier. Several community leaders arrived and told the crowd that no decision had been reached, and by 8:30, the crowd began to disperse. However, rumors that turned out to be untrue were spread that Student Nonviolent Coordinating Committee speaker Stokely Carmichael's plane to Louisville was being intentionally delayed by whites. After bottles were thrown by the crowd, the crowd became unruly and police were called. However, the small and unprepared police response simply upset the crowd more, which continued to grow. The police, including a captain who was hit in the face by a bottle, retreated, leaving behind a patrol car, which was turned over and burned. By midnight, rioters had looted stores as far east as Fourth Street, overturned cars, and started fires. Within an hour, Mayor Kenneth A. Schmied requested seven hundred Kentucky National Guard troops and established a city-wide curfew. Violence and vandalism continued to rage the next day, but had subdued somewhat by May 29. Business owners began to return, although troops remained until June 4. Police made 472 arrests related to the riots. Two black teenage rioters had died, and two hundred thousand dollars in damage had been done. The disturbances had a longer-lasting effect. The riot would have effects that shaped the image that whites would hold of Louisville's West End, that it was predominantly black (Kenneth H. Williams, "'Oh Baby ... It's Really Happening': The Louisville Race Riot of 1968," *Register of the Kentucky Historical Society* 3 [1988]: 57–58).

Kennedy taking part. I read some excerpts from *To Seek a Newer World*, material taken from the public speeches of Senator Robert F. Kennedy—especially Alfred Lord Tennyson's "Ulysses":

> *... Come, my friends,*
> *'Tis not too late to seek a newer world.*
> *Push off, and sitting well in order smite*
> *The sounding furrows; for my purpose holds*
> *To sail beyond the sunset, and the baths*
> *Of all the western stars, until I die.*
> *It may be that the gulfs will wash us down:*
> *It may be we shall touch the Happy Isles,*
> *And see the great Achilles, whom we knew.*

When I got home, I had a phone call from Washington asking me to come to the funeral in New York City, but I couldn't go. A wire came at home asking the same thing, signed, "The Kennedy Family." I wrote in my journal, "I wish I could go—but my job is here. Yet my life will never be quite the same again." The autographed picture had just come, and I hung it below the one I had of JFK.

William V. Shannon, a writer for the *New York Times*, wrote an article about the Kennedys, "Said Robert Kennedy, 'Maybe We're All Doomed Anyway,'" where he described the Kennedy family as rationalists. He said that they challenged life and went above and beyond any limits they faced.

RFK's theology reaches me when I despair as I did at his death. He wrote that we must acknowledge that human beings and our accomplishments are fragile, but that life should be lived with hope. RFK believed that we all have a purpose and have to make some contribution to society. There are injustices all around us and we need to speak against them and do something to change them. RFK wanted to make a positive impact on society and to take a stand against the unfairness in our country and around the world.

May he rest in peace and may light perpetual shine upon him.

Christopher Buckley, in *Losing Mum and Pup*,[113] writes: "Right after JFK was shot, Mary McGrory[114] said to Daniel Patrick Moynihan, 'We'll never laugh again,' to which Moynihan responded, 'Mary, we'll laugh again, but we'll never be young again.'"

---

113. Christopher Buckley, *Losing Mum and Pup: A Memoir* (New York: Twelve, 2009), remembers the loss of his parents, Bill and Pat Buckley, who died within eleven months of each other in 2007 and 2008.

Quogue, Long Island, New York

At the meetings of the Standing Liturgical Commission, Jonathan Sherman, bishop of Long Island, and I both liked a cigar after dinner. The SLC usually met again after dinner, and they quickly banished Bishop Sherman and me to the outside with our stogies. That was one of the pivotal times in my life because Bishop Sherman said to me one night, "Estill! Where is your summer place?" I admitted that we didn't have a summer place and he said, "How would you like to take charge of one of my summer chapels on Long Island for a month?" I nearly bit my cigar in half and answered, "I'd love it! Where is it?"

It turned out to be the Church of the Atonement in Quogue. Later that year we were at a party in Louisville and someone asked, "Bob! Where is your summer place?" I spoke up with pride and said, "Quoog [*sic*], New York." A man's voice behind me said, "That's pronounced 'Quogue'!" He was Henry Shroeder, who worked and lived in Louisville but grew up in Quogue. His mother still lived there year round and turned out to be the main pillar of the little chapel. In fact, her house was only a short distance from the church and bore the name Kirklea (which means near the church). She was one of the first persons I met, and she was standing on the altar in her stocking feet, dusting the stained-glass window behind the altar.

Not only did Quogue become our summer place but we soon moved from July to August and stayed through Labor Day. After thirty-five years, I felt it was time to retire before someone asked me, "When?" On the last Sunday at the offertory, the convener (the equivalent of senior warden of a vestry) came forward and presented Joyce and me with a key (on a Chanel key ring) to the lovely house they provided the summer clergy, with the standing invitation for us to visit each year after the church closed after Labor Day.

After several years I was invited to come up early or stay after Labor Day (we chose to come a week before Quogue) and be the preacher at the Dune Church, St. Andrews, the summer chapel at Southampton situated on the ocean and the site of a former Coast Guard station.

St. Andrew's Dune Church has a departure prayer:

Heavenly Father, grant that we who worship together where glorious dunes meet your unfathomable sea, be always mindful of your gifts to us of material beauty, always respectful of your great power and mystery. As you have long dispatched rescuers to go forth from this Station armed through prayers with thy strength, send forth today this congregation to aid all those who founder, that our lives, infused with the spirit, will bear witness to the blessings of this community and bring glory to thy name, through Jesus Christ, our Lord. Amen.

Except for Mrs. Shroeder, we didn't know anyone at Quogue, but on one of the first weekends, Joyce and I were walking on the beach and we passed a couple and said, "Hello." We walked on a few steps until it dawned on me—and apparently on him—that we knew each other. It was Edwin Wilson, a classmate from EHS days. Ed was now the drama critic for the *Wall Street Journal* and taught at Hunter College in NYC. We became fast friends, and our friendship included visits to their July summer place in Linville, North Carolina, and of course, seeing them for the month at Quogue. They met us in England during one of our sabbaticals, and we stayed with friends of theirs in their country home and went to the Royal Ascot races.

Tailgating at the Royal Ascot.

We dressed in rental finery, which I thought made me look like Rex Harrison. When the pictures came back, I realized I looked more like Jackie Gleason!

Our month at Quogue opened up regular trips on the Hampton Jitney into the city, and for over twenty years, a week or so upstate at Saratoga. "Saratoga in August," as they say in their brochures, "is the place to be." My day began at dawn with a trip to the track to watch the morning workouts, then breakfast at one of the traditional eateries, and back to the hotel to freshen up and sit on the porch, studying the *Daily Racing Form*. Around noon, it was back to the track and the clubhouse, where you could reserve a table for lunch and watch the races the rest of the afternoon. My honorary membership in the Thoroughbred Club of America came in handy and gave me free entrance.

After the races it was back to the hotel for a shower and a change of clothes for the polo matches. They took place in the fields below Skidmore College in the late afternoon—as the Prayer Book puts it, "as the shadows lengthen and the busy world is hushed." On Wednesday nights, the Philadelphia Symphony performed in the outdoor theatre.

On one of my Saratoga trips I took alone, I spent the night in the city seeing *On the Town* in Central Park with Chic and Ed Wilson. We sat right in front of Jessye Norman, who, as I reminded her, had received an honorary degree at the same time I did from the University of the South at Sewanee.[115] We had lunch together after the ceremony and talked opera. I still think she is my favorite Wagnerian.

The next morning I took the train to Saratoga and looked forward to finishing John Irving's great novel, *The World According to Garp*. I had a window seat, and a man sat next to me on the aisle. After a brief "hello," I buried myself in the book. He seemed to want to talk, but I ignored him and read on. We shared a taxi at Saratoga, and I finished *Garp* just as we got to my hotel. On Wednesday night, the Philadelphia Orchestra was doing an all–Aaron Copeland program, with Aaron Copeland conducting. When the lights in the pavilion dimmed and the conductor came on the stage, it was the man who had been sitting next to me on the train—Aaron Copeland! I had missed a rare opportunity to talk with one of the great composers of all time. Since then I've used the story in a sermon illustrating how we often miss the great moments God gives us by our own blindness or at least by sticking to our own agenda.

In the evenings we would go to the trotting horse track for a night of harness races and dinner at a table overlooking the track. What a great day, if you love horses and racing!

Various family members and friends accompanied me to Saratoga, but before long, most of them had too much horse and left me to go alone.

For several summers, Alan O'Neil, a friend from seminary days who had a church in Hartford, would meet me at the Rip Van Dam Hotel and stay in a separate room. After one of the last summers when I was checking in at the desk, one of the old ladies who ran the place and knew me as a regular said in a seductive voice, "Mr. O'Neil is waiting for you upstairs!" I think she thought we were gay.

---

115. The seven who received honorary degrees from the University of the South on May 20, 1984, apart from Jessye Norman and myself were the Right Reverend B. Sidney Sanders, John M. Templeton, the Reverend Thomas D. Bowers, Loren B. Mead, and Andrew F. Brimmer.

"What's that thing he's putting around its stomach?"

Allen didn't know horses, but he was good company. Another friend from Quogue, John Griffith, came with me several times, and we would drive, stop along the Taconic State Parkway, and eat delicious egg salad sandwiches prepared by Jane, his wife. John knew even less than Allen about horses and would often read some financial paper at the clubhouse table. I took him with me into the paddock one time and told him to walk right by the guard at the gate like he was an owner. My Thoroughbred Club pin got me in. We were standing watching in silence as a groom was saddling a two-year-old when John broke the silence and in a loud voice asked, "What's that thing he's putting around its stomach?" I thought we might be escorted out. But we were, thankfully, able to move off into the crowd around another horse.

Another year when Joyce and our Westie, Duncan, were along, we took a walk and passed John Gaines's house—he being an old friend from Kentucky and the one who first envisioned the Breeders' Cup. He was on the porch and asked us up for a morning coffee. Duncan seemed to love the Gaines's big Victorian house and ran in the door and upstairs. As we were about to leave, I called him and put him back on his leash and we left. Later, at a party, John admitted that Duncan had left a big dump in their bedroom. Since John's fortune was made in Gaines dog food, he took it very well and Duncan continued to eat Gaines.

My cousin-in-law Alex Campbell and one of his partners, W. T. Young, were regulars at the sales and the races, and once they asked me if I'd like to fly down to Monmouth Park for the fifth race in their private jet. I declined. W. T. Young's horses did quite well. He especially benefited from the success of his home-bred stud, Storm Cat,[116] a Northern Dancer grandson and a leading sire. Storm Cat began his stallion career at a thirty-thousand-dollar fee and by 2002, it was five hundred thousand dollars. Overbrook Farm became famous, and Storm Cat was pensioned in 2008. Tabasco Cat won the Preakness and Belmont Stakes in 1994. Bill Young Jr. announced in 2009 that he would disperse Overbrook's horses (two hundred or so) at the Keeneland September sales. Bill Young's Timber Country won the Preakness in 1995, Grindstone won the Derby in 1996, and Editor's Note took the Belmont in 1996. Alex's horses never did as well. One of his last ones he named Awesome Ashley after Ashley Judd, the actress, an ardent UK fan. Bill Young died in 2004 of an apparent heart attack.

After several summers of seeing Bill Young at Saratoga, Keeneland, Belmont, and Churchill Downs, Bill said to me one morning at the track, "Bob, have you left the ministry?"

Those summer days at Saratoga were wonderful, and I miss them still. It certainly is the place to be.

Quogue was also the place to be. Helen went off to college to the University of Arizona after three or four years at Quogue and didn't come anymore, but Bobby and Elizabeth grew up there, attending the fine junior sports program and learning to sail and surf, play tennis and

---

116. Storm Cat (February 27, 1983–April 24, 2013) was an American Thoroughbred stallion whose breeding fee during the peak of his stud career was five hundred thousand dollars, one of the highest in the world, the highest being his Grandsire, the Canadian champion, Northern Dancer, at one million dollars (with no guarantee; 1984–1987). As such, he was one of the few horses with a twenty-four-hour armed guard. Peppermints were Storm's favorite treat.

golf, and ride bikes. They made good friends and enjoyed our occasional trips to the city.

One of Elizabeth's best friends was Tracy Mullen, who invited Elizabeth to her debut in New York City. She had a grand time, and when she got home she said the most exciting thing was when the boys who were their dates just stood on the curb and hailed a taxi to take them wherever they wanted to go. I think she thought the taxis were free.

On one of our city trips I performed a wedding at the Church of the Heavenly Rest (for Susie Peck's daughter), and Joyce and I stayed at the Colony Club. Much later, I had the sad task of preaching the homily at the funeral of Denny and Susie Lewis's only son, who was killed in an automobile wreck in Argentina. He was an outstanding young man. His whole class from Groton came to the funeral at St. Thomas's, along with the headmaster. I had an illustration from William Sloan Coffin whose son died at an early age, and it was the central part of my homily. The headmaster of Groton was asked to say a few words just before the homily—and he used my illustration! I had to do a quick rewrite during the hymn before the sermon.

We drove out to Quogue for the interment in the lovely little Quogue Cemetery and had a chance to see a number of our friends at a reception afterward in the Quogue Library.

Bobby would get in shape for football by running around the Rectory, as they officially called the house for the clergy. It was a fine A-frame house with three bedrooms, each with twin beds. There were two full baths, a kitchen, living room/dining room, study, TV room, and a lovely patio overlooking Bert Eggers's Sand Acres.

Almost our first weekend at Quogue, the Eggers invited us over to Sand Acres for drinks. They had all the old crowd there, most of whom came to the Church of the Atonement on Sundays. We had drinks, and as we were saying our good-byes, Mr. Eggers said, "Why don't you stay, and after everyone leaves, we'll go out for supper?" That sounded good, so we had another drink, piled into Bert's—we were calling him that by now—English taxi, and went to one of Quogue's best restaurants, the Ambassador. Bert ordered another round of drinks and said to the waiter, "Ask the chef to come here!" When the chef arrived, they had a long conversation as Bert ordered a special dinner. We all had another drink. When the food finally arrived, I found I could hardly feel my chin. I looked across the table, and at least two or three guests were having trouble keeping their elbows on the table. All I could think of was, *Here I am, the new minister at the little church, and on my first night out on the town, I'm drunk! Or at least nearly so. If the whole month is going to be like this, I'll need a liver transplant!*

Over our years at Quogue, our dogs enjoyed it as much as we did. We were a short walk across Sand Acres from Money Bog Creek and quite near the ocean itself. The dogs learned to lie belly down on the lush, cool grass as we had drinks on the terrace in the early evening. Elizabeth and I played doubles tennis and nearly beat the Gardeners—who played all the time. Elizabeth had great summers and grew up right before our eyes. She was and is beautiful, too—and knows it in a quiet, unassuming way. "May our sons be like plants well nurtured from their youth, and our daughters like the well-hewn corners of a palace" (Psalm 144:3).

One year shortly after arriving at Quogue, Dave Keptner and I stopped in Southampton on our way to play golf to call on Mrs. Schroeder in the nursing home. I got the room number, went over to her bed, noted that she had declined a great deal since last summer, and told her who I was. Just then, Dave appeared in the door and waved his arms and said, "That's not Mrs. Schroeder!" I made a hasty retreat and saw the real Mrs. Schroeder, who looked quite the same as last summer. As we were leaving, we passed the room of the first lady who was being calmed by the nurses and the staff, and she pointed at the door and cried, "There they are!" We beat an even hastier retreat to the car.

We had lots of visitors during our summers at Quogue. Two couples, the Enholms and Johnsons, came from Dallas. Thanks to my old friend

Jack Darneille from Washington, he made it possible for Bill Johnson and me to play the famous Maidstone Course in East Hampton. Just the two of us played, and neither of us was on our game. Jack had said he'd meet us afterward and was very interested in how we would do. We decided to rig our scorecard in his honor, so when we finally double bogeyed in, we handed Jack a card attesting to the fact the Bill shot two over par and I broke 80. He was so impressed and pleased, he showed the card to the pro and to several of his friends as we had drinks in the nineteenth hole.

Speaking of drinks, the Darneilles took all six of us to dinner at Maidstone, and when it came time to order the wine, Jack's wife ordered one bottle of white wine. The Enholms alone could put down a couple of bottles, and we had a lot of laughs when we got back to Quogue.

My friend Bowie Kuhn, former commissioner of Major League Baseball, died in Florida in March 2007.[117] I played golf with Bowie at Quogue each summer, and while he was an ardent Roman Catholic (went to daily Mass), his wife, Louisa, was very active in the little Episcopal Church and at home in Florida.

We always had a one-dollar bet on the nine-hole course at Quogue, and I gave him quite a few strokes but still won the dollar most days. Sometimes he would disappear behind the hedge on the ninth hole, taking his dollar with him, and go home. His house was just a sand iron away.

Our usual foursome consisted of my old Episcopal High friend Ed Wilson, then the drama critic for the *Wall Street Journal*, and Julian Goodman, former head of the National Broadcasting Company.[118] One

---

117. Bowie Kent Kuhn (October 28, 1926–March 15, 2007) was an American lawyer and sports administrator who served as the fifth commissioner of Major League Baseball from February 4, 1969, to September 30, 1984. He served as legal counsel for Major League Baseball owners for almost twenty years prior to his election as commissioner.

118. Julian Goodman (May 1, 1922–July 2, 2012) was an American broadcasting executive and journalist. He was born in Glasgow, Kentucky. Goodman took a hard stance in support of the First Amendment. Goodman was known for never asking for a raise or promotion. He started his career as a reporter working for three dollars a week for the

day we were looking for a ball in a clump of bushes when wasps swarmed up out of the bush and stung us. Bowie, who had escaped being stung and whose ball was the one lost, said, "Don't worry! If you're allergic you'll be dead in fifteen minutes!"

One of our friends at Quogue saved his copies of the London *Spectator* for me each summer. I especially liked the editorial essays by Paul Johnson and the gossip column by Taki Theodoracopulos, who also wrote for the *New York Press* weekly.[119] I often found quotes that were usable in talks and sermons. On one visit to the Dune Church in Southampton, where for years I had been one of their guest preachers, I quoted Paul Johnson along with Fred Buechner.[120] After the service, who should come through the line but Taki himself? He was in the company of Eddy Ulmann.[121]

Later in the summer, in his September 14, 2002,"High Life" column

---

Glasgow Daily Times. After serving in the army, he moved to Washington. Here he met William McAndrew, director of NBC network news, and was given a job for the night news desk. He served as president of NBC from 1966 to 1974. Goodman helped establish Chet Huntley and David Brinkley as a well-known news team and led the network from 1966 to 1974. While working for NBC, he negotiated a $1 million deal to retain Johnny Carson as host of *The Tonight Show*. Goodman was included on the master list of Nixon political opponents.

119. Taki Theodoracopulos (born August 11, 1936), originally named Panagiotis Theodoracopulos and best known as Taki, is a Greek-born journalist and writer living in New York City, London, and Gstaad, Switzerland. His *High Life* column has appeared in *The Spectator* since 1977, and he has also written for other US and UK publications. In 1984, Taki served three months in Pentonville Prison for cocaine possession. He documented his prison experiences in *Nothing to Declare: Prison Memoirs* (1991).

120. Carl Frederick Buechner (born July 11, 1926) is an American writer and theologian. He is an ordained Presbyterian minister and author of more than thirty published books. His work encompasses different genres, including fiction, autobiography, essays, and sermons, and his career has spanned six decades.

121. Edward Foote Ulmann, known as Eddie to his friends, died in Southampton on May 4, 2013. He was seventy. After his retirement as chairman of Allied International Corporation in New York during the 1990s, Ulmann began a career in writing for the *New York Press*, a weekly publication, under the pseudonym "Classicus." When the *Press* folded, he began writing on a regular basis for *Quest*, *Avenue*, and *Taki's Mag*, a website run out of London with more than a million viewers.

in the Spectator,[122] Taki wrote about his weekend in Southampton. He wrote that Eddy took him to my Church before doing anything else. He was excited to hear me quote The *Spectator*, especially because Fred Buechner was his English teacher many years ago. Taki mentioned meeting me in his article and described me as "a very good-looking man." Evidently, he was inspired by my sermon and even wrote that he would try to attend more services outside of his Greek Orthodox religion.

122. "High Life: Inspiration on the Dunes," *Spectator*, September 14, 2003, p. 61.

Washington, DC

My friend John Harper had told me I was being considered for rector of St. Alban's Church, situated on the cathedral close at the juncture of Massachusetts and Wisconsin Avenues. While I was attending the Church and City Conference at the College of Preachers—where, incidentally, one of my heroes, Senator Moynihan, was our speaker and leader for three days—Millard West, senior warden of St. Alban's, called and asked if Joyce and I could fly up and meet with the vestry and calling committee at St. Alban's.

I had breakfast that morning with my friend Paul Moore, who had been elected suffragan bishop of Washington, DC, and he urged me to accept if called. We were deans together when Paul was in Indianapolis. This was January 6, 1969, and on January 14 Millard West called to say the call was unanimous.

A trip to Phoenix for a meeting of the Liturgical Commission gave me some time to think and pray about the call. I wrote in my journal that night, "During a long evening walk, Washington seems so in the center of things I am most interested in—the Church, politics, problems of the cities, etc. Perhaps I have been at home in Kentucky too long."

After a weekend in Washington to see St. Alban's in action, and lunch with the retiring rector, whom I had known for a long time, Felix Kloman, I felt I should accept the call and did, on January 18, 1969.

I agreed to come in May (after the Derby!) with my first service on May 4.

Meanwhile, I had a heavy schedule to honor, which included preaching at the cathedral in Jacksonville, Florida (and staying with Cumberland Island friends, the Hillyers); Savannah, Georgia at Christ Church; Augusta, Georgia, at the Church of the Good Shepherd and St. Paul's, plus a meeting as chair of the editorial committee of the Standing Liturgical Commission in New York. Massy Shepherd, my teacher at seminary and a longtime member of the SLC, was just back from Rome with the new translation of the Lord's Prayer—agreed upon by Roman Catholics and Protestants—

> *Our Father in heaven*
> *Glorify your Name*
> *Your kingdom come*
> *Your will be done*
> *On earth as in heaven.*
> *Give us this day our daily bread*
> *Forgive us our sins as we forgive those*
> *Who sin against us.*
> *Save us from the time of trial*
> *And deliver us from evil.*
> *For the kingdom, the power, and the glory*
> *Are yours now and forever.*

Some minor changes were made before it was put in the new Book of Common Prayer.

After accepting the call I took my belongings to Washington since I would be there for a month before Joyce and the children came. I stayed with the newly elected senior warden, Don Griffin, a retired admiral who has been commander of NATO in the South Atlantic before retirement. They had drinks and dinner, and their guests were Admiral and Mrs. Arthur Radford. Admiral Radford was then head of the Joint Chiefs of Staff. Quite a night for an ex–seaman second class!

On our last Sunday in Louisville, a nice reception was held, and we were given a color TV, a lovely silver coffee urn, a book on Kentucky, and many kind wishes—especially from Booker Robinson, my loyal senior warden and friend, whom I knew I would miss dearly.

Appropriately, for a native Kentuckian, we were at the Kentucky Derby with Louis and Dotty Hermann. I met Scotty Reston and Kay Graham, who will be one of my parishioners at St. Alban's. I kissed Joyce, ran down the steps at the end of the race, and caught a taxi for the airport. I shared the taxi with three others, and someone asked me where I was from and I answered, "Washington, DC." So it was and yet, "The sun shines bright." It's not easy to leave home.

I was asked on May 30, 1969, to preach the Baccalaureate Sermon at Episcopal High—where I had gone nearly twenty-five years before. Being asked to preach the Baccalaureate shows you don't have to have made it through first Latin to be invited back! I tried to challenge them to "turn on" rather than "turn off"—and to identify God where he is, "where the action in life is." After the day at the high school, I drove to Middleburg and spent the night with my cousin Al Shands and his wife, Mary (Norton), at their country place, next to Rattlesnake Mountain and the Kennedys' country place.

June 3 was a great, if somewhat sad, day as I was back in Louisville to drive the family to Washington and our new home. Our arrival in DC got off to a fine start with lunch at Kay Graham's with Lally and Yan Weymouth. Tom and Mireille Johnston, Senator and Mrs. John Sherman Cooper, and the Joe Alsops. The only downer was when I overheard Joe Alsop across the table refer to someone as "plain as a parson's wife."

I spent the rest of the lunch trying to get him back with cracks about newspaper writer's wives. He didn't realize that I was offended, probably because he was used to offending people every day.

Arthur Schlesinger Jr., in his *Journals* (1952–2000)[123], upon hearing

123. Arthur Schlesinger Jr., *Journals 1952-2000* (New York: Penguin, 2007)

of Joe Alsop's death in 1989 wrote, "Relations with Joe had their ups and downs. He got very mad at me over Vietnam ... attacked me in columns and was cold and irritable when we met...." But he concludes that after Alsop gave up his column, they became friends once again, showing that "friendship mattered far more to him than political agreement."

On June 22, I was formally instituted as rector of St. Alban's by Bishop Moore, with Frank Sayre (now our nearest neighbor on the close) preaching.

Joyce's first official party as first lady of St. Alban's came in late June at the Ghanaian embassy. Ambassador Ehah was a member of St. Alban's and very nice to us. The party was held in the embassy garden on one of those sweltering Washington evenings, and the garden felt like a tropical rain forest. Several Ghanaians wore their tribal clothes with bare shoulders, and at least one had the skin of a leopard on his back with the head over the back part of his head. The party was in honor of the ambassador from Upper Volta, who E. M. Debrach, Ghana's ambassador in Addis Ababa says, can, by stopping the Volta River, "cut off my water in Ghana at any time!" Joyce noticed that the silver on the tables was the same as our pattern.

One of the best clergy support groups I have ever been in consisted of my cousin Al Shands, Tom Bowers, Bill Swing, Ed Romig, John Harper, Jim Fenhagen, Earl Brill, Ted Eastman (when he was in Washington before going to Pennsylvania), Jack Smith (EHS chaplain), and Bennett and Ed Sims.

We met twice a month and made it almost obligatory to attend.

My friend Bill Swing (later bishop of California) was at St. Columbas when I was at St. Alban's. One of his parishioners was the chairman of the Special Olympics, which held its opening session in RFK Stadium with over fifty thousand people present. He asked Bill to give the invocation. Bill said he arrived early, got up on the platform, and found a seat with his name on it. Just before the festivities began, an usher handed Bill a program.

He opened it to see when his invocation would come, and to his horror he read, "The National Anthem, sung by The Reverend William Swing"!

Just as he looked frantically for someone in charge, the microphone came on and the person presiding said, "Now, now, now [the mike was acting up], the, the, the, Reverend, Reverend, Reverend, William, William, Swing, wing, wing will sing the National Anthem, anthem, anthem...."

Bill says he took a deep breath and on the way to the microphone tried to remember whether it was "the rockets red blare, or glare or whatever"...and also that he should start it low. He took the mike and said, "Please join me in singing the National Anthem," and began as low as possible. "Oh..." It was too low and he had to start again. He swore that not one person in the crowd of fifty thousand joined in, and he finally finished his solo and flopped back into his seat. Even the band had remained in stunned silence.

The cathedral grounds offered a very visible place for demonstrations. In fact, Washington itself almost always had some group or another demonstrating for their cause. Just off the cathedral grounds on Massachusetts Avenue, the Vatican embassy was a prime spot for disgruntled Roman Catholics to air their views. One lady in particular became a regular tourist attraction and a distraction for daily commuters and neighbors. Apparently, her son had petitioned the papacy for permission to annul his marriage and remarry. It had either been turned down or denied. At any rate, his mother, a rather formidable lady went into action. She made

One demonstrator became a regular tourist attraction.

a large sign that said, "F— the Pope" (the f— word was spelled out). I assume the courts had ruled in her favor, and she made it every day but Sunday right at rush hour!

Another, less spectacular group of protestors ended up in our backyard for three nights and had our permission to use St. Alban's bathroom facilities. They were students from the University of the South at Sewanee, twenty young men and one young woman, and were there to protest the Vietnam War! Joyce asked the female student if she wouldn't prefer to use our bathroom (and shower!), but she politely declined. Many other groups came but the Sewanee group was unique. After they returned to Sewanee, we received twenty-one thank-you notes.

As I have noted before, our rectory was only one of two separate houses on the cathedral close. Hence we were in an ecclesiastical fishbowl. One afternoon as I was dressing to go out to dinner, I looked up from tying my shoes to see a rather elderly lady in a fur coat with one of the cathedral maps in her hand. She looked at me and said, "Isn't this the Bethlehem Chapel?"

"Isn't this the Bethlehem chapel?"

Living in Washington throws you in with all sorts of people. I was asked to baptize Stewart Ross's daughter in the Children's Chapel of the Cathedral. Afterward, I put in a quick visit to a reception at the Ross's home and had a long talk with a very friendly and talkative woman who turned out to be Linda (Johnson) Robb (the daughter of President Lyndon Baines Johnson)—Chuck was there, too. At a prayer breakfast sponsored by the National Association of Manufacturers Business Lobby Group, I gave the invocation and sat next to George Shultz (then secretary of labor under Nixon, and later secretary of state under Reagan). After my invocation, he commented on the fact that blacks were demanding reparations from churches and said in a rather sour way, "You're getting what you deserve. How does it feel?" In fact, that past Sunday, one of the more radical black groups had come to the cathedral during the main service and had grabbed the mike to interrupt the service and make their claims. Whether right or wrong, the cathedral electrician simply turned off the power to the microphones—leaving the "takeover" almost inaudible to all but those closest to them in the vast building.

Senator Brock Adams (Washington State) was a member of St. Alban's and came by the rectory, often late at night after a difficult day in the Senate, to talk about the particular issue or bill that was on the floor.

George Reedy was another parishioner, and he had been press secretary and later a staff assistant for Lyndon Johnson. Nancy Harrison was a vestry member and a great supporter of our efforts to have outreach programs, especially for youth. Her husband, Gill, was the editor of the *New Republic*. Another supporter was Nancy Symington.

I taught a class at the National Cathedral School, where Helen was a student. Vice President Agnew's daughter was in Helen's class in their senior year and was accompanied by a Secret Service person (a young woman).

Al and Mary Shands had bought a lovely estate near Middleburg called the Mill House. It had a separate building that had been made into a guest house, and they generously gave us the use of it. It was a much needed place to which we could get away from the fishbowl existence on the close. On Christmas Day 1970, we took Joyce's parents, who were visiting us, to the Mill House. Al and Mary were in Kentucky, and a light snow fell that night. It was a snug and relaxed two days. I taught one of Al's ponies to jump!

Another escape for me was having one of my best friends, Buddy Buckner, a West Pointer and army officer, assigned to the Pentagon. We played squash there, and one day as we were playing, a soldier knocked on the door and shooed us off for General Westmoreland! It developed later that he didn't show. He probably was hiding away because of his premature (and wrong) statement that we were winning the Vietnam War. Years later he was in the congregation at Linnville when I preached. He was a hero there (!) and was called "Westie."

The British Embassy was always very friendly and included us in the annual Queen's Birthday party with strawberries and cream to go with champagne.

My first Christmas at St. Alban's we had the usual midnight service with a packed church, despite competition from the cathedral's service. I was pretty worn out afterward and had arranged for Dick Peard and Bill Davis (my assistants) to do the Christmas day service, which, I was told, usually had only a few older parishioners who couldn't get out at night, organ and hymns only, and generally a brief service.

Early Christmas morning, I got a call at the rectory asking me for the time of the service and saying that the British ambassador and his family and the Embassy staff would be coming. "Could we reserve some seats for about fifty people?" I shamelessly got vested and took part in the service, greeting the ambassador and his group at the door.

Another Christmas had its exciting moments. About an hour before our midnight service at St. Alban's we got a call from the head usher at the cathedral to inform us that our dog, Duncan, was loose in the cathedral and running about in the crowd gathering for their service.

We hurried to the south transept and an excited (and peeved) usher informed us that Duncan was just seen in the Children's Chapel. As we started in that direction, a message came over his walkie-talkie, informing him that Duncan was sitting in front of the Lincoln Chapel gazing up at the figure of the president. Again, we were too late, finding from another usher's phone that he had exited from the north transept and was last seen heading for Wisconsin Avenue.

"He's heading for the Lincoln Chapel!"

Elizabeth finally found him resting from his exertions under the corner mailbox. "He seemed," she said, "to be very proud of himself."

My predecessor, Felix Kloman, couldn't have been more supportive, and with the help of Millard West, Dr. Alan Walker, Cary Winston, and probably others, I was admitted as a clergy member of Burning Tree Golf Club and (with the help of John Harper) the Metropolitan Club. Bishop Creighton was also a member of Burning Tree, and we shared a locker.

One day at Burning Tree, I was playing in a twosome and another twosome came up behind us.

We asked them to go through, but they suggested we form a foursome and play on together. That was fine with us, and we all introduced ourselves. One of them said, "I'm Barry Goldwater." I had to admit afterward that he couldn't have been nicer and was fun to play with. In fact, I told him our daughter, Helen, was applying to his University of Arizona. He took out a pencil and on the back of his scorecard wrote down her name and asked a few questions and a few days later sent me a copy of a lovely letter of recommendation he had written. Needless to say, she was accepted! On another occasion I took Romer McFee (writer John McFee's brother) out to play. He told John about it, and John, unbeknownst to me, went out and wrote down license plate numbers, looked up the owners, checked to see what was happening on the floor in Congress at that time, and published a short article in the *New Yorker*, naming names of those luckless Congress members who were "loafing at Burning Tree." For weeks afterward, his article was a matter of discussion at the Burning Tree lunch table. I kept a low profile, especially when I heard someone say, "If I could find out who got him in, I'd bust them out of their membership!"

On June 3, 1971, while we were at the National Gallery for a cocktail party for docents of the Junior League (Joyce was one), we received word that Joyce's father had died of a heart attack. Jess (the children called him "Deedee") was a gentle, quiet man who had a bad heart for years. He had to stop hunting and playing golf and always had his emergency pills at hand.

In May, with the Shands and Fergusons we attended the gala opening of the John F. Kennedy Center for the Performing Arts. What a night! I spoke to Ethel Kennedy and asked about Tom Johnston. She introduced me to singer Andy Williams. After a lavish dinner we danced to the music of Meyer Davis, Lester Lanin, and Peter Duchin and got home at 4 a.m. At midnight there were fireworks, and I joined several people who stood

on tables for a better view. A rearview picture of me was on the front page of the *Washington Post* the next day.

Millard West was my guest and partner for Burning Tree's Member-Guest Tournament. We played with Congressman Paul Rogers and his brother from Florida. Deputy Attorney General Richard Kleindienst, fat, soft-looking, and dressed in all white (with a white golf bag, too), was in the foursome behind us. Bobby Kennedy would never have hired him. Millard and I didn't win anything, and I felt like Lee Trevino, who said, after a bad round, "I feel like Tarzan, I'm swinging like Jane, and I'm hitting the ball like Cheetah."[124] Later at Burning Tree I did better and won the second flight of the club championship!

On my forty-fourth birthday, Joyce and I went to the preview of Leonard Bernstein's *Mass*, which would formally open the Kennedy Center. A packed house gave a twenty-minute standing ovation. Bernstein wept and then went on stage and embraced all the cast. Senator and Mrs. Ted Kennedy were there as well, as was Danny Kaye.

Writing on October 18, 1971, I noted that Dean Acheson died the previous week, and an article in the *Washington Post*, mentioned his admiration for Lord David Cecil's interpretation of Joseph Conrad's view of life. Cecil and Conrad believed that man should live life nobly and virtuous even if they don't know why they are doing so. They believed that it was better to live life on the beautiful side, rather than the ugly.

Joyce and I had a reunion of sorts in Cambridge where I was vice president of the alumni association at ETS. Ben Arnold (shortly prior elected suffragan bishop of Massachusetts) was the president and our old friend Milton Saville was the secretary. The Harpers were there, too, and we left after the meeting to take a two-day rest. John dropped the bottle of Makers Mark bourbon I had brought as a hostess present. It smashed to pieces on the steps of Washburn Hall, and we just left it there. The last I saw of the remains, a

124. *LIFE*, July 2, 1971. William Burns, "The Mad Golfer is the Best." 35.

little group of seminarians had gathered around it in a kind of wake. At least we christened the new hall with the best Kentucky bourbon made.

On November 19, 1971, we began what would be the first of a dozen cruises on which I would serve as Protestant chaplain. This is made possible by being on a seminary faculty where we can get off at times like Thanksgiving and Christmas. This cruise was on TS *Breman* sailing out of NYC, so we had drinks and supper the night before sailing with Ed and Chic Wilson and went to the Met to hear *Carmen*.

We sailed late Saturday and were off Hatteras in very rough seas by Sunday morning in time for church services. I had taken a Dramamine, so no mal de mer, but the rest of the passengers seemed to be sick. As the Roman Catholic chaplain came out of his service (ours was to follow) he said, "Don't take an offering."

I said, "But I thought they told us to take one up for the benefit of the Seaman's Institute."

He replied, "I know, but I threw up in the alms basin!"

"Don't take up an offering . . . ulp!"

I held the service, and during it several people got up and left. I hoped it was seasickness rather than my sermon. We did not take an offering.

Helen left for college on August 19, 1972—far away at the University of Arizona. I wrote her a note, "to be read aloft," with some advice and much love. Joyce took her out to Dulles to see her off. I couldn't bring myself to go and worked out a good excuse. My, how we would miss her. It's hard to see the nest thin as the first one flies away and tries her wings. But Yevtushenko is right, and I quoted him in my note to Helen:

It's dangerous to go out
Into this nightmare world
But it's still more dangerous
To hide in the woods.

We ended the day with a lovely evening at Wolf Trap with the New York Philharmonic doing Mahler's Fifth Symphony.

On December 15, 1974, one of my heroes died at age eighty-five: Walter Lippman. I thought him to be a great man, and it always seemed right to have him living just on the other side of the cathedral close on Woodley Road. It seemed to balance the place. He had a photograph he had hung on his wall of an inscription on a Charleston, South Carolina, tombstone. It was that of James Petique in 1863. The epitaph read in part:

Unawed by opinion
Unseduced by flattery
Undismayed by disaster
He confronted life with an antique courage
And death with Christian hope.

"There's a beautiful thing," Lippman had said to a visitor. "There is the essence of the best American spirit."

Ruth Harwood Cline, PhD, in her history of St. Alban's (1854–2004), wrote, "Estill served during the administration of President Nixon...a turbulent time in U.S. history."[125] Vietnam, new proposed liturgies, women's ordination, youth lifestyles (hippies), rock music, narcotics—all impacted life in Washington and St. Alban's. There was a widening gap between the old establishment and the young. A diocesan fund drive

---

125. Ruth Harwood Cline, *Church at the Crossroads: A History of St. Albans' Parish, Washington, DC, 1854–2004* (Chevy Chase, Maryland: Posterity Press, 2009).

called the Missionary Development Fund was also a divisive factor. I made a big push to have the vestry accept St. Alban's quota in full, but though the vestry finally went along, a majority of the parish were anti-diocese and national church.

Our coffeehouse brought hordes of young people onto the close every Friday night, thanks to Dick Peard's leadership. The noise, some bad behavior, and the obvious use of drugs by a few caused tensions with the cathedral. We had as many as two hundred young people on any given Friday. We also established in 1972 a very successful day care center to accommodate working mothers and their needs.

———————

Several Kentucky friends had put my name up for bishop of the Diocese of Kentucky; Bennett Sims and Herb Donovan were also on the list. Meanwhile, our Diocese of Washington elected John Walker as suffragan. I was for him all the way and was the only rector of a cardinal parish to sign a letter of support, which went on before the election. David Reed, missionary bishop of Columbia, was elected in Kentucky. At Morning Prayer the next day, the New Testament lesson was Jesus saying, "A prophet is not without honor, save in his own country."

In February 1973 Cecil Woods, dean of Virginia Theological Seminary and a friend of long standing, called to see if we could have lunch. When we met, he said that the search for a director of the Continuing Education Center (started by my friend and support group member Bennett Sims), was on. I began thinking about who would fit that important job when he said, "I want to offer you that job!"

With the approval of St. Alban's vestry, I had taught an evening class in liturgics at VTS for three years. I had also been asked to give the Annual Kellogg lectures, so I knew the seminary and was known by the faculty and many students. I had been in the parish ministry for over twenty years and had experience in small, medium, and large parishes; knew a great many clergy; had national exposure as a member of the Standing

Liturgical Commission; and was one of the founding members of the Clergy Association in Washington, DC.

So after a time for prayer and reflection, I said yes and was formally elected. I tendered my resignation to the vestry effective May 31, 1973.

My leaving St. Alban's was not handled well on my part. Ruth Harwood Cline quoted me, "I regret that neither the Vestry nor I knew the proper procedure for saying goodbye." Those dynamics came out in later studies, some of which we developed at VTS. It is just as important to have a time for good-byes as it is for hellos. I confess that in a mistaken effort to keep the focus on St. Alban's and not on me, I saddened and in some cases angered the people who had been my best supporters.

Later, when interviewed by Dr. Cline, I said, "I now see that what St. Alban's needed was an interim rector at the time I was elected rector." Long tenures like that of Dr. Kloman raise points that need to be considered before a new rector comes. I can see that my four years were, in that sense, interim years that hopefully paved the way for the next rector.

On May 20, 1971, I was carted off to the Washington Hospital Center in an ambulance from my doctor's office with what turned out to be an acute gallbladder attack. After three days in the intensive care cardiac unit, I gave up my gallbladder. I was reminded of St. Francis, who called his body, "brother ass." Joyce entertained thirty people for dinner the night I was laid out in the hospital! It was our good-bye for Al and Mary, who were moving to Kentucky. After several drinks, someone asked Joyce, "Where is Bob?"

A night or so after Cecil's offer, Joyce and I were at the Fenhagens in Georgetown for dinner. The Brills and the Shands were there as well. Before dinner as we were having drinks, Jim called Al, Earl, and me into the kitchen and said, "I've got to share this with you because I'm so excited. I had word from a friend at VTS that the search for the continuing education director has come down to just two, and I'm one of the finalists. No one seems to know who the other person is, but they say it's a person who didn't go to VTS." Cecil, after offering me the job, had pledged me to silence. Since he had the formal duty of presenting his choice to the board, I could tell Joyce but no one else. Here I was in the home of one of my best friends and couldn't tell him anything. I finally dropped all ethics and protocol and blurted out, "I am the man!" Jim and I hugged, and I said I'd withdraw, and he said, no, he would withdraw.

Of course, the board had not yet met. We agreed to stay in the process, and I was relieved that I didn't have to tell him that Cecil had already made his choice. "All things work together for good," however, since shortly after my election, Jim was asked to head a similar program at Hartford Seminary. The VTS politics were such that I really think Jim would have been at a disadvantage right off the bat. They really needed an outsider, and I was the man.

———————

Yours in Truth: A Personal Portrait of Ben Bradlee by Jeff Himmelman is an interesting portrait of one of the most interesting persons of our time. We met Bradlee through Kay Graham when we lived in DC. He, of course, with Kay brought the *Washington Post* into being, with the *New York Times*, one of the two most influential papers in the country, if not the world. Bradlee was very profane, and in one of his letters he came up with a word that was included with a string of ugly words describing his reader as a "retromingent"—a person who urinates backward.

I looked the word up in my OED, and sure enough it is exactly what the word means. If the person Bradlee described had looked it up, he or she would have been proud to be in the royal company of retromingent animals—the lion and the elephant, for example! I wish I would have had that word to send along in answer to some of the ugly letters I got during the civil rights conflict in Kentucky.

Virginia Theological Seminary and the Continuing Education Center

As I drove up the Holy Hill to begin my new life at Virginia Theological Seminary on April 24, 1973, I thought of the psalm appointed for the day: "Send out your light and your truth, that they may lead me, and bring me to your holy hill and to your dwelling" (Psalm 43:3). I was convinced that this was God's call to me at the midpoint of my ministry. I hoped to do a good job and to be renewed myself. Bennett Sims started this program to answer the mid-career crisis that many clergy have. It was a six-week experience in residence in the new Continuing Education Building and in the midst of seminary life. There was a weeklong "return" built into the program after the first year.

As a VTS alumnus, Bennett had definitive views of "his program" in relation to the seminary. That didn't make him or the program very popular with the powers that be. I had the advantage of being a graduate of a different seminary and enjoyed a close relationship with President Cecil Woods and most of the faculty. I attended daily chapel and encouraged our continuing education members to do the same. I also attended the regular faculty meetings and continued to teach the undergraduate course in liturgics. We invited several faculty members to speak on theological topics, and we melded in with students at meals and after chapel.

I went through the six-week program as a participant, which helped me understand the dynamics and pick out some areas I might want to change. Chris Bryan, an attractive and bright New Testament scholar, remained as my assistant for the first year before going to Sewanee to teach. That helped greatly with the two return groups that had gone before and knew Chris.

One great bonus is that Bobby had transferred from St. Alban's School to Episcopal High School, which, of course, is right next to the seminary's Holy Hill. (When I was at EHS, as I said earlier, we called it the "Hilly Hole"!) I was able to manipulate my schedule to attend all of his football games (he was the starting wide receiver on the varsity). Before one of Bobby's away games (in Lynchburg), I was leading a retreat for the women of the Diocese of Washington and Virginia at Airlie House in Virginia. The retreat began Friday night, and I gave two talks that night and two Saturday morning. I designed the retreat to have all of Saturday afternoon be quiet and to enjoy the grounds of Airlie House. I put the ladies into what I called "the great silence," jumped into my car, headed for Lynchburg, and got there just in time for the game. I saw Bobby briefly afterward and headed back to the retreat, arriving right on schedule for the evening session. I hadn't said anything to anybody about my trip. But when I went to the podium to begin my talk, there was a note written on a paper towel in lipstick that read, "Who won?"

My feeling was that his life and my life are too short to miss sharing these moments. Elizabeth would soon transfer to St. Agnes in Alexandria, so everyone was relocated. Elizabeth took up right away with friends, including Margo Helfenstein—whose father was the admissions officer at EHS and in school with me.

On one of my western trips to attend a church meeting, I stopped to visit Helen at the University of Arizona in Tucson. She needed a car, and so, accompanied by a boyfriend, we went shopping. At each dealership she and Steve, the boyfriend, would lie down and look under the car at the motor. It was over a hundred degrees that day, and I stayed in my rental car in the air conditioning at the first few stops. I felt guilty not getting into the spirit of the event, even though I was paying for whatever we got.

Finally, at the Volkswagen place, I got out and laid down under one of the models, only to have Helen and Steve ask, "What are you doing?" I was under the front end—and it turned out that Volkswagens had their motors in the back.

I got back in the air conditioning and leafed through my checkbook.

We took Elizabeth with us on our next Christmas cruise aboard a Greek ship, the TJS *Queen Anna Maria*. Helen was going to California with friends from Arizona, and Bobby wanted to stay at the seminary to be near his new love, Maggie—whose father was head of St. Stephen's School. Elizabeth was a good sailor, except for one rough day when she threw up in the elevator. We sailed out of Norfolk to New York and then to the Caribbean. While in New York we saw a friend from Quogue, Howdy Goodwin, who asked us to come to lunch with him where the Salvation Army was singing Christmas carols. We politely declined since we'd promised Elizabeth we would take her to the Palm Room at the Plaza. As we were moving on, Howdy said, "I'm so sorry, they only come once a year to 21!" The 21 Club was an American traditional cuisine restaurant in mid-town Manhattan. We had missed our chance. Two years later, I wrote in my journal,

I'm convinced I am doing more in the Seminary than I could be doing anywhere else right now. To have a deep sharing in the lives of the men who come through our program—and to share in strengthening their ministry all over the Church in the USA, in Britain and Japan and New Zealand, is really rewarding.

My own continuing education was part of the experience of each term. Also, I received word that I was accepted in the doctor of ministry program at Sewanee/Vanderbilt, which takes place in the summer.

One of the additions to the program I made was a field trip to Capitol Hill and visits with members of Congress. Andrew Young was one of the best and gave us a lot of quality time in his office. The Revered Mr. Young, a Congregationalist minister and at the time Congressman from Georgia's 5th Congressional district, was a close friend and supporter of Martin Luther King, Jr. in the civil rights movement. At one point there was a vote called, and he took off down the hall on a bicycle to cast his vote. We also visited various models of ministry like the Church of the Savior.

Al Shands and I continued teaching a Wednesday night class for seminarians on the liturgy, and Charles Price and I went around Virginia, Maryland, and DC, talking about the proposed new *Book of Common Prayer*.

The off time when we didn't have groups coming through the program gave me time to study, read, and use the seminary library. Bobby and I also got into the horse business by buying a small Welsh pony for Elizabeth. We named him Joe Graves and boarded him at a small farm near the seminary. When the owner died we had to move him, so we built a stall off the back of our house and tethered him during the day. I ended up being the groom, mucking stalls, and bringing water and feed. The only city ordinance having to do with keeping a pony was that its manure pile had to be one hundred yards from any domicile. That was no problem since we backed up to EHS and a corner of their property they had left wild.

Joe Graves could hardly keep up with the demand for manure from the various gardeners. One morning I happened to look out and see a limo pulled up next to the pile with a man standing watching his driver shoveling "our" manure into a garbage can in the trunk of the car. I walked over and said, "Good morning, I'm Bob Estill, and that's our manure pile." The man who was watching the loading said, "Good morning, I'm Gerald Ford, and this is public property" (all while his man kept shoveling!). Who was I to turn down the vice president of the United States?

Cecil Woods returned from his sabbatical, and Bill Blood, the business manager, who had opposed our having a pony on campus, couldn't

Joe Graves

wait to tell him about our violation. I beat him to it, got Cecil to come with me, and introduced him to Joe Graves. Cecil's eyes filled up and he said, "I had a Welsh pony when I was a boy!" and added, "I think this adds a touch of class to the seminary!"

When we went to Quogue, my friend Cooper Dawson at EHS asked if Joe Graves could come to Camp Allegany, which Cooper had run for years. For two summers, Joe Graves went camping and came home fat as a pig, having been fed treats by the girls at Camp Allegany.

Fortunately, I had an escape clause in my purchase of Joe Graves, so when we finally left the seminary I gave him back to the people who had sold him to us. His time with us was a blessing, and he became famous, both at the seminary and at EHS next door.

I'm sure his manure offerings greatly enriched the seminary's and Gerald Ford's gardens. I even gave a sermon (delivered to the seminary community) on how life can sometimes be like a manure pile—yet rich things can grow out of it. It seemed to go over better than many of the faculty sermons.

Once, at the Woodberry game, they announced over the PA system, "Mr. Estill, your pony is loose and is running up Seminary Road!" Herb Donovan, my friend from Louisville days and an EHS grad, heard the news and caught Joe Graves and returned him to his stall. I sat tight and watched Bobby catch a touchdown pass in the end zone. No wonder Herb was later elected bishop of Arkansas.

I always tried to be on hand to greet the new class of fellows to the six-week program. Afterward, I went by their room with a schedule and some helpful maps and to check to see if their room was okay.

One of the fellows arrived right after lunch at 12:30 p.m. He was a nice-looking guy with a bushy hairdo that was kind of off-color yellow.

At 1:45 p.m. I made my way to his room on the second floor, knocked, and the door opened to a bald man I had never seen before (or at least I didn't remember). I apologized for being at the wrong room until I realized it was the man with the bushy hairdo! Fortunately we had a good laugh, and later, after the whole group had gathered for introductions, he brought the whole thing up and even removed his wig for all of us to see.

We had several other interesting moments over the next few years, but no wigs. In fact, we would become so close that one of the fellows felt secure enough to point out that my cigar offended him. (I only smoked one after supper, and the whole group either smoked cigarettes during our sessions or at least put up with the smoke. This was years before our greater awareness of "killer tobacco," when most of us stopped completely.)

As I remember it, I thanked the fellow for his honesty and willingness

to count on our new friendship gained in this program, and I'm almost ashamed at this day and time to admit it, but I still lit up.

The program was open to any ordained person and was theologically ecumenical. We usually had a good mix of denominations, but sadly, in those days, no women. We were always sensitive to our rules and regulations, and although we had a happy hour most evenings before supper in the seminary dining room with the students, some spouses of students, and some faculty families, we always had alternate choices of beverages for those who did not drink liquor.

At the closing happy hour after one of the six-week programs, a Baptist clergyman said, "You all seem to enjoy drinking liquor. In honor of this last night I'm going to join you! So fix me a drink of your hard liquor." Several of us went to the makeshift bar and winked at each other. We poured him a drink made up of a jigger of bourbon, one of Scotch, one of gin, and added some white wine and ice. Everyone gathered around, and we handed him the drink. He raised it high and gave a toast and then took a man-sized swig of the awful mixture. There was an expectant silence, and then he broke into a grin and announced. "Damn, that stuff is really good!" Needless to say, as we recovered the drink and poured it out, that was his first and I hope his last drink.

On a happier note, at the mid-weekend of the six-week program, we invited the wives to join their husbands for a long weekend. Our continuing education program had a splendid building, and each fellow had a private room and bath with two beds. We assisted in the expenses of travel, and it was usually a joyful and relaxed weekend. One element was an hour with just the wives and our staff. We gave them an overview of the program and answered any questions they might have. This was a new feature in the program, and as we gathered I felt we should take a moment to go around the circle and have each wife reintroduce herself and maybe say a word or two about what it was like back home without her husband.

The first woman got through introducing herself and suddenly burst into tears. Suddenly, the whole room was crying and beginning to share with each other some of the problems they were having being clergy wives.

The hour went by, the husbands were outside the door, and after another hour of really in-depth sharing, I called a halt and we arranged a schedule whereby each wife could have some time with my assistant or with me. From that beginning, we always arranged more time for the wives, and nearly every session brought out the same response.

I learned a lot from this and carried it over into my pastoral relations with the clergy and their spouses with the help of our excellent team of pastoral counselors.

In addition to running the continuing education program, I served as adjunct professor of liturgies on the VTS faculty. My friend and colleague Fitz Allison, who had been teaching at the seminary for years, warned me that there would be many committees—most of which wasted valuable time. He had worked out a way to deal with it and shared it with me. "Whenever there is a new committee or task force formed," Fitz said, "volunteer to be on it. Then when it meets, be late for the first one, volunteer again if there are subcommittees and don't go to their meetings, or if you do, ask some irrelevant questions or make long speeches that have nothing to do with the business at hand. After a year or two of this," he said, "you'll find that they don't put you on committees, or if they do, keep up my advice!"

Actually, I headed a committee that was to develop a doctor of ministry program for the seminary, and with Dick Reid, the subdean, and Cecil Woods, the dean and president, on it, I had to work pretty hard and had an excellent excuse for not joining other committees.

I loved being at VTS and spent my free time and three weeks of summer vacation on the campus at the Vanderbilt seminary and in the Virginia library.

When it came time for my doctoral thesis, I submitted to my committee at Vanderbilt a proposed title: "Doggie Stories Help Children Know

Jesus!" I was going to illustrate it and do research on doggie stories. I could hardly wait to hear from the committee, and finally the word came. "We liked your idea for your thesis and it certainly meets the criteria and is, as a doctoral thesis should be, new ground. However, we believe your title should be, "Zoomorphic Forms Enable Children to Reach the Numinous"! I knew all was lost, so I wrote back and suggested I write on the subject, "Liturgy and Existentialism." They, I think in relief, adopted that idea and told me to "press on."

In March 1976 Fred Curry and Tom Luce, members of the search committee at St. Michael and All Angels (SMAA), Dallas, came to Alexandria. They had asked if I would let my name be considered as rector nearly a year earlier, and I had said no. We were just starting the doctor of ministry program, and I felt obliged to see it established and off to a strong start. During that year they had called John Harper, who declined and Dudley Calhoun, later rector of St. Paul's, Winston-Salem, who also said no. This time I said that I would allow my name to be put in again, and I agreed to bring Joyce and visit Dallas.

Dudley and I had been friends since the Sewanee summer school, and he had been called to St. Ann's, Atlanta, where Bishop Claiborne had put my name, though I couldn't consider it at the time. Then I'd been called to St. Paul's, Winston-Salem (after Tom Fraser was elected bishop coadjutor of North Carolina), and again had declined. Dudley was then elected. Now Dudley was to say no to SMAA, and as I say below, I accepted. Four and a half years later I was ordained and consecrated bishop coadjutor of North Carolina and was elected at the diocesan convention that met at St. Paul's, Winston-Salem! Small world, the church.

On our visit to Dallas we were met by Chandler Lindsay (Elliott Roosevelt's daughter), stayed at the Fairmont, had dinner with the search committee and vestry with question and answers afterward, and on Sunday (Palm Sunday) attended services (five of them!) and looked at some possible housing with Dick and Noreen Haynes—no kin of

Joyce's. We flew back to Dulles with a lot of excitement and good feelings about SMAA.

The next week I was the Lenten preacher in Newport News, Virginia. Newport News seemed very backwater after our visit to the Big D, and yet right across from the tired old Warwick Hotel where I stayed was the Victory Arch (a replica of the **Arc de Triomphe**). I copied the words on the arch: "Greetings with love to those who return. A triumph with tears to those who sleep." This was the debarkation point, this silent backwater of the James River, of the Spanish/American War and two world wars. Over a million soldiers passed through the arch from 1942 to 1945, many never to return. "A Nameless Grave" by Longfellow is there for an unknown casualty of the *Merrimack/Monitor* battle!

> *Thou unknown here sleeping in the sea*
> *In thy forgotten grave! with secret shame*
> *I feel my pulses beat, my forehead burn,*
> *When I remember thou hast given for me*
> *All thou hadst, thy life, thy very name,*
> *And I can give thee nothing in return.*

I had a terrible feeling about the possibility of leaving VTS and the Washington area, but a great feeling about SMAA. I missed being with laypeople and the parish ministry.

On April 15, 1976, I called Cecil Woods and then Earl Forsythe, senior warden, to accept the call to SMAA, effective June 1, 1976. That day I had lunch at the Metropolitan Club to tell Cecil.

Millard and Doris West, who had a party for us seven years before at their home in DC, had a lovely by-the-pool dinner party to say good-bye. They were great friends and supporters at St. Alban's.

On my last day in Virginia I jogged on Greenway—just outside our back door, saw where Bobby had caught touchdowns in Hummel Bowl, fought off some tears, and later in the day Joyce—who would stay until school was out—and I drove to Dulles, where Braniff carried me off to the Lone Star State. I wept not so much for leaving but for the shortness of life and seeing life going by so fast. I was entering the second half of my ministry.

Braniff bumped me up to first class (a good omen!), and I overcame the tears and readied for a new life and a new ministry for our Lord and his church.

Dallas, Texas

Three Texas jewels from a woman
newspaper writer named Sherrod:
"Don't squat with your spurs on."
"When you're in a hole, stop digging."
"Never kick a cow chip on a hot day."

Starting in a new place without Joyce and the children wasn't ideal, and I wrote in my journal how surprising it was to find how much I missed my old ways and Virginia. Of course, there was the excitement of the new place, but there was a sense of life passing, of the finality of the chapters of one's life. I had a feeling that nothing is lasting, or (perhaps in my darkest moments) even worth the effort.

The prayer from Compline in the *BCP* (p. 133) was comforting:

Be present, O merciful God, and protect us through the hours of this night [was this the dark night of the soul I was going through?], so that we who are wearied by the changes and chances of this life may rest in your eternal changelessness; through Jesus Christ our Lord.

Many writers, poets, and teachers make an effort to put heart into their work. Indeed, many others join them in an effort to wrestle with the beauty and brevity of human existence. I thought about this during those first days in Dallas. I thought, "Thus it is! The beauty and brevity of human existence." Another Collect from the Book of Common Prayer came to mind, "Grant us, Lord, not to be anxious about earthly things, but to love things heavenly, and even now, while we are placed among thing that are passing away, to hold fast those that shall endure."[126]

Helen came up from Tucson, and this would be a whole new chapter in her life, too. We were staying in a rented condo until our house was ready, and Helen for the time being was first lady of Saint Michael and All Angels. Helen's old, beat-up VW Bug was parked out front alongside the Mercedes, BMWs, and Cadillacs that belonged to the swell people in this condo. When she first arrived, she had a lot of stuff tied on the roof with a clothesline! She was not the first lady of the parking lot.

When Joyce came for a long weekend, I took the two of them to lunch at the Royal Coach Inn—for old times' sake. That's where the Standing Liturgical Commission had a lot of its meetings since Dallas was halfway between coasts and had its great Dallas–Fort Worth and Love Field airports. I have to admit that flying into Love Field, going right to the Royal Coach Inn (a fake Tudor English building), and back to the airport did not give me a very good view or experience of Dallas. I would come back to Dulles and the lovely drive along the Potomac, back into the district, and say, "Dallas is about the ugliest place I've ever been. Plus, they killed my president."

I learned to have a different view after living in Park Cities in Highland Park, and loving the great zoo and the museums, Dallas Cowboys football, the Texas Rangers baseball team, the surrounding ranch country, and of course, the people. I found, with my Kentucky background, I could say "ByBul" just like any Texan.

The weather in Dallas was interesting. The temperature could change

---

126. This was translated from the Leonine Liturgy and was used for Ascension Day.

almost instantly. You could start a golf game in a regular short-sleeved shirt, stop at the turn to get a sweater, and by about the twelfth or thirteenth hole, have to come in because of the cold. On the other hand, summer and fall days routinely hit the hundred-degree mark. We had a screened-in porch and sleeping porch in our new house, and most of the time couldn't use them because it was either too hot or too cold. One native Texan told me, "There's nothing between the North Pole and Dallas except a barbed-wire fence!"

Once when the Standing Liturgical Commission was meeting, it was the weekend of the Texas/Oklahoma football game. We were working over Prayer Book texts when the door of our meeting room burst open and two Oklahoma fans, very drunk, stood in the hall, waving their banners and tilting their glasses. When they saw our rather somber group, some with clerical collars, they sobered up on the spot, and you could see the alcohol drop out of their faces like the gas falling out of those old gas pumps with the glass tops. I think we put a crick in their weekend, and on top of that, Texas won!

Bobby was with us in Dallas when we celebrated his twentieth birthday. (He was born on February 26, 1957.) I felt then that if I could wish one thing for Bobby—Elizabeth and Helen, too—it would be that they

might find a strong faith and a deep sense of God's purpose for their lives. I feared that I'd failed to bear the kind of witness to that—at least in such a way that it is contagious.

One of the strong points of SMAA was that we were able to draw some of the best minds to speak to or lead adult education programs. Norman Pittenger preached and spoke to the adult class.[127] Malcolm Muggeridge visited in conjunction with talks at the University of Dallas,[128] and the newly retired archbishop of Canterbury, Michael Ramsey, was our guest for a long weekend.[129] We had a great celebration of the Eucharist with our eighty-voice choir, some members of the Dallas Symphony, incense, bells, and all the liturgical trimmings. As the archbishop of Canterbury passed the pew where Mrs. Ramsey and Joyce were sitting together, as His Grace passed in procession, Mrs. Ramsey genuflected! I never could get Joyce to do that for me.

We had lunch with my friend John Kirkham from England, who married a Raleigh woman and who was an area bishop[130] of Salisbury and suffragan for Her Majesty's Armed Forces. John told me that at one point in his career he was chaplain to Archbishop Michael Ramsay. He had some

---

127. William Norman Pittenger (July 23, 1905 - June 19, 1997) was an Anglican priest, teacher, and theologian. He wrote about and promoted process theology and became one of the first acknowledged Christian defenders for the open acceptance of homosexual relations among Christians. He served as vice chairman and chairman of the Theological Commission of the World Council of Churches from the mid-1950s through the early 1960s. He lived most of his life in the United States, though from 1966 until his death he lived at King's College at Cambridge University as an honorary member of the university.

128. Thomas Malcolm Muggeridge (March 24, 1903–November 14, 1990) was a British journalist, author, media personality, and satirist. During World War II, he worked for the British government as a soldier and a spy. As a young man, Muggeridge was a left-wing sympathizer, but he later became a forceful anticommunist. He is credited with bringing Mother Teresa to popular attention in the West and stimulating debate about Catholic theology. In his later years he became a religious and moral campaigner.

129. Arthur Michael Ramsey, Baron Ramsey of Canterbury, PC (November 14, 1904–April 23, 1988) was English Anglican bishop and the one hundred archbishop of Canterbury. He was appointed on May 31, 1961, and held the office until 1974.

130. In the Anglican churches, the term applies to a bishop who is an assistant to a diocesan bishop.

wonderful stories about him. Someone once asked him if he believed in
the Assumption of the Blessed Virgin Mary. He replied, "If she's not in
heaven, then where in the hell is she?"

Our ETS professor Frederick W. (Dilly) Dillistone[131]—a renowned
scholar, especially on the Atonement, and then retired in Oxford—also
visited us, as did Marshall McLuhan,[132] Jacques Barzun,[133] Mortimer
Adler,[134] and Henri Nouwen.[135]

We had lots of Sunday services (8 a.m.; two services at 9:00 a.m.;
three services at 11:00 a.m.); parishioners could attend services that had a
guitar, Mass, services in the chapel, services in the main church.... Because
of the variety of the services we were divided on Sundays into six congregations. The adult class numbered around three hundred as an average,
and there were two other adult education offerings at the same time. We
were high church and often added incense to our bells and genuflections.
I learned to genuflect without holding onto something! The choirs were
excellent, and the eleven o'clock choir numbered about eighty singers and
often sounded better than the Mormon Tabernacle Choir. We also had a
daily Eucharist at 7:30 a. m. in the small chapel.

---

131. See note 59.

132. Herbert Marshall McLuhan, CC (Ordre du Canada; July 21, 1911–December 31, 1980),
was a Canadian philosopher of communication theory and a public intellectual. His
work is viewed as one of the cornerstones of the study of media theory, as well as having
practical applications in the advertising and television industries. McLuhan is known for
coining the expressions *the medium is the message* and the *global village*, and for predicting
the World Wide Web almost thirty years before it was invented.

133. Jacques Martin Barzun (1907–2012) was a French-born American historian. Focusing on
ideas and culture, he wrote about a wide range of subjects, including baseball and classical
music, and is best known as a philosopher of education.

134. Mortimer Jerome Adler (1902–2001) was an American philosopher, educator, and
popular author. As a philosopher he worked within the Aristotelian and Thomistic traditions. He lived for the longest stretches in New York City, Chicago, San Francisco, and
San Mateo, California.

135. Henri Jozef Machiel Nouwen (1932–1996), was a Dutch-born Catholic priest, professor,
and writer. His interests were rooted primarily in psychology, pastoral ministry, spirituality, social justice, and community.

Learning to genuflect
(without holding on!)

I did a lot of Lenten preaching—going to St. John's Lafayette Square and Christ Church in Lexington, Kentucky; a two-day lecture at the Seminary of the Southwest in Austin; and at the cathedral for "Monday Preaching" in Houston.

At my first diocesan convention, Suffragan Bishop Robert Terwilliger[136] got up and said there was no scriptural authority or historical precedent for ordaining women. I was aghast, and I asked for the floor and apologized for this being my first contribution as a newcomer but said I disagreed with our suffragan and that I had just come from being on the faculty of our largest seminary and that it and all but one—the exception being Nashotah House—disagreed with him, too. I sat down with a small round of applause from our delegation and was never elected to do anything at any of the following conventions.

It turned out that a number of clergy agreed with me but were not willing to go against the bishops and probably the majority of the convention.

Later, I was asked to lead the annual retreat of the men of the diocese and also became one of the leaders of the Cursillo Movement.[137] But SMAA was such a time-consuming job that I didn't have time, or the inclination, for involvement in the diocese. The bishops remained friendly, but Bob Terwilliger got even by preaching for forty minutes when he came for confirmation. We had over a hundred waiting for him to get on with it and confirm them!

At the Evergreen Conference Center in Colorado I also led a three-day

---

136. Robert Elwin Terwilliger (1912–1991) was suffragan bishop of the Episcopal Diocese of Dallas from 1976-1986.

137. The Cursillo Movement consists of proclaiming the best news of the best reality: that God, in Christ, loves us—as communicated by the best means, which is friendship toward the best of each one, which is the person and his capacity of conviction, decision, and constancy.

workshop on the liturgy. Joyce was elected as a trustee of the National Cathedral Foundation and went frequently to Washington for their meetings.

The calling process to St. Michael's and All Angels had consisted of only one visit to Dallas and a call after that, and as far as I know, none of the six resident clergy had been considered, although each had a group backing their candidacy.

When I was elected rector, these same six clergy were on the staff, and I believe all six had hoped to become rector. Only one of them kept up a negative campaign against me, and he left for another job in the diocese. Several years later he left the Episcopal Church and, I believe, was deposed. Bill Power, who taught at Perkins, became a loyal and helpful colleague and brought his support group along, as did Henry Coke, a native of Dallas, although some of his followers still wished he had won. Father Westover was loyal, somewhat withdrawn, but much loved by a small group, especially members of the Altar Guild. He never called me anything but "Father Estill" (his Christian name was Clarence). It was only when we got on the golf course—he was a very good golfer—that he then called me "Bob." Steve Swann was soon elected head of the Episcopal High School of Dallas and always remained a friend. Our parish grade school was overflowing and had a waiting list. It was a major supplier for the Dallas Episcopal High School.

SMAA had Saturday morning confessions, which took place in a real confessional box at the rear of the nave in the main church. Fr. Westover told me how to use it, and he wisely suggested that I take a book to read since not many penitents came for the formal confession. I put my cassock on, got a book, entered the priest's side, turned on the green light, and waited. Soon I heard high heels coming from the front of the chapel and heading for the confessional. I opened the screen, and a woman entered and said, "Father Estill, Joyce is on the phone!" It was our receptionist, Lola Nix. What a letdown for my first formal hearing of a confession.

I brought Jim Frensley, who was inactive but lived in Dallas; John

Akers from Kentucky; John Drake, who had been rector of the Advent in Spartanburg, South Carolina, but after his wife's death had withdrawn and was working at Sears; and Bill Clarkson, newly ordained and a Duke graduate. So we were well-staffed, and with so many services, everyone had a chance to preach and celebrate nearly every Sunday.

The profile for the new rector had as its top priority the recovery of a strong Christian Education program. At one of my first vestry meetings I commented on this as something we should get to work on. Henry Beck, in answer to my analysis of the situation in which I said we need some highly qualified adults to set a program in motion, said, "How much do you estimate that will cost?" I took a guess out of the air, and I think I remember saying, "About thirty thousand dollars each." Henry replied, "I'll underwrite that for two," and another vestry member said, "I'll take one," and so on until we had the whole sum pledged. That's the way things get done in Texas!

Cursillo is big in Dallas, and a lot of SMAA members were actively involved, so with some reservations I signed up and went to Grapevine Conference Center. Being a veteran of church-sponsored retreats and conferences, I took along a bottle of bourbon, and it is a tribute to the quality of Cursillo that I never even had a sip.

If I had had one reservation, it might have been that there was a strong biblical fundamentalism evident. But the emphasis on prayer in all its aspects and the Sacraments—especially the Eucharist—more than made up for it. I was reminded of a quote from Ronald Goldman on Christian Education. He tells of a student who came home from a Hebrew school and told his mother he had a great day at school. She said, "Johnny, what did they teach you?" He replied, "Well, the Jews were escaping from Egypt, and the Egyptians had them trapped at the Red Sea. Moses quickly ordered engineers to build a pontoon bridge, and the Jews got across and then they mined the bridge. There were helicopters circling overhead to dive-bomb the pontoon as soon as the

Israelites successfully crossed the bridge. Moses ordered them to dive-bomb the pontoons and all the Egyptians fell and got drowned." His mother asked in amazement, "Johnny, is that really what they taught you in Hebrew school?" He answered, "No, Mom, but if I told you what they taught me, you wouldn't believe me!"

Cursillo turned out to be a kind of Anglo-Catholic retreat/renewal event, and I had a great experience. Jim Rose, a layman from SMAA, was the leader, and all the talks—except the one on the Sacraments—were made by laypeople. We visited the Blessed Sacrament, which would have caused Virginia Seminary apoplexy, but seemed very much in place here and helpful spiritually. "Cursillo" means "short talks" (or "short course"). That was the only misnomer. They seemed to use the North Korean torture system, which kept us awake, exhausted, and yet exhilarated. I took along a number of books to read if things got dull.

The final service was attended by several hundred people who had gone through Cursillo and was a wonderful celebration. So now I was a "Cursillisto" and would, and did, recommend it as a very positive renewal vehicle.

Our daughter Elizabeth was happily enrolled in Highland Park High School. Helen lived nearby, and Bobby—after a six-month break to surf in Hawaii—was at Texas Christian University in Fort Worth and on the varsity football team.

One day I had a man in my office who went on and on about his son who had dropped out of school. I listened, did some counseling, and as he was leaving, who should come down the hall pushing a broom but Bobby? He had an interim job helping Leon Farmer, our wonderful property manager. I didn't have the heart to introduce him.

Meanwhile Helen was working as a receptionist at the famous Parkland Hospital, where President Kennedy died. It was in a tough part of the city and operated a very active emergency room. One day a disgruntled patient came in the lobby, pulled out a pistol, and started firing. Helen hid under her desk until the guards grabbed the man and took his gun away.

Leon Farmer managed our maintenance staff, and the business manager, who had served under the former rector Don Henning, continued in his job until we found he was laundering money for people. He would take a check made out for ten thousand dollars, give one thousand dollars to SMAA, and then send the nine-thousand-dollar balance to the school their child was attending, allowing the donor to take a full ten-thousand-dollar tax deduction! High Texas finances. I let him go.

Our choir held an annual choir camp in Colorado at the Evergreen Conference Center near Boulder. Our choir director, Paul Thomas, drove up, but his wife, Joyce, did not want to take that long drive, so she chose to go with me on American Airlines. She had never flown before and was quite nervous. We got her on the plane (she was badly overweight) and discovered that the seat belt wouldn't go around her! We ended by fastening it around her leg. I had visions of her body flying forward, leaving me with only her leg strapped into the seat. We arrived in Boulder safely, and Paul met us. While he went to get his car from the parking lot, I saw an old Lexington friend, Baylor Van Meter, who had been visiting his sister Louise (who was married to Pete Widener and had a ranch in Colorado). We chatted until Paul pulled up in his car, and I had to call Joyce from her seat in the terminal. Baylor thought she was my Joyce, and I'm sure he told everyone in Lexington that Joyce Estill had put on a lot of weight. I didn't have a chance to set him right.

Evergreen was such a nice and convenient place to hold meetings that we returned with our clergy and Christian Education staff for a weekend retreat and employed John Westerhoff,[138] then at Duke Divinity School, to be our leader.

Later, when I was a nominee for bishop of the Diocese of North Carolina,

---

138. The Reverend Dr. John H. Westerhoff III (b. 1933) was a United Church of Christ minister, and later an Episcopalian priest and professor at Duke University Divinity School for twenty years. He advocated through his writing, teaching, pastoring, and editorial work an enculturation model he called "catechesis" or Christian formation.

I thought I had at least one clergy vote in John, who had become a friend. I found out after the fact that he was not canonically resident and could not vote! When I became the bishop, he was the first clergyperson I accepted as a canonical resident. John had a pet rabbit that sat with him on the sofa each night watching television. How could you not like a guy like that?

The Dallas–Fort Worth Airport was a wonderful asset in coming and going. You could always get an earlier flight home at the end of a meeting, or on short hops Southwest operated out of the old Love Field, which was right in our neighborhood. On January 16, 1979, I flew to Austin and gave a prayer at the Inauguration Prayer Service for Bill Clement, a member of SMAA and our new governor.[139] He and I were probably extreme opposites politically. George H. W. Bush and John Connolly were there, along with Dr. Criswell,[140] pastor of the First Baptist Church in Dallas. I watched future president Bush and John Connolly during the inauguration—and they, like I, were thinking of other things, their minds far away. We had bar-b-que Texas style on the capitol grounds, and I flew back to Dallas.

At a meeting of the Dallas Clergy Association held at the First Baptist Church, I asked Dr. Criswell how many people were members. He said twenty-five thousand. I think he had more church buses than we had people (actually, SMAA had five thousand)! It interested me that the five largest churches in their denominations—Baptist, "Christian," Presbyterian, Methodist, and Episcopal—were in Dallas.

A lot of Texans go west to California on vacation, although many frequent

---

139. William Perry "Bill" Clements Jr. was the forty-second and forty-fourth governor of Texas, serving from 1979 to 1983 and again from 1987 to 1991. Clements was the first Republican to have served as governor of Texas since Reconstruction.

140. Wallie Amos Criswell (1909–2002) was an American pastor, author, and a two-term elected president of the Southern Baptist Convention from 1968 to 1970. Supporters have described him as one of the twentieth-century's greatest expository preachers and the patriarch of the conservative resurgence within the SBC.

the ski slopes in Colorado and Utah in the winter. During one vacation, we joined Donnie and Bob Enholm and flew to San Francisco after church and rented a car to drive to Carmel. We stayed at a lovely inn that was snuggled into the hillside overlooking Carmel Bay. One night we had dinner with the Larry Harts from Dallas, whose house hangs out over the sea and the no. 10 hole at Pebble Beach. He served a vintage Margaux red wine.

Though she said I misunderstood her, Donnie was the one who came up to me at the reception in my honor and whispered in my ear (she had a throat problem), "I'm going to be your wife's best friend!" I made a mental note to warn Joyce; she was still in Virginia, waiting for the end of Elizabeth's school. Despite my fears, Donnie and Bob did become, and are to this day, best friends.

The Enholms were interested in the possibility of investing in part of a vineyard, so we visited several, sampled their vintage, and saw their storage areas. We also visited the William Randolph Hearst castle in San Simeon while driving down the breathtaking seaside highway. Among other things we could see was the Soledad Prison where Sirhan Sirhan, who killed Robert Kennedy, was imprisoned.

We ended our California trip in San Francisco, and as we were leaving a lunch place near the cathedral, who should we run into but Bill and Mary Swing?[141] They were there to be interviewed for bishop, and later he was elected. In the afternoon I left for Berkeley and the winter meeting of the National Board of Examining Chaplains, and Joyce and the Enholms left for Dallas. I've always enjoyed visits to Berkeley and walks on the University of California campus, but this time the whole place looked down at the heels, and the excitement I had felt in the air before seemed gone.

---

141. William Edwin Swing (b. 26 August 1936) is a retired bishop of the Episcopal Church in the United States. He was the bishop of California, based in San Francisco, from 1980 to 2006. Swing was ordained a deacon at Huntington, West Virginia, on June 11, 1961; he was ordained a priest at Wheeling, West Virginia, on December 20, 1961, and consecrated as the seventh bishop of California at Grace Cathedral, San Francisco, on September 29, 1979.

Back in Dallas my phone at home rang about eleven-thirty at night, and a woman's voice said, "Father Estill, you'd better come over. I've just shot my roommate." Needless to say, I did go right over and stepped over her late husband's body at the foot of the stairs. Bill Powers, a longtime friend of the couple and my staff colleague, had also been called, and while I sat with her, he dialed the Park City police. The couple were younger than we, but we had often been at parties together and had been in their home and they in ours. They were active members of SMAA. We knew they were having marital problems and that they partied a great deal.

They had come home from a formal party, and she had gone upstairs to her bathroom and had taken a pistol out of a drawer and put it to her head. But as she looked into the mirror, she told us she thought, *I'm shooting the wrong person!* She exited the bathroom just as her husband—in his black tie—was coming up the steps with a glass of after-dinner drinks in each hand. She shot him five times.

She spent the night in jail as a precaution against a possible suicide. There was a hearing, and she went, as they say, scot-free.

She began coming to our regular weekday Eucharist (7:30 a.m.), and we had talks, as she also did with Bill Powers. After several months she came in and asked me if I would appoint her to the Altar Guild. At SMAA the rector appointed the members of the Altar Guild. I thought about it for a day or two, prayed some, and said yes. As soon as that happened, three members of the Altar Guild came to see me and said they were resigning. I tried to dissuade them by pointing out Jesus's attitude toward sinners, etc., but they were firm in their decision. Finally, one of them said, "Our husbands are making us resign!" I guess they were afraid she would teach them some new tricks!

By this time Elizabeth was happily enrolled in Highland Park High School and had already made friends. She was in a carpool, and the first day the mother who had the duty pulled up for her in a huge convertible with the top down and the air-conditioning on! She had also made some

THE SUN SHINES BRIGHT

boyfriends. She and the girls in the carpool, who dressed to the nines, when they got to school would rush into the ladies' room for a final grooming.

After we had been in Dallas for a few months, one of her steady boy-friends asked her to invite us to meet his parents, who dutifully called and invited us to dinner.

When we arrived they called me "Father Estill" and Joyce "Mrs. Estill" until we asked for "Joyce" and "Bob." They asked if we would like a glass of wine, and I noticed they had a fully stocked bar, so I said, "I'd really like a vodka martini, and Joyce would like a bourbon and water." That broke the ice (pardon the pun), and the rest of the evening was relaxed and, I think, a great relief for them. As we were leaving, they came out on the porch to wave good-bye and, confused by some driveway lights, I drove off over their front lawn. They became good friends, and we liked their son a lot—as did Elizabeth.

As I've said earlier, one of the exciting things about Dallas was the constant stream of interesting people who came to speak. Early in March 1979, I had dinner with Marshall McLuhan, Jacques Barzun, and Mortimer Adler. I was disappointed with McLuhan, who seemed pompous, full of himself, and something of a showoff. Malcolm Muggeridge was there, too—and, in my opinion, much superior to McLuhan. He remembered his Easter visit with pleasure.

Later, the next month, Norman Pittinger was in town (again). He really was a lovable old guy and always brought a breath of fresh and more liberal air to the place. We needed it! We take the *New York Times* and, believe it or not, the *Wall Street Journal,* which is more liberal than our daily the *Dallas Daily News*—imagine that!

The Standing Liturgical Committee met in Dallas, and it brought the presiding bishop, Jack Allin,[142] and two anti–Prayer Book revision

---

142. John Maury Allin (1921–1998) was the twenty-third presiding bishop of the Episcopal Church. He was ordained a deacon in the Episcopal Church in 1944 and a priest in 1945. He was elected bishop of the Diocese of Mississippi in 1961 and served until he was elected presiding bishop in 1974. He retired in 1985.

clergy—Bill Ralston and Logan Jackson—to debate and to air their objections. Bill is the son of my first and beloved senior warden in Middlesboro, and I even preached the sermon when he was ordained deacon. He had really gone conservative—especially with regard to the Prayer Book. I knew Logan when he was in seminary, and of course, Jack Allin, who consecrated me bishop. Bill and Logan were both very bright products of Sewanee, as was Jack. I was disappointed to find Jack had sold out to the anti-Prayer Book group. He fought the new Prayer Book all the way. Fortunately, he wasn't much of a leader, and the Prayer Book revision went on without him.

On May 27, 1979, I received the doctor of ministry degree from the joint program of Vanderbilt and Sewanee. I put up my father's brass shingle, "Dr. Estill," on the door of my office. He had it on his door for over forty years. Now there was another "Dr. Estill."

My staff and many parishioners began to call me "Dr. Estill," which I liked much better than "Father." One afternoon I was out making calls, and a good friend, Dick Humke from Louisville, was in town and came by to see me. My secretary told him that Dr. Estill was out but would be back around four. Dick almost broke up with laughter over the "Dr. Estill" bit and promised to return at four. When I got back a little before four, Barbara

Peeler, my secretary, told me about Dick's reaction, so we set him up. When he came in, Barbara said, "Dr. Estill is back and is expecting you. Follow me." She then took him into a side room where we held meetings, turned on the lights, and said, "If you'll take off your clothes, Dr. Estill will see you in a minute!" Humke never got over that experience.

August came again, and on the first, Muzzy, our springer, and I left Dallas

Dr Estill.

for the long drive to Quogue, a good way to unwind before our month away. We got as far as Nashville the first night, and after supper we had a walk on the nearly deserted Vanderbilt campus, where I'd spent several summers working on the joint doctoral program with Sewanee. I picked a magnolia blossom for old times' sake. Their aroma always reminded me of Vandy. We drove straight on the next day, arriving at Quogue at 2 a.m. I had two calls to pray about that summer, as I'd been asked to consider putting my name up for bishop in North Carolina and also Rhode Island. We were certainly happy in Dallas, and yet I'd always considered myself a "man under orders." My task then as always was discerning what God was telling me to do.

I had a little rubber boat just big enough for Muzzy and me, and most of the summer, or shall we say most of August, I spent floating in Money-boque Bay, looking for God's will.

Rhode Island seemed out, but North Carolina was a different matter. So I said no and yes, respectively, and that I would go to High Point, North Carolina, for a meeting with their search committees along with the other semifinalists—Ted Eastman, Allan Bartlett (both of whom followed me in Washington and Louisville, respectively), Bob Ladehoff, Will Spong (brother of Jack), Gordon Charlton, Raby Edwards, Dan Matthews, Martin Tilson, and Doug Burgoyne. We all stayed in the same motel but met with the search committee separately—a good process.

Looking for God's will

They asked us to wait until they had boiled down their list to five and then to make a decision that, if all things were equal, we would say yes. They carefully took down our schedules, and as promised they reached me on the way home to Dallas in Hagerstown, Maryland, and said I was one of the five. That gave Muzzy and me two days to drive, consider the call, and respond to the chair of the committee. If all things were equal, if elected, they wanted to know whether I would accept. I had a yellow pad in the car and had drawn a line down the middle of the page with "stay" on one side and "go" on the other. I would write down the pros and cons as we sped along toward Texas. The lists were almost equal in length!

As we reached the long stretch of road just over the Arkansas line into Texas, I said in my prayer, "Lord, I can't seem to get anywhere in this. Can you please help? I can't do it myself." Nothing happened, but after a few miles with only an occasional car passing us, in the distance I saw a tiny speck coming toward us. It grew bigger and bigger, and it was obviously one of those giant trucks. As it came on, I suddenly saw, above the cab, written in giant blue letters, one word: CAROLINA.

I called the committee and said that I'd say yes. The other four turned out to be Ted Eastman, Dan Matthews, Martin Tilson, and Doug Burgoyne. There would be two open hearings in October—one in Raleigh and one in Salisbury.

While in Dallas we made two visits to Sea Island with friends to play golf, eat, drink, and be merry. We stayed at a house owned by our senior warden's wife, Patty Beck. Patty won the house in a blackjack game! I asked her what she put up, and she said, "My airplane." Dallas is full of such stories.

North Carolina

In the fall of 1979 I was in Denver at the General Convention to appear with the Standing Liturgical Commission for the final vote on the proposed Prayer Book. It was passed overwhelmingly. Joyce was with me. We stayed at the Brown Palace Hotel, and we took one night off at the invitation of the North Carolina deputation to meet them for cocktails. As usual, she is my best foot forward!

Our long years of work were finally ended, and we now had the 1979 version of the *Book of Common Prayer*. I'm sinfully proud to have been on the commission that wrote one of the Prayer Books for the Episcopal Church in the USA.

The North Carolina process finally came to an end on November 2, 1979, with the Special Convention Meeting in Winston-Salem at St. Paul's Church. Coincidentally I had been called to be their rector after Tom Fraser was elected bishop coadjutor. Just before lunch, my friend and apparent supporter Dudley Calhoun called to say I had won the Lay Order on the first ballot and nearly so on the Clergy Ballot. They had cast a second vote and adjourned for lunch. Dudley felt certain I would win.

John Akers and I went to lunch, and when we came back, the staff met us in the hall with a paper miter, balloons, and cheers to say that Dudley had called and I had been elected on the second ballot. During all that bedlam, hugs, and tears, Alfred Purrington Sr., the chancellor of the Diocese of North Carolina, called and gave the official call. Bishop Fraser and Jake Viverette, president of the standing committee, were on

Elected Bishop on the second ballot.

the line as well. I called Joyce, who was serving as a volunteer in the lunch room at Highland Park High School, so she was able to tell Elizabeth, a rising senior.

I wrote in my journal that night, "Just like that, my life and the lives of a lot of others were changed and altered and things past and present ended with new beginnings."

I had prepared a list of people to call, beginning with the other four candidates, and spent the rest of the day doing that. Bobby and Helen were first on the list.

I wrote in my journal, "I must stay very close to my Lord in these hours and in the days ahead. I have a great sense of joy—even in the midst of sorrow over having to leave this wonderful parish, staff and people."

I remembered an old saying: "If you could only be elected bishop and have your mother know it, and then retire—how easy it would be!"

Texans can never understand why anyone would want to leave Texas. Still, on January 21, 1980, the parish celebrated our night with a dinner and a marvelous musical show written by Doug Perry, titled *Bye Bye, Bobby*—a delightful spoof with enough love and tears to make it a fine evening for the parish and for us. Chris Walters-Bugbee, the communications director for the Diocese of North Carolina, was there.

Chris was very impressed and remarked afterward that SMAA had more people at that event than they have in North Carolina for the diocesan convention! On January 24 I was back in North Carolina and had the privilege of giving a talk after the banquet at the annual convention in Charlotte. Chris was a little off in his numbers, since North Carolina had over five hundred people at its convention!

All the preliminary things to be done brought me back to Raleigh. One of the most important was the hiring of a secretary. The business manager had placed an ad in the paper, and the waiting room outside of my new office was crowded. I interviewed all day—and it seemed to me that each aspirant felt God had called them to this particular job.

When I got to the airport that night to fly back to Dallas, I called Lucille McKee—Bill Clarkson's mother-in-law, one of the few people I knew in Raleigh. I told her how unqualified the women I had interviewed were, and she said, "What are the things you're looking for?" I said, "I'd like for her to be attractive, happily married, preferably without children, an Episcopalian if possible though not if she measures up to my other needs, and hopefully a member of the Junior League." This last thing, I explained, would show me that she was involved in the city and the issues of the day.

Lucille called me in a day or so and said, "I've got the right girl for you! The only thing I forgot to ask if she could type!"

That was Libbie Ward, and in addition to all my other standards, she could type up a storm. She was just perfect! We served seven years together, until she had her first child and went into full-time motherhood. I felt like I'd lost a daughter.

Ordination and Consecration

$\mathcal{M}$ arch 15, 1980, was a beautiful spring day, and with all three children, Joyce and I drove to Durham and the Duke Chapel for the ordination and consecration. I blurted out in the car that this was "the happiest day of my life," before realizing, and being reminded at once, that our wedding day and the days our children had been born must have been more important and happier.

The night before, twenty-eight bishops and a few of their spouses along with our family had cocktails and dinner at the Velvet Cloak Inn in Raleigh.

At the consecration, a large contingent from Lexington, another from Middlesboro, and over eighty from Dallas were present, and the Duke Chapel was packed. I asked my former bishops to be co-consecrators: William Moody, Gresch Marmion, Don Davies, and Tom Fraser. Neither Washington bishop could be there. Presiding Bishop Jack Allin was the chief consecrator. John Harper, my longtime friend from our days at Episcopal Theological School, preached, and Allen O'Neal, another friend from ETS days, read the litany. My lay presenters were Donnie Enholm, James and Lucille McKee, Joseph Blount Cheshire IV (whose grandfather was onetime bishop of North Carolina), and Jack Darneille from Washington. The five convocation deans were the clergy presenters: Downs Spitler, Frank Vest (later my suffragan bishop), Rowland Whitmire, John Campbell, and Dan Sapp. Page Bigilow—who had served

Who? Me?

"For a bishop, as God's steward, must be blameless; he must not be arrogant or quick-tempered or addicted to wine or violent or greedy for gain; but he must be hospitable, a lover of goodness, prudent, upright, devout, and self-controlled."
(Titus 1:7-8)

with me on the Standing Liturgical Commission—Bill Powers, Bill Clarkson, Bill Brettmann, John Akers, Erv Little—all former assistants and colleagues—and Cecil Woods, dean at Virginia Seminary, were my attending presbyters and concelebrated at the Eucharist. They caused a bit of a stir when they came forward and included a woman priest, the Reverend Page Bigilow!

Among the presenters, Joe Graves gave me Bishop Burton's pectoral cross—which Hendree Milward, his grandson, sent me. Bishop Burton wore it when he baptized me at Christ Church in Lexington.[143] Paul Thomas, the organist and choirmaster at St. Michael and All Angels, played the prelude and postlude on the organ, and choirs from the small churches of the diocese sang.

My family present, in addition to the children and Joyce, consisted of Revell; her husband, Barrie, and son, Barrie Jr.; and Aunt Eugenia Whitridge, professor of sociology who had taught at Duke and retired to Hillsborough. The flowers were in memory of Joyce's father, my parents, and our son Julian II. My sister hadn't been in church for so long, she wore a hat! She asked me what she should call me now that I was a bishop.

143. Bishop Lewis William Burton was the first Episcopal bishop of the Diocese of Lexington, Kentucky, which was organized in 1896. His father, Lewis Burton Sr., was at St. John's Parish in Cleveland, Ohio, a position that Bishop Burton later acquired. Lewis William Burton was born in 1852 and attended the public schools of Cleveland and Kenyon Grammar School, a preparatory school for Kenyon College, Gambier, Ohio, which he entered in 1869. He graduated from Kenyon in 1873. In 1874 he entered the Philadelphia Divinity School. In 1877 he was ordained to the diaconate. After ordination to the priesthood, he served as rector of All Saints Church until 1880. He became assistant to his father, and then his successor at St. Mark's Church, Cleveland. In 1884 Burton accepted a call to St. John's Church in Richmond, Virginia. On October 1, 1893, he became rector of St. Andrew's Church in Louisville. He was forty-three years old when he was consecrated bishop of Lexington on January 15, 1896, where he served as bishop from 1896 to 1929.

I replied, "Most Precious One." She believed me! Over eighteen hundred people attended, plus two hundred bishops and clergy.

After the grand consecration service, it was quite a change to visit a small church with a choir of five and an old pipe organ. This was to be my responsibility while coadjutor—the churches with fewer than three hundred parishioners. That included 75 percent of the churches in the diocese.

You are the first person I have ever confirmed.

For my first Sunday as a bishop I drove to Scotland Neck. After vesting, I met the one child who would be confirmed, and clad in my new array, I bent over and said, "You are going to be the first person I have ever confirmed." She took one look at this apparition clad in a cope and miter and threw up! So I was off to a flying start.

Bishops—at least in the Diocese of North Carolina—are dressed in an alb, a chasuble, a cope, and a miter. And they all wear a ring with the diocesan shield on it, a pectoral cross, and they carry a staff. Bishop Richard Baker,[144] bishop before Tom Fraser, called and gave me his ring. A Baptist layman in Middlesboro carved my staff out of wood from Virginia, Tennessee, North Carolina, and Kentucky.

I wrote in my journal, "I feel something like Frodo in the *Lord of the*

144. The Right Reverend Richard Henry Baker (July 8, 1897–April 13, 1981), bishop coadjutor of North Carolina, 1951–1959; bishop of North Carolina, 1959–1965. During World War I, Norfolk-born Richard Henry Baker left Virginia for France and was awarded the Croix de Guerre by the French government for extraordinary heroism as an ambulance driver. He returned to graduate from the University of Virginia and Virginia Theological Seminary, priested in 1924, and served as chaplain at Virginia Episcopal School. Baker served churches in Louisiana and Virginia before beginning his twenty-year-long rectorship at Baltimore's Church of the Redeemer. As bishop of North Carolina, Baker supported funding for local diocesan programs and for the Mutual Responsibility and Interdependence program promoted by the national church.

Rings, having taken the ring of a bishop. Tolkien writes, 'A great dread fell on [Frodo]...longing to rest and remain by Bilbo's side. "I will take the ring," Frodo says, "...though I do not know the way."'"

Dick Baker, who had been the bishop before Tom Fraser, had also gone to Episcopal High School, years before I did, and we had known each other from provincial meetings and had played golf several times at Kanuga. He usually beat me, which I found out later was partly due to the fact that one of his legs was shorter than the other, and he could negotiate the mountain course better than I! So—perhaps he owed me! He called on the phone after I was elected and said he'd like for me to have the ring and then pass it on to the next bishop. I thanked him warmly and had just hung up when the phone rang again, and Dick said, "My wife said that was really chintzy of me! 'You should give it to him and not have him pass it on.'" We had a good laugh, and I thanked him and her again. Unfortunately, he was not up physically to be at the consecration service.

With all this stuff, it's no wonder that little girl threw up! It is said of the poet W. H. Auden that "he had a saving sense of the ridiculous." One look in the mirror should remind bishops of "the ridiculous" and of the need for a healthy sense of humor and perhaps even some humility.

The best thing to that point about being a bishop was visiting each congregation. I tried to have a pre-visit a week or two before the official

They thought I was John Wayne.

one—with the clergy, vestry, and any other leaders. Then the big day came, and one was welcomed. The feeling of being part of a larger church was shared, and when possible, I got to baptize and confirm as well as preach and preside at the Eucharist. The inevitable covered-dish supper or lunch followed, and I could feel my Episcopal presence growing beneath my pectoral cross.

On January 1, 1983, Tom Fraser retired, and I became the bishop, My responsibilities increased as I began to visit and get to know the larger congregations.

The dean of the divinity school at Duke, Dennis Campbell, set up a class in Anglicanism for the twenty or so Episcopal students, and Peter Lee, then at the Chapel of the Cross in Chapel Hill, taught it at first. When he was elected bishop of Virginia, I was asked to take it over. Dennis and I became good friends and often had lunch together. He later became the headmaster of Woodberry Forest School in Orange, Virginia. Dennis told me of receiving a paper from a student in his class on the Atonement. The student's paper had this typographical error: "Jesus came into the world and took our quilt [sic] away." Dennis wrote next to it in the margin when he returned the paper, "Don't worry: He promised to send a comforter!"

Late in January I received a phone call from one of my oldest and closest friends, Buddy Buckner, to tell me he had an inoperable cancer. I broke down at the end of our conversation and simply wept.

At the beginning of my episcopate, another friend, George Graves, died with the same thing. I flew to Fort Lauderdale and conducted his funeral as I would in a year or so with Buddy. How is it that some of us live and others die at the same age! Surely, life is short and uncertain, and we should live every minute to the fullest possible extent. I am reminded of Jorge Luis Borges's tanka poem:

> *Not to have fallen*
> *like others of my lineage*
> *cut down in battle.*
> *To be in the fruitless night*
> *he who counts the syllables.*

In the service for the ordination of a bishop in *The Book of Common Prayer* (1979), in the "Examination," the presiding bishop says, "With your fellow bishops, you will share in the leadership of the Church throughout the world."

That comes true right away. In addition to all the diocesan, interfaith, and civic duties, there are frequent trips to House of Bishops' meetings, committees, and convocative responsibilities and conferences here and there across the country and abroad.

I found that new bishops were mostly to be seen and not heard. At my first House of Bishops' meeting, I introduced a motion of some sort (which I have chosen to put out of my mind). The vote came back against it, 321-1! I went into the men's room to get over the shock, and as I left to go back to my seat, my hero and former colleague when we were both deans of cathedrals and he was then suffragan bishop of Washington while I was there—Paul Moore—passed me and said, "Nice try, Bill."

Later, after a year or two, I was named to the Board of Theological Education and later chaired it, and later also the Board of Examining Chaplains and chair of the House's Liturgy Committee, so my early defeat was forgotten even by Paul Moore.

The greatest event was the 1988 Lambeth Conference held on the campus next to Canterbury Cathedral, with bishops from all over the world in attendance. Robert Runcie, the Most Reverend and Right Honorable Lord Archbishop of Canterbury, was our host.

One of the highlights was the Queen's Garden Tea Party at Buckingham Palace. The spouses wore garden party hats, and the bishops their purple cassocks.

All the spouses wore large hats.

All of the royals were there, and Joyce and I were introduced to the Queen by Archbishop Runcie, who read our tag and said, "Your Majesty, I present the bishop of North Carolina and his wife." We were told not to speak unless spoken to, and the Queen said, "I have never been in North Carolina." That gave me the opening to say, "Your Majesty, we are both Kentuckians and just came from Lexington where we saw your brood mares at Will Farish's farm." She threw up her hands and said, "How were they?" I replied, "They were fine, but they miss you!" She threw up her hands again and the archbishop tried to pull her along, but she stayed put, so I said, "I especially liked the Bustino mare," to which she replied, "Oh, I do, too!" With that the archbishop pushed the bishop of Vermont to the front, and they moved on.

We moved on to Princess Diana. She said, "I love your purple cassock." I was ready to give North Carolina back to her!

To my great surprise—and do I add delight?—a picture of me patting a giant seventeen-hand-high police horse appeared on the front page of the *Times*. Bishop Jack Spong, who always sought publicity, was green with envy.

Previously when I was on sabbatical in England, Italy, or Spain, I had preached at Canterbury Cathedral as well as the Episcopal Church in Florence. Most of the congregation on that Sunday at Canterbury were tourists. All of the Brits were at home in bed. On

Petting a police horse.

that occasion Archbishop Runcie was in the congregation and afterward invited us to tea later in the afternoon at the archbishop's palace. He had held the annual ordination service, and all the new clergy and their spouses were there.

All of the US bishops gave extra money so that the bishops from developing countries could attend Lambeth. We also shared housing with those bishops and their spouses. Our new friends were from the Sudan, and along with their people, they were suffering from a long drought and lack of food. The bishop's spouse, when she thought no one was looking, plunged her fingers into the sugar bowl. It was a sobering experience for us. He told me that on his last visitation to one of his villages before coming to Lambeth, no one came to the service. They were too starved and weak to leave their huts.

Later, as part of the conference, we gathered in the crypt of the cathedral near the spot where Becket was murdered and watched a production of T. S. Eliot's *Murder in the Cathedral*. We were sitting behind Archbishop Runcie when the famous line was given by one of the knights in the way of an apology for killing Becket: "When you come to the point, it does go against the grain to kill an Archbishop, especially when you have been brought up in good Church traditions." Runcie laughed a bit nervously with the rest of us.

One of our most memorable experiences during our first visit to Canterbury several years before Lambeth was going into the cathedral at night with the only light coming through the stained-glass windows from the street lights outside. We were staying on the close with one of the senior canons and his wife and had their little Corgi with us. We left him outside the cathedral, and just as I was about to sit in the famous Bishop's Chair, the Corgi burst through the door and ran around the nave looking for us!

St. Augustine's chair was saved!

At the Lambeth Conference I thought Runcie was an excellent presider and host. He met the special train from London with a lot of us on it—and was there with his wife to bid us good-bye as well. Some of the speakers, like Desmond Tutu, were memorable, though the small group discussions, and even the group Bible studies, were boring and not very productive. I think it was at that meeting that Bishop Tutu said, "The missionaries came to Africa and gave us Bibles and taught us to pray. When we closed our eyes in prayer and then opened them, they had our land and we had their Bibles." The free time was the best part, and our meals together gave us a chance for informal talk. Most events took a recess at 4 p.m., and I got to jump on the train and go to the races at several tracks nearby—getting back in time for dinner.

The long daylight makes it possible to race well into the evening, and of course racing in England is a wonderful experience. I didn't get to any steeplechase events, but the flat racing on the natural turf was racing as it should be. I even picked a few winners. Joyce, meanwhile, was involved in the wives' meetings and events organized for the spouses.

Back in the diocese, the addition of Jim Lewis to the staff as diocesan Christian social ministries director, was waking things up. At the diocesan convention shortly after he had come, I asked him to be speaker at the banquet the first night. I was in a wheelchair to dramatize the issue of accessibility for the handicapped.

Jim opened by saying that I had asked him to say a word about himself, to keep it light since the delegates had been meeting all day, and to describe his plan for Christian social ministries (CSM). He said that after talking with some of the members of the commission, he had decided to use the time to be even more specific about how he saw his work in the diocese. He admitted that he had had some doubts about coming to North Carolina where "people had voted for Jessie Helms as their senator." I noticed several delegates sinking down at their seats. He added that he had prayed about it—and that he was convinced that it was God's will and that "*She* approved"! More delegates sank in their seats. The rest of the talk was, I thought, brilliant. Jim is a superb communicator, and he worked in his credentials along the way. Washington and Lee grad, All-American lacrosse player, Marine officer with service in Vietnam, lacrosse coach at the Naval Academy while curate at the church in

A doctor from Duke.

Annapolis—and happily married to a Sweetbrier girl. It was quite an evening, and he got a very warm reception from most of the audience.

One of the first events Jim Lewis designed was a prayer vigil for those living with AIDS. Our diocese followed this with the first church-sponsored AIDS Conference that had been held in North Carolina. The only light moment in an otherwise glum and painful day at the AIDS Conference was when a doctor from Duke, addressing mostly people my age, said, "Think back over your last ten sexual partners."

Another first for our diocese was the ordination of a woman to the diaconate and later the priesthood. That opened the door for those who had been waiting and hoping. In addition to that first, we began the diaconate program. I brought my friend from Washington days, Earl Brill,[145] and made him the chaplain to our students at Duke and the director of our new Deacons' Training Program. Earl was one of the brightest persons I knew, and as soon as he opened shop, we had a fine group of candidates ready to go. Sadly, Bishop Fraser was opposed to the idea of a perpetual diaconate; so, although I said I would start such a program when I was one of the nominees for bishop, I waited until Tom retired and until I moved from coadjutor to bishop.

Jim Lewis organized an excellent Department of Social Ministries, and soon we were involved in such wide-ranging projects as helping unionize the chicken workers at a plant in Siler City; establishing with the Diocese of East Carolina a farmworkers' ministry; and enabling a

---

145. Earl H. Brill, in more than forty years of service to the Episcopal Church, displayed a commitment to campus ministry, training for deacons, orientation for new clergy, and continuing education for laity and clergy. He served the church and academia in a variety of capacities, most notably as the director of studies at the College of Preachers in Washington, DC, and a canon of the Washington Cathedral from 1974 through 1983.

great deal of new work by accessing the Jessie Ball duPont Fund.[146] Over the years we received over a million dollars from the fund. We also were one of the sponsors for the establishment of the Self-Help Credit Union in Durham, which has grown into a multimillion-dollar credit union.

As soon as I retired as bishop, my successor, the Right Reverend Robert Carroll Johnson Jr. fired Jim, who was hired almost immediately by the Diocese of Delaware, where he pitched himself against the poultry business, the most powerful industry in southern Delaware and the neighboring Eastern Shore of Maryland. As Jim had done in Siler City, North Carolina, he organized poultry workers into unions, publicized woeful working conditions inside chicken processing plants. He took on major companies like Purdue Farms, Inc., and Tyson Foods. He is now retired and living in Charleston, West Virginia on Lee Street!

We helped establish a chapter of Integrity at Duke to reach out to gay men and lesbians, and with the help of some of those students, I held late afternoon sessions in my office to listen to their concerns and to attempt ways of helping them.

Another great addition to our team came with the election of Frank Vest as my suffragan bishop.[147] Frank was rector of our largest parish, Christ Church in Charlotte, and we had been friends even before I came to the diocese. I felt the people of the diocese should be able to elect their own suffragan instead of having assisting bishops appointed by me. I had appointed two retired bishops—John Burgess,[148] the second African

146. The Jessie Ball duPont Fund, "Florida's leading national foundation," is a charitable foundation that issues grants to organizations that received support from Jessie Ball duPont during the years 1960 to1964, inclusive. When she died on September 26, 1970, the bulk of her estimated forty-two-million-dollar estate, one of the largest in Florida history at that time, became the Jessie Ball duPont Religious, Charitable and Educational Fund.
147. Frank Vest (1936–2008), suffragan bishop of the Diocese of North Carolina (1985–1989), bishop coadjutor of the Diocese of Southern Virginia (1989–1991), and bishop of the Diocese of Southern Virginia (1991–1998).
148. John Melville Burgess (March 11, 1909–August 24, 2003) was the twelfth bishop of the Episcopal Diocese of Massachusetts in Boston from 1970 to 1975 and the first African

American bishop to serve in North Carolina, and then Fred Putnam[149] during the interim after Tom Fraser's retirement—but now we had our own elected suffragan, and a superior one at that. I also thought the suffragan should live in Raleigh and operate out of the diocesan house, where we would be just down the hall from each other. In fact, we shared a bathroom! Frank and I were on the same wavelength, and we worked together as a team.

One of the few things about which we differed was churchmanship. He was a "Virginia low," and I often said I was a "closet Anglo-Catholic." Frank had a great sense of humor, and he once said, "Closet, hell." Nonetheless, he went along with wearing high-church vestments, and I told him he looked dashing in a miter.

On March 11, 1987, Caroline Allen Estill was born to Bobby and Cindy Allen in Boston. Bobby, who was a sportscaster for the CBS affiliate, put it on television, so nearly a million people saw her before we did!

And on June 27, 1987, Elizabeth and John Battle Robertson II were married in Christ Church in Raleigh. Dan Sapp, the rector and a long-time friend, assisted me, and the happy couple left in a horse-drawn cart

---

American to head an Episcopal diocese. After beginning his ministry in his home parish of St. Philip's Episcopal, a Colored Episcopal Mission in Grand Rapids, and then Cincinnati, Ohio, Burgess became the Episcopal chaplain at Howard University in Washington, DC, in 1946. In 1951 he became the first African American to serve as canon at Washington National Cathedral. In 1956 Burgess moved to the Episcopal Diocese of Massachusetts as an archdeacon of Boston's parishes and missions and superintendent of what became named the Episcopal City Mission. He was the first black archdeacon in New England. In 1962 Burgess was installed as a suffragan bishop of the Episcopal Diocese of Massachusetts, becoming the first African American to serve the Episcopal Church as spiritual leader in a predominantly white diocese. When Burgess was consecrated as diocesan bishop in 1970 he became the first African American to head an Episcopal diocese.

149. Frederick Warren "Fred" Putnam Jr. (June 17, 1917–June 7, 2007) was the first Episcopal bishop of the Navajoland Area Mission. He also served as suffragan bishop of Oklahoma and assistant bishop in Minnesota.

for the City Club and the reception. The only slip in the service was when I mispronounced John B's last name, "Robinson" [*sic*]. Elizabeth, in a loud stage whisper, corrected me and hissed, "Daddy, it's Robertson!" I also had the pleasure and privilege of presiding at Helen and Steve Foote's marriage and Cindy's marriage to Bobby in Winter Park, Florida.

As we had for the previous twenty summers, we spent August at Quogue where I was the priest in charge through Labor Day. As usual, I spent a few days at Saratoga—that year with John Griffith. I also had a meeting in Boston, so I was able to see Bobby, Cindy, and Caroline. I took the Estill Jrs. to the Ritz Bar and then to Lochober's, the restaurant where Joyce and I had been thirty-five years before! Bobby arrived at the Ritz without a tie, and the head waiter took him aside to lend him a tie from their supply. I took Cindy to our table in the bar, and as I seated her, I saw good friends from Dallas, Dan and Betsy Shea, sitting in the far corner. Betsy's back was toward us, and Dan waved discreetly and kept talking with Betsy. When Bobby appeared, Dan broke into a smile, pointed us out to Betsy, and the two came over to say, "Hello." Dan admitted that his first thought was that I was stepping out with a blonde. What a loyal friend!

Back in Raleigh, September 19, 1987, was a big day. We embarked on the largest financial campaign in the history of the diocese—the ACTS campaign—"A Celebration Through Stewardship." Our goal was $6.6 million. Ward, Dresham, and Reinhardt were our outside fund-raising counsel.

Old mapmakers wrote at the edges of their maps: "Beyond here, there be dragons." At the time, I wrote journal, "I have a feeling that, beyond this campaign there 'be' a new sense of mission and ministry for the diocese."

We ended the year with a visit to the Boston Estills and a chance to be in a New England Christmas snowstorm with a wind-chill of minus twenty degrees. In addition, as 1987 ended, I would like to think that I had measured up to the highest compliment the Quakers ever pay anyone: "Friend, thee has been used."

On February 15, 1988, one of my heroes died—Richard P. Feynman, arguably the most brilliant and influential of the postwar generation of theoretical physicists.[150]

In many of his books and articles, Feynman discussed uncertainty, saying he would rather not know something than have the wrong answer. Feynman knew he was a curious character: he taught himself everything from fixing radios to speaking Portuguese, and from drawing nudes to deciphering Mayan hieroglyphics.

He coined the phrase "cargo cult science" to describe modern psychology. He said that some Pacific Islanders built their own runways and manned them using wooden headphones and bamboo antennas, so that cargo planes would continue to arrive after WWII. Feynman compared this to cargo cult scientists, who he said go through scientific investigations but something is constantly out of place. They cannot get an answer, just as the Pacific Islanders could not get planes to land.

I agreed to serve on the board of General Theological Seminary in New York to support my old friend Jim Fenhagen, then dean of the seminary.[151] They had a difficult financial problem in that their plant was old and demanded a lot of money simply for maintenance and renewal (the main boilers that heated the place were ancient and in need of repair or replacement). My visit afforded me a chance to visit with the seminarians

---

150. Richard Phillips Feynman (1918–1988) was an American theoretical physicist known for his work in the path integral formulation of quantum mechanics, the theory of quantum electrodynamics, and the physics of the superfluidity of supercooled liquid helium, as well as in particle physics for which he proposed the parton model.

151. The Reverend Canon James Canon Fenhagin (1930–2012), a nationally esteemed church leader and theological educator, is probably best known for his fourteen-year tenure (1978–1992) as dean and president of the General Theological Seminary in New York City, where, in addition to administrative responsibilities, he taught subjects related to Christian spirituality and the practice of ministry. Ordained in 1954, Fenhagen served both rural and urban Episcopal congregations in Maryland, South Carolina, and the District of Columbia before becoming director of Christian Education for the Diocese of Washington, DC. Following his tenure as dean of General Theological Seminary, he directed the Cornerstone Project of the Episcopal Church Foundation.

from our diocese and take them out to lunch. When I was in seminary, my bishop never visited me at all.

I tried to "keep the shop" and be in the diocese and available as much as possible. Yet in the ordination service for bishops, I was charged to "share with my fellow bishops in the leadership of the Church throughout the world," and I answered, "I will, by the grace given me."

So...I tried to be faithful to that call. For example, in February 1988 alone, I was in New York for the General Seminary Board Meeting and in Atlanta, at the airport, for a meeting of the bishops of the province—for a total of four days that month out of the diocese.

Later in the year, I was at Sewanee for the meeting of the board of trustees—of which I was a member—and to call on our seminarians; then back up to another meeting of the General Seminary board in New York; at the Province IV Synod Meeting at Kanuga; in Detroit for the July 1988 General Convention for eleven days, and in England for the Lambeth Conference (which meets every ten years); at Quogue for the month of August; at Kanuga again for the board of directors—of which I was then chairman—and the board of visitors; in New Haven (Yale) for a meeting of the National Board of Theological Education, of which I was chair, and visiting seminarians; in Virginia for a day speaking to the Huguenot Convention; in Honduras with our Companion Diocese Committee, and in Belize to do their confirmations; and finally (December 12–13) in Delray Beach, Florida, at the Duncan Center, to meet as a member of the Presiding Bishop's Select Committee of Bishops and Deans.

When I was interviewed by the search committee of the diocese—and later, in talks before the delegates who would vote in the election of the bishop—I emphasized the establishment of a program to train people for what was then called the "perpetual diaconate." Tom Fraser died October 20, 1989. His last words to me were, "I wish I could give you this pain!" He had been opposed to the diaconate, and I made it clear that we disagreed, and that while I respected his position, when I became bishop I would push it through. So, in 1983, when I became the diocesan bishop, we started the program. I especially emphasized the part in the ordination service for the diaconate in the Book of Common Prayer (1979) that states, "You are to interpret to the Church the needs, concerns, and hopes of the world," and "at all times, your life and teaching are to show Christ's people that in serving the helpless they are serving Christ himself."

As I mentioned earlier, I called my old friend Earl Brill to be the chaplain to Episcopal students at Duke and be the director of the Deacons' Program. I had known Earl, who had been on the staff of the College of Preachers at the Washington National Cathedral, when I was at St. Albans. Weekend classes were held at the Episcopal Student Center at Duke, and we were able to use faculty from the Duke Divinity School, its library, and from time to time, take advantage of visiting speakers and lecturers. Some of our own clergy—several with PhDs—also taught the weekend classes.

After the program was well under way and a number of men and women ordained, I began taking deacons with me on Sunday visitations so that all our congregations could see a deacon in action and hear from me an explanation of our program. Often the deacon would drive the car while I would answer mail on my tape recorder or, between visits, get in a nap. Chuck Oglesby was my driver on several occasions, and I was dictating letters into my machine as he drove on—keeping an appropriate deadpan tone. So I made up a letter telling some imaginary recipient that I would consent to their request to be married to someone of the same sex (this was years before that issue came up in the church). Chuck never blinked an eye, so I finally shut off the recorder and I said, "Dammit, Chuck! I know you're listening!" He had to admit he was, and then I told him I had fooled him into confessing. As of the last lists from the diocesan convention in 2006, there were thirty deacons now canonically resident in the diocese.

Once or twice a year I enjoyed a hunting trip with my hunting buddies, John Bratten, Gene Hardin, and Bill Sigmon. John had restored an old family farmhouse and four-hundred-acre farm in South Carolina near Florence. On one of our visits, Ely, an old black man who had worked for Bernard Baruch on his hunting estate nearby, came for supper and told us of all the important people who came there to hunt or simply relax. The most famous in Ely's opinion was Winston Churchill, who came several times when he was in this country. Ely would meet his train and drive him to the lodge. Ely said Mr. Churchill would always check on the brandy supply and would take a bottle to his room after dinner. He would also call Ely to come up for a nightcap! Eisenhower and Clare Boothe Luce were also guests, and Ely told us Mrs. Luce could outshoot all of the men.

I especially enjoyed these hunts because we would ride horses until the dogs would point, then get off, unsheathe our guns, shoot at the covey, then remount. What a way to go!

John Bratten was a perfect host, and on one dove hunt at his Quarry in Raleigh I got my limit fairly soon and laid the birds out in front of me so that I could be sure not to go over the limit. John—the perfect host—came by in his pickup dispensing soft drinks and ran right over my birds.

I started hunting in Texas as a way to have time with Bobby, and at one point we wanted to do some quail hunting but didn't have a dog. Our receptionist, Barbara Peeler, who was divorced, said, "My ex-husband has a wonderful dog named Lucy. He never hunts anymore, and Lucy just sits in his backyard in a pen. Call him!"

I guess I wasn't thinking clearly, but I did call him and asked if we could "borrow" Lucy. There was a brief silence on the other end until he said, "Father Estill, I wouldn't lend Lucy to God if he asked me!" He quickly recovered and said, "I'd love to take you and Bobby out—and I'll bring Lucy!" And he did. His idea of quail hunting was to locate a covey on the ground and shoot as many as possible. He then announced, "Now we've got our supper! Let's hunt!"

I always ate anything I shot, with three exceptions, when I had a taxidermist stuff and mount a wood duck shot at Orten Plantation near

Wilmington while hunting with our host, my old EHS classmate Lawrence Sprunt; a Canada goose, shot from a blind at Lake Mattamuskeet in the company of Bill Sigmon, Gene Hardin, and John Bratten; and on another hunt, a mute swan. I finally gave up "blood sports."

Robert Caro—in the second volume of his LBJ biography[152]—describes Coke Stevenson, onetime governor of Texas, who was on a hunting trip with several fellow legislators and a lobbyist. They were hunting on a friend's ranch, and Stevenson was asked by his friend to stop in one of the back pastures and destroy a horse, an old family pet, which had grown old and infirm. "Stevenson agreed," wrote Caro, "and as the car with the hunters was passing the horse (the others didn't know of the owner's request), he asked the driver to stop and got out of the car. 'I think I'll just kill that ol' horse,' he said, and taking aim, shot it in the head. His companions, unaware of the rancher's request, stared in amazement. 'Why did you shoot that horse?' the lobbyist finally asked. 'I always wondered what it would feel like to shoot a horse,' Stevenson drawled. Pausing, he stared hard at the lobbyist. 'Now, I'm wondering what it would feel like to shoot a man!'"

It's fortunate that before I gave up hunting I found my bishop's ring in the pocket of a pair of quail-hunting pants. I had lost it once before for several hours when it flew off my finger into a wastebasket on a bitter cold night at our conference center. I finally retraced my steps and found it with the carton I had fried chicken in from a drive-through.

The last loss came shortly after I retired, and for nearly two years into retirement it was gone. If I had put those hunting pants away with my other hunting gear, I might never have found it.

I've always tried to keep active in ecumenical matters and was president of the Kentucky Council of Churches and president of the North Carolina

---

152. Robert Caro, *Means of Ascent.* (New York: Knopf, 1982)

Council as well. In that capacity I often met with North Carolina's governors—especially when we hoped for a governor's decision to give a life sentence to someone scheduled to be executed. We didn't have much luck, though Governor Jim Martin did come through at least once. I also met with then senator Terry Sanford, one of North Carolina's finest, who was helpful in some problems in Central America when we had companion relationships with Belize.

Years ago when I was in Louisville I met Saul Alinsky, one of the great organizers of the 1950s and '60s. Later I attended through the Church and City Conference a two-day workshop with him in Chicago. In the fine biography of Alinsky by Sanford D. Horwitt,[153] Horwitt wrote, "Alinsky defied every power that robbed poor people of their dignity." "This," Alinsky said, "was ultimately an act of preserving my own!" He worked around the concept that the American system functioned best when power was evenly distributed throughout society and, conversely, was headed for trouble if some segments were relatively powerless. For him, "Change means movement, movement means friction, friction means heat, and heat means controversy."

I've also known some impressive and powerful women during my career.

Mother Teresa came to Charlotte to open one of her convents, and I was invited to meet her along with other judiciary heads and sit with her on the platform as she made a speech. When she came into the room she went up to each of us and had a few words. One of her Sisters followed closely behind her. When she came to me, she looked up (she was a tiny person) at my purple shirt and said, "You are a bishop?" I told her I was an Episcopal bishop, and for some reason I added, "I have six granddaughters!" She threw up her hands and turned to the Sister who was

153. Sanford D. Horwitt, *Let Them Call Me Rebel: Saul Alinsky, His Life and Legacy.* (New York: Knopf, 1989).

about the same size and said, "Let me have six medals!" She took them in her hands and said, "I bless these for your grandchildren." I believe our youngest grandchild swallowed hers, so she was twice blessed.

At the end of our time with her, we had a picture taken for the paper. The photographer lined us all up with Mother Teresa in the middle. He said, "Mother Teresa, will you stand up?" She answered in her thick accent, "I am standing up!"

I was thrilled to meet her, but her address was a letdown and I wished I had not been on the podium seeming to agree with her. Almost the whole talk had to do with what she called "the sin of abortion." She said, "If you don't want your babies, give them to me."

Probably the most influential woman I have been privileged to know was Katherine Graham, then owner and publisher of the *Washington Post*. Joyce and I had met her daughter, Lolly Weymuth, on Cumberland Island, and Lolly, I'm sure, must have asked her famous mother to "be nice to the Estills." In fact, Kay was an inactive member of St. Albans and when her son, Donny, was married, I performed the service. Kay included us in many of her parties, and we would come home bragging about sitting next to Walter Cronkite or Tom Brokaw or one of the Alsops. Joyce, at one party, ended up next to Dustin Hoffman. We even spent a weekend at her place in Virginia—Glen Welby Farm. I believe Clayton Fritchey was there, too.[154] I was her partner when we played tennis, and I distinguished myself by serving a ball that hit her between the shoulders and broke her bra strap.

Helen Shoemaker, widow of my cousin Sam Shoemaker, was another strong person, and her books on prayer and her work in the Faith Alive movement influenced a lot of people. After Sam's death, Helen would call me from their home in the Green Spring Valley, and we would meet

---

154. Clayton Fritchey was a syndicated columnist who also had a long career in public service at the White House, the Pentagon, and the United Nations.

at her club in Georgetown for lunch. To save on parking, I would pick
her up at our rectory and take her to lunch. We talked and talked—and
usually the parking fee was more than the lunch tab. She had grown very
conservative in her later years, and we often disagreed about things once
we got beyond prayer.

When Helen Estill graduated from National Cathedral School, she
headed the student committee to choose a graduation speaker. They
chose Gloria Steinem! She came, spoke well (there were a few s— words,
and I believe I heard one f— word), and wore blue jeans while the graduates were in white evening dresses and carried red roses. She came to our
rectory afterward and had a Coke out of one of our silver cups. She spent
some time on the phone talking to her mother. As Kay Graham pointed
out, "Gloria's theme was that there is a kind of authentic self in there that
is a guide if it's not too squelched, and if we're not too scared to listen
to it." That insight came to the young ladies at the National Cathedral
School, thanks to Helen Estill. The Steinem silver cup remained on our
mantle until Helen left for the University of Arizona.

Anne Harrison—whose husband, Gil, was editor of the *New Republic*—was an influential member of St. Alban's and a great supporter of
what we were doing with young people at St. Alban's and beyond.

My distant cousin Mary Breckinridge was another creative and influential woman whom I got to know when I was in Middlesboro. She was
founder of the Frontier Nursing Service based in Hyden, just over the
mountains, deeper in the coalfields. She asked if I would come have communion for her community of nurses and fieldworkers. My father was the first
pediatrician to visit the Frontier Nursing Service headquarters in Hyden.
He held a clinic and also a refresher for the nurses and staff. I remember
hearing him say that he was not too popular with the mountain folk who
brought their children to him because he didn't prescribe a lot of pills!

We had a wonderful visit, although I found that cousin Mary really
preferred the 1662 English Prayer Book and insisted on doing the service

"her way." Nevertheless, her work in the mountains cut the infant mortality rate down to practically nothing, and her book *Wide Neighborhoods* deeply touched me.[155] Joyce was elected and served on the FNS board and, at this writing, was an honorary member of the board.

While I was in Lexington at Christ Church after retirement doing a four-month interim between rectors, Supreme Court Justice Sandra Day O'Connor came to Lexington and was the guest speaker at Christ Church. We had a reception afterward, and I had a long talk with her and was more impressed than I thought I would be. She turned out to be the important swing vote on the Court—and, as with my impression, much more liberal than I had expected.

In Christ Church there is a pew with a plaque reading, "Here worshipped Henry Clay." I was tempted to write under it, "But not much!" Still, Clay was a great man and was baptized and confirmed rather late in life. Justice O'Connor spoke of him and seemed to have done her homework. The whole Fayette County Bar Association was there, along with US representative Ben Chandler.

Since this section of my memoir is centered on the fact that I have been privileged to know some remarkable women, I would count among them Queen Elizabeth, about whom I wrote while describing our Lambeth trip, and of course, Princess Diana! And while not in the same league, but arguably the "Queen of Saratoga," Mary Lou Whitney was another celebrity I got to know. She and Sonny Whitney had a lovely house on their farm in Lexington and came for an extended stay during the time I was rector of Christ Church. They came to church, and at the door she asked if I would call on her to talk about preparing her daughter for confirmation, which, of course, I did. I found her to be surprisingly well read and interested in the issues of the day and not at all the Eurotrash sort I had expected.

---

155. *Wide Neighborhoods: A Story of the Frontier Nursing Service*, published by the University of Kentucky Press. Still in print.

In the course of preparing her daughter, I found that Sonny had never transferred his letter to any church and wanted to do so at Christ Church. He had not a clue as to where it might be. I traced it clear back to Groton, where he had been confirmed while a student.

Another important woman, Barbara Harris, an African American clergyperson and a friend and colleague at many civil rights affairs, was ordained and consecrated suffragan bishop of Massachusetts—the first woman bishop in the Episcopal Church.[156] I had to miss the service because of a detached retina operation on that same day. My operation went well, and I talked with Barbara on the phone and wished her Godspeed.

May 1989 was a travel month. First I was in Asheville, North Carolina, for Bob Johnson's consecration as bishop of Western North Carolina. Then I went to New York to chair a meeting of the Board of Theological Education—with a night at the theatre to see *1964*, preceded by a cocktail hour at the Yale Club with Preston Kelsey, the executive secretary of the BTE. Next was a meeting at the Roman Catholic Mercy Convent in California (near San Francisco), then with Bill Swing and the Joint Commission on Health, which he heads, and via shuttle to visit Bobby and Cindy in San Diego—with a chance to be with Caroline, too, and then up to Tomecula Creek Inn to see Helen, Steve, and two other California granddaughters, Jessica and Elizabeth. Finally, Joyce and I were back in Dallas where I performed the wedding service for Joannie Kohler (Donnie's daughter) and Bob Enholm's stepdaughter and preached at St. Michael's at the 8:50 and 11:00 services.

As I've noted before, when one takes the vows at ordination, the promise is made "to take part in the Councils of the Church." That taking part eats up a lot of time, energy, and money, as well as time spent out

---

156. Barbara Clementine Harris became a suffragan bishop of the Episcopal Diocese of Massachusetts in 1989 and thus the first woman ever to serve as a bishop in an Anglican church anywhere in the world.

of the diocese. I'm not sure some of the councils of the church are that important, or for that matter relevant. They do generate air miles, though!

One happy solution to all the travel and public exposure and perpetual giving out is to have a place for taking in, and in November 1992 we purchased a condo at Dunescape on Atlantic Beach. It has three bedrooms, two and a half baths, a kitchen, dining area, and living room, as well as two porches—one screened in. It's on the first floor overlooking a swimming pool and, beyond the dunes, the ocean.

Lynn Harold Hough wrote in *The Interpreter's Bible*,[157]

As men grow older, they often lose their eager desire to communicate. The eager outreach for fellowship with other minds somehow ceases. Too often age builds its own walls of isolation. The Christian (who continues to experience the quality of his religion) has found the fountain of youth, because he is always eager to communicate.

Oliver Wendell Holmes in "The Voiceless" wrote in the same vein:

Alas for those that never sing,
but die with all their music in them.

These are good reminders when one retreats too often and good reminders that one never really retires.

Hough, in her commentary on the book of Revelation in the *Interpreters' Bible*, writes, "There is an old story of a man who was weary of battling with the sea. He put an oar on his shoulder and set out with the intention of journeying inland until he reached people who knew so little of the sea that they asked him what strange thing he carried on his shoulder."

---

157. *The New Interpreter's Bible Vol-12,* commentary by Lynn Harold Hough (Nashville: Abingdon, 1998)

I feel just opposite about the sea. I need to be in it and by it at least some of the time.

James Thurber, one of my favorites, wrote, "I suppose at our age we all have bruised and flattened batteries and bearings, but we will all keep running for years, with certain engine rattles and body squeaks."

And in a letter to E. B. White, Thurber wrote from England, "Over here everybody turns Catholic when anything is the matter and perhaps you should try that. T. S. Eliot turned Catholic and so did Evelyn Waugh and they look fine."

Thurber also wrote, "In America, most male writers fail to reach the age of 60, or, if they do, they have nothing more to say, but occasionally say it anyway."[158]

On October 26, 1992, with my good friend John Claypool in Louisville, I read prayers and interred the ashes of Helen Haynes, Joyce's mother. She had lived for the past few years at the Penick Home in Southern Pines, where we could be near her as Alzheimer's slowly took her away. It was a lovely day in Cave Hill Cemetery, Louisville—and we laid her ashes next to Joyce's father's grave. The Hermanns, Tafels, and Jane Stough, all old and dear friends, were there at the graveside.

Helen always had a well-worn (and read) Bible by the side of her bed.

Herman Wouk in *This Is My God*, wrote, "Dead end or no, a man wants to praise God for the marvels of life, and to ask to be spared its terrors if possible—and to give thanks for what he has in hand, in health, family and work. He wants to, that is, if a sense will not leave him that God is there."[159]

Huckleberry Finn, on the other hand, prayed for a fishing pole and got a pole and no hooks, whereupon he gave up religion as an economic recourse.

---

158. Excerpt from correspondence from James Thurber to Herman and Dorothy Miller, Copyright © 1948. Excerpt from correspondence from James Thurber to E. B. White, Copyright © 1937. Excerpt from correspondence from James Thurber to Ronald and Jane Williams, Copyright © 1955. Reprinted by arrangement with Rosemary A. Thurber and The Barbara Hogenson Agency, Inc. All rights reserved.

159. Herman Wouk, *This Is My God* (New York: Little, Brown and Company, 1987), 91.

Late in 1993 I was making my last official visits to congregations. So far, I'd been given a golf putter, bread, chutney, preserves, numerous T-shirts, letters from Sunday school children, caps of all sorts, and special music at Elkin—in the foothills of the mountains. They inserted in their service leaflet, "During this weekend in October in the Blue Ridge, when the leaves are at their peak, the barns are full, and the chickens are stewed, it seems fitting to say farewell to our Bishop by acknowledging and saluting our Southern spiritual heritage in this series of Preludes based upon 'The Sacred Harp.'"

I commented at sermon time that I didn't know the chickens in the Blue Ridge had a drinking problem.

Allard Lowenstein,[160] whom I met while campaigning for Bobby Kennedy, in his biography by the Duke professor William H. Chafe, wrote, "As you go along, you build a life in which you do many different kinds of things. But it all has a common denominator that gives it some sense, some direction—the sense that your total activity is going to make a better situation for people to live in. The question should be, 'Is it worth trying to do? Not *can* it be done?' You don't just set goals and when you reach them, find that they equal happiness…. Within the quest itself, much of the fullness of life exists."[161]

At the end of 1993 I flew to Boston on a clear, cold day to be met by Sister Margaret Ann and Mother Adele Marie of the Sisters of St. Margaret.

160. Allard Kenneth Lowenstein (January 16, 1929–March 14, 1980) was an American Democratic politician, including one term (1969 to 1971) as a US representative for the 5th Congressional District in Nassau County, New York. His work on civil rights and the antiwar movement has been cited as an inspiration by public figures including US secretary of state John Kerry, Barney Frank, and Gary Hart, among others. He was a graduate of the University of North Carolina. In 1949 Lowenstein worked as a special assistant on the staff of Senator Frank Porter Graham, and he was a foreign policy assistant on Senator Hubert H. Humphrey's staff in 1959.
161. William H. Chafe, *Never Stop Running: Allard Lowenstein and the Struggle to Save American Liberalism* (New York: Basic Books, 1993)

Not a bad way to get through the tunnel from Logan Airport where, with Sister Margaret Ann at the wheel, the man in the toll booth—apparently a good Catholic—waved us through without paying, saying, "No charge, Sister! Have a nice day!" Frank Vest would have been impressed.

I spent the morning at the convent talking with the Mother Superior about one of our postulants, a deacon, who wanted to enter the order and become a Sister. I also visited with one of our seminarians making a retreat at the convent and then was driven to Cambridge and the monastery of the Society of St. John the Evangelist, where, after supper, I ordained Brother Eldridge Pendleton to the priesthood.

One of the losses in our diocese around this time was the closing of St. John's House in Durham. I brought them to the diocese, and they were a great presence for nearly ten years. It was their decision to concentrate on their work in Massachusetts. I remain an associate.

On December 4, 1993, in a special convention, Bob Johnson was elected 10th bishop of the Diocese of North Carolina. Later, at his consecration in the Duke Chapel, I handed over the diocese, figuratively, by handing him the diocesan bishop's crozier. More to the point, after the service and the reception, I handed over the keys to the bishop's car! I explained some of its features, including the sunroof. Connie Johnson told me later that on the way to Charlotte after the service, she pressed the button in the ceiling that activated the sunroof, only to have the button break off, leaving the roof open with no way to close it. She said they arrived in Charlotte with their hair standing, literally, on end.

Bob's first official act was to fire Jim Lewis, my excellent—and controversial—social action director. I guess it was a campaign promise and inevitable.

On February 17, 1995, our younger daughter, Elizabeth, went into Rex Hospital for biopsy surgery to take out a lump in her breast. She had found it by self-examination, and our friend and doctor, George Paschal, performed the operation. Sadly, he found a growth "about the size of a black-eyed pea" and confirmed it was cancerous. That began for Elizabeth a long and awful regime of chemo and radiation therapy, with daily shots and trips to Chapel Hill and Rex Cancer Center. We were especially fortunate to have a friend, Dr. Joe Pagano—who at that time was married to one of our women priests[162]—who was head of the University of North Carolina Lineberger Cancer Center in Chapel Hill. He kindly arranged an almost immediate appointment with their excellent team.

Throughout the whole ordeal, Elizabeth was her usual upbeat, optimistic self.

One of the few downers came early on when we (Joyce and I) attended a group meeting of people who were new to the program who would be going through various forms of treatment. Elizabeth was the youngest patient in the group. The pastoral counselor on the team led the session and started by asking the group how they felt about discovering they had cancer. One rather obese woman, who must have been in her fifties, spoke up and said, "If Jesus wants me to have cancer, then I'll have it." Elizabeth, to my surprise (and agreement), spoke out at once and said, "I don't believe that!" And, although I had on a necktie, I spoke up, too, and said, "Neither do I! And I'm a bishop!" For the first—and I believe the only—time during the ordeal, Elizabeth burst into tears.

I can't remember now how the counselor handled the situation, but long afterward I now think I handled it badly. I should have, as I did, come to Elizabeth's aid, but I probably should have added something to the effect that if her outlook enabled that poor woman to handle this dreadful disease, she should go for it.

It was especially fortunate that I had just retired and had the time to be Elizabeth's primary caregiver. The chemo treatments were bad enough and had to be done in Chapel Hill. We almost never made it all the way

---

162. Anna Louise Pagano.

back to Raleigh without having to stop while Elizabeth was sick and threw up. It was not long before her hair began to fall out. Still, her spirits remained high, she took her treatments in a room with several others, and would talk and encourage them as well as the doctors and nurses. One nurse in particular became such a friend that we invited her to go to our place at Dunescape for a weekend with her family and friends.

We used the wonderful prayer in the *Book of Common Prayer* (p. 459)

Strengthen your servant Elizabeth, O God, to do what she has to do and bear what she has to bear; that accepting your healing gifts through the skill of surgeons and nurses, she may be restored to usefulness in your world with a thankful heart; through Jesus Christ our Lord. Amen.

Years ago I bought a little wooden crucifix in Rome and held it up when Pope Pius XII gave his blessing in St. Peter's Square. We've used it every time someone in the family was hospitalized or has had a baby. The Christ figure has long ago broken off, and the cross is a bit worn—but it is an important symbol for us and one I treasure. For this period it was with Elizabeth.

So, for us, March had come in like a lion—but we are sustained by the Lamb!

Elizabeth underwent another operation at the UNC Hospital in Chapel Hill with a member of her team performing it. They removed some lymph nodes to be sure the cancer had not spread—and thanks be to God, it had not. Her surgeon was Dr. Cance, and I noted that he needed a final "R" on his name to be a cancer surgeon. He and her primary doctor are younger than she.

The radiation treatments were done on an outpatient basis in the Rex Cancer Center, and although they left her very weak and easily tired, radiation was nothing compared with the chemo. My experience in the navy in World War II came in handy, and I gave her a daily shot, alternating between "in the tummy and in the fanny." I told her what the chief said when I told him I'd never given anyone a shot: "Hell, man, it don't hurt you none!"

Her hair began coming back, and she never liked the wig she had to wear. One day I was at a stop light in Raleigh, and she pulled up beside me and doffed her wig! She looked as beautiful as ever, even with short hair.

On Good Friday, I joined several hundred people at the capitol in Raleigh and gave the opening meditation on the Way of the Cross. We prayed for peace in the world and the removal of the death penalty, for the homeless and for racial harmony. We have done this each year since I've been a bishop. This year a street person named Gregory attached himself to us as we processed. He especially was drawn to the Sisters in their habits, and to those of us in clerical collars. He wanted money for food. I finally challenged him to let me take him to the Shepherd's Table at the Church of the Good Shepherd—just across the street from the capitol. After some unsuccessful efforts at getting money, he did go with me, and they reopened the soup kitchen for us. He and I ate a sandwich and had a paper cup of soup sitting outside the church on the steps. I went to the last of the three-hour service at Christ Church, but Gregory declined to join me. He's a Baptist!

On May 20, 1995, in a celebration at our conference center—The Summit—I received the Lifetime Achievement Award from the Jessie Ball DuPont Fund. The diocese had received to that point over two million dollars in grants. The award was fifty thousand dollars, and I could designate forty thousand for diocesan projects and another ten thousand dollars for personal discretionary use. Jim Lewis was one of the key players in getting the grants and expanding our outreach programs nearly 100 percent. He and some of our programs were controversial, especially our help in organizing labor at the Siler City chicken processing center. But I believe we were the moving force behind a number of parish programs, too.

Shortly after receiving the DuPont award, I had a chance to hear a great lecture by one of my heroes—Robert Coles, who was at the North Carolina Museum to talk about his research on children.[163] I came away inspired and convinced that we should be doing all we can in matters that really count in human rights.

I spent a lot of time defending Jim Lewis and the programs (or, at least, some of them), and it was worth every minute spent.

Sabbaticals

One of the programs we introduced to the diocesan clergy was a sabbatical program. While I was directing continuing education at Virginia Seminary I dealt with clergy burnout. Not only had most of the clergy not had a sabbatical, but many never took a day off or time for themselves and their families. Few set aside study time, and even fewer were enrolled in study groups or took classes in seminaries or graduate programs. We had to make the point that you cannot give out all the time without having time to take in.

So with the help of a Jessie Ball duPont grant we set up a program and gave scholarship aid whereby, after five years of service, a clergyperson was entitled to a two-month sabbatical. If they already had a month's vacation time, their sabbatical could be as long as three months.

Joyce and I took two sabbaticals during my fourteen years as bishop, though we did not use the Jessie Ball duPont funds. We did use funds allocated by our Diocesan Sabbatical Study Team, made up of clergy and

---

163. Robert Coles is a child psychiatrist, professor at Harvard University, and author of more than fifty books. He is best known for his explorations of children's lives and books that explore their moral, political, and spiritual sensibilities. He is also known as an eloquent spokesman for voluntary and community service—the subject of his book, *The Call to Service* (Boston, Massachusetts: Houghton Mifflin Co., 1993)

laypeople I appointed. They were available to anyone taking a sabbatical and helped greatly to clarify goals and to help with setting realistic expectations.

ASSISI

One of the most memorable of our sabbaticals was a six-week stay in Assisi, walking in the steps of St. Francis. Friends from our Washington days had a place in Assisi and a driver, who met our plane in Lucerne and, after a night on the lake, drove us to Assisi. Our hotel overlooked the Arno Valley, and each night, aided by a bottle of Averna, we would sit on our balcony. When a train came into the valley each night at the same time, we would finish off our after-dinner Averna and go to bed.

I have to admit that as we were leaving Assisi, our hotel manager heard our story and announced that there were no trains at night. That Averna must have more kick than we thought.

During our six weeks we took the train (a day train!) to Florence, where we were welcomed by the priest in charge of the Anglican church (built by J. P. Morgan) where the next day I preached and presided at the Eucharist.

Later in the month we spent several days in Rome and afterward had a special tour of the Villa de Este, my kinfolks!

FLORENCE

We spent the rest of our visit in Galleria degli Uffizi, awed by the art and sculpture that practically engulfed us: Giotto's *Madonna Enthroned*, Fra Filippo Lippi's *Madonna and Child with Angels*, Botticelli's *Birth of Venus* (sometimes called "Venus on the Half Shell"), Raphael's *Madonna with the Goldfinch*, and the more secular *Venus of Urbino* by Titian, complete with a snoozing lap dog. Of course, we also saw Michelangelo's *David*, the fourteen-foot, three-inch-high masterpiece and the crowning exhibit of the Uffizi—much like the *Mona Lisa* of Leonardo Da Vinci is at the Louvre in Paris.

While we had been in Florence before, the feast of art sent us back to Assisi with new memories and awe. Being co-creators with God, is an amazing fact and a mighty witness to his gift of grace.

During another sabbatical, we stayed in Oxford and had the use of the famous Bodleian Library. Among other projects I delved into some of the material having to do with my family history. Imagine my surprise when one of the bloodlines led into the d'Este family and, through that, the infamous Borgias.

Lexington Interim

*D*on Wimberly, bishop of Lexington and a friend of long standing, invited me to be an interim at Christ Church as they looked for a new dean. After talking with Joyce I accepted for four months.

One of the things retired clergy can do is serve as interims in churches without a minister during the time they are in the search process. I really did not want to do that kind of ministry and had turned down a couple of calls (one from Calvary, Pittsburgh) to do so. Then, as often happens, I got a call to do a four-month interim at Christ Church in Lexington. How can you say no to that?

So, I found myself downtown in one of the penthouse condominiums atop the Radisson Hotel with a view that includes West Second Street and the Lexington Cemetery—a view from my beginning to my ending. Joyce would come along later and the children for at least a long weekend now and then. Sadly, no dogs. I was "home" for my sixty-ninth birthday!

Family Visit during the Interim

One of the highlights for me was a long weekend with Joyce, Bobby and Cindy, Elizabeth and John B., and Helen. I got the Christ Church VW van and met them at Bluegrass Field. They stayed at the Radisson with our daughter Helen with us in our penthouse and the others in rooms on a lower floor overlooking Rupp Arena.

John Milward had very thoughtfully arranged for me to have an out-of-town membership in the Lexington Club, so after unpacking, we lunched there and spent the afternoon sightseeing. Cindy and John B. had never been to Kentucky, and Bobby and Elizabeth had left Lexington long ago when we moved to Louisville.

We had a special tour of Three Chimneys Farm and got to see Seattle Slew in his pasture. Afterward, we drove down the Pisgah Lane and toured Aunt Laura's former farm, now a state-of-the-art horse farm named Win-Star. I think they were more impressed than they would have been if they'd seen Haltura—Aunt Laura's farm, which was a "real" farm, with cattle, sheep, chickens, pea fowls, mules, and tobacco.

On the way back from Keeneland, we drove through Calumet, and as we passed the breeding barn a stallion was just being led in. Ten minutes or so later, as we passed the barn again, he was coming out! Everyone was impressed with the speed of the encounter, and Bobby swore that he

saw the stallion smoking a cigarette as he was being led away.

Ann Estill Campbell, my cousin, invited us to her farm for an elegant, seated dinner. Alex her husband was out of town, but we saw him the next morning at Keeneland along with Ted Basset—who was at that point president of Keeneland.

We were able to watch the early morning workouts, visit some of the stables, and have breakfast at the track kitchen with all the jockeys, stable hands, some owners, and exercise boys and (now) girls.

Later that morning we took a walking tour of Gratz Park, West Second Street—with a photo op of the house at 421 in which I was born.

We had lunch at the Idle Hour Country Club with my cousin Naomi Estill Vance. This interim gave us a chance to become close friends as well as close kin.

We found the Iroquois Hunt Club that afternoon and toured the Kentucky River hunt country before going back to the Mill for drinks and dinner and back to the Radisson fairly early in order to be up for church Sunday.

The service at Christ Church gave Elizabeth and Bobby a chance to see where they were baptized (Helen was baptized in Middlesboro at St. Mary's). We had a fairly quick lunch at the Radisson and went back to the airport. They all wanted to move immediately to Lexington! I hated to see them go, and the penthouse seemed pretty quiet after their visit.

There were lots of faces from the past, but also lots of faces missing after being away for thirty years. Cardinal Newman's great hymn "Lead, Kindly Light" came to mind:

And with the morn those
angel faces smile
Which I have loved long since,
and lost awhile.

Each morning, after an early exercise walk, I showered, ate breakfast, and left the hotel. My walk to the office took me along Main Street to Cheapside, where Saturday horse and mule (and probably slave) sales were conducted in the early days. I passed the statue of John Cabell Breckinridge, whose great-grandson, Dr. Scott Breckinridge, and my father attended my mother at 471 West Second Street when I came into the world. Dr. Breckinridge's death at an early age was one of the first I can recall, and I remember seeing my father in tears. They had been in medical school together at Physicians and Surgeons in New York at Columbia University. My father encouraged him to come to Lexington to practice, and they were best friends. He was one of my godfathers, the other being Clinton Harbison, later my senior warden and mentor at Christ Church. My godmother was Betsy Battle.

One of the habits I always had as a parish priest was having lunch with people who worked downtown. One notable lunch in Lexington came with Jeb Magruder of Watergate infamy, who had become the pastor of the First Presbyterian Church. We were in Washington at the same time and talked about that—but not Watergate.

The governor of Kentucky, Brereton Jones, had pardoned him at the request of W. T. Young, but he was still a felon in most states. He seemed a bit jumpy and somewhat disheveled, but the people at First Presbyterian liked him and said that his sermons were getting better.

Two funerals came along near the end of my interim. One was for my good friend Bunny McKinlay's daughter, who committed suicide, and the other was for Liz McDonald, an old friend, the daughter of Bishop Dandridge of Tennessee and wife of Angus, who was my senior warden for one term. It was good that I was here instead of a stranger, but it is still especially hard. Liz was a died-in-the-wool low-church person and looked with disapproval as we introduced some high-church things like Eucharistic vestments. She finally accepted them when I assured her that her father had worn them in his diocese when he visited the University of the South at Sewanee!

As a Lexingtonian I've always admired Henry Clay, "the Great Compromiser." In one of the biographies of Henry Clay it makes the point that he waited to be baptized until he was out of politics because he felt he could not be a Christian and a politician. What bad theology! I used this story when Sandra Day O'Connor came to Christ Church and sat in his pew.

When Henry Clay died (1852) at age seventy-five, Thomas Watson of Richmond wrote a poem that ended,

> *He sleeps, yes, let the Mighty Statesman sleep.*
> *His name shall live while time shall count a day*
> *Columbian's children shall, for ages keep,*
> *The great and glorious name of Henry Clay.*

Henry Clay is buried in the Lexington Cemetery near the Estill family lot. A large monument marks his grave, and there is a figure of him on the top. When I was a child there was a story going around that if you would approach his tomb and say, "Whadda ya say, Henry Clay?" he would answer, "Nothing."

Bishop Dandridge, former Bishop of Tennessee and father of Liz McDonald, an active member of Christ Church and a good friend, had retired to Lexington and lived with the McDonalds and attended Christ Church. He did not want to do anything but "sit in the pew." He sat there, a constant supporter and mentor and a lovely man. He died slumped over his Prayer Book in the little office the McDonalds had provided. He had been reading Evening Prayer.

One of the talented young men who came to Christ Church, Lexington while I was rector was Bob Horine. At that point he was a journalist for the *Lexington Herald-Leader*. Later he talked with me about ordination and was consequently ordained a deacon and then a priest. Among other ministries he wrote a regular column for one of our national church magazines. One of his best had to do with St. Patrick. He told me that he had found a story about St. Patrick and the Druid King Aengus. Patrick had converted the King and baptized him on top of the Roch of Cashel. Patrick had grown old and feeble and in order to steady himself, he drove the spiked point of his pastoral staff into the ground and accidentally through the King's foot. "The King," Bob said, "did not cry out in pain and later he revealed that he thought it was part of the ritual!"

One of my earliest pastoral calls was on Hendree and Jane Milward at the Woodland. Hendree had Parkinson's disease but was still bright and alert. When I looked up their apartment number at the desk, I saw Rebecca Milward's name below theirs. She was the widow of Emmit Milward, one of my senior wardens. I asked the man at the desk if I could see her. He replied, "She's not here anymore." I asked, "Has she moved?" and he said, "No, she passed away."

Later, as I was leaving I ran into my old friends Sam Walton and Joe Houlihan. When I explained my mistake, Joe said, "You're on the wrong end of Main Street!" (The Woodland is on East Main, and the Lexington Cemetery is on *West* Main.)

One of my visits to the past was a trip to the cathedral domain (actually, a camp and conference center in the foothills just short of the Estill County line). In its early days the toilet facilities were outside in three-hole privies, one on the boys' side and another on the girls' side. The dining room and offices were in a building between the two sides. At a conference or some other function, the camp director and I rigged a microphone under the women's privy. We'd wait in the office until we saw someone go in, then count to ten and say over the microphone, "Lady! Would you move over to another hole? We're painting down here!" The resulting screams and hasty exit were always worth all the trouble.

There was some action on the men's side, too. One of our rotund clergyman was sitting on one of the holes smoking his pipe. Unfortunately he knocked out his pipe into the hole next to him and caused a gas explosion that went *whump*! It sent him running out the door, pulling his pants up as he ran. The advent of indoor plumbing stopped our fun.

Since I was the youngest priest in the diocese, the bishop appointed me director of the Diocesan Youth Program. This happened while I was

The end of the ladies outdoor privy.

in Middlesboro, so I had time to visit most of the diocese's youth groups and meet with those that had been directing a very limited program. I reappointed several of the people, arranged for some budget requests, and scheduled youth conferences at the domain.

The conferences were almost an instant success. The domain has trails, several hills to climb, caves to explore, a swimming pool, and lake and adequate space for games—plus the cathedral itself, which a local man observed, "is the largest tobacco barn in Lee County!"

On my last Sunday in Lexington as interim, they gave a nice reception after the service and presented me with a Kentucky julep cup. It was engraved, "Christ Church Cathedral, Rector 1955–1961, Interim Rector and Dean 1996."

During the reception Joe Graves spoke.

> *Robert Estill has many gifts.*
> *Would you agree that one of his greatest gifts is a*
> *marvelous sense of humor?*
> *How many people do we know who have even a*
> *comparable sense of humor?*
> *Is he a better teacher and preacher and Bishop because*
> *he can tickle our funny bone?*
> *Is there a message here for each of us?*
> *Should we lighten up?*
> *Should we try to create more smiles?*
> *Bishop Estill*
> *Thanks for creating smiles and laughter*
> *Thanks for touching each of our lives in such a*
> *meaningful way.*

I enjoyed being in Lexington, but I knew it would be good to be home in North Carolina again.

Retirement

When we were at Virginia Seminary, I wrote several cruise companies and sent a resume asking if they used chaplains on their ships. I pointed out that, being on the faculty, I could be free on holiday times, such as Thanksgiving, Christmas, and Easter, and when regular clergy with churches could not be. I got back some letters saying they didn't have chaplains (except for Roman Catholics), or that the captain held the Sunday services, but I did get one or two that said they would keep my application and two—the Cunard line and Holland America—that gave me the name and address of their agent, who hired chaplains along with other "entertainers"!

As a result, Joyce and I went on cruises to the Caribbean with two different lines and had to regret one because of moving to Dallas.

Just before retirement I wrote another letter to the same cruise companies and got in touch with the agents and again began to get jobs. I got to go free as did my "guest," Joyce. Usually we had a nice cabin and little work to do (we ended up taking sixteen cruises). We visited nearly every island

Cruise and vacationing.

Tour leaders numbers 1 and 2

in the Caribbean and sailed out of Amsterdam, Rome, London, New York, Seattle, Miami, Fort Lauderdale, Tampa, and Athens.

In the midst of this retirement career, we got a call from the Cunard agent, who said, "Have I got a deal for you! How about a seventy-eight-day cruise around the world?" It was a once-in-a-lifetime opportunity, and we flew to Greece and caught *The Royal Viking Sun* for the beginning of the cruise.

Rather than take a lot of pictures, I wrote and illustrated a book on each of our cruises. I hoped our children (and maybe grandchildren) would enjoy those someday.

At each port of call, Joyce and I acted as ship's host and hostess to the passengers on the land tours, so again, those for us were free. Our duties consisted of being sure each person on our tour got back on the bus.

We also handed out wipes and water, and watched out for those who were physically challenged. I got a cheap laugh from my bus when I introduced myself as their host and that I was also the Protestant chaplain on the *Royal Viking*. "They must have thought this busload needed a chaplain!"

As tour guides in a museum.

My journals tell in some detail of our stops and life aboard ship. I held eleven Sunday services plus two holiday services on the round-the-world cruise, and I have published a book about that experience. A rabbi and a Roman Catholic priest were on board, too. The rabbi had more work than either the priest or I, and one night he was called to go to a particular cabin where he was told a man had died.

He dressed and went to the cabin, knocked on the door—no answer. He knocked again, and finally a woman with her hair up in rollers opened the door.

The rabbi said, "I'm so sorry to hear about your husband." She whirled around to look back into the cabin and cried, "What's wrong with him?" The rabbi was at the wrong cabin.

None of my flock died, though I did visit one man who was waiting in the sick bay to be offloaded to a hospital. His trip in a small boat to the shore may have either killed or cured him.

The last day of the cruise, coming into San Francisco I was in the elevator with a lady who I had noticed had been on for the entire seventy-eight days. She was filling out her post cruise questionnaire, and I asked how she had liked the cruise. (I had on an open-neck sport shirt and had packed my chaplain's name badge.) She replied that the one complaint she had was that they didn't have a Protestant chaplain (!). I said, "Oh yes, we did, and he was wonderful!" I watched as she erased her remarks and prayed that no one would blow my cover.

"We didn't have a Protestant Chaplain."

Inscribed in the front of our *Round the World Cruise*, I quoted Joachim du Bellam (*Les Regrets*, 1559): "Happy he who like Ulysses has made a glorious voyage." And Psalm 77:19: "Your way was in the sea, and your paths in the great waters."

Retired and Contented

May 14, 1994

It's hard to believe that I've been retired over twenty years at this writing (1994–2014). Fourteen of those years were spent in our home on Landor Road in Raleigh, and now we're in our sixth year at The Cypress of Raleigh (2008–2014), a continuing care community.

As I have written in these pages, the first retirement years were marked by being the primary caregiver for our daughter Elizabeth in her fight against breast cancer. Another portion, which I have also recorded here, was taken up with cruises and travel.

Just for the record, I believe I left the Diocese of North Carolina even stronger than it was when I came in 1980. We developed and built an excellent camp and conference center, which was completely paid for and debt-free (my current successor sold it!). Among our accomplishments: the conference center helped renew our ministry to youth; fourteen new congregations were started where none had been for the past ten years; fifty women have been ordained and are canonically resident (there was none in 1980); a fine Deacons' Training Program with twenty-two graduates and a full-time director and residency in our student center at Duke; an introduction into the Diocese of the Monastic Order of Saint John the Evangelist with a house in Durham; the addition of two more college chaplaincies; a larger number of resident clergy (250) when the number was 186 in 1980; a dynamic social ministry program that generated over two million dollars in grants and was led by Jim Lewis (later fired by my successor); the most successful capital fund drive in the history of the diocese (over five million dollars). Now it's nice to be fallow for a while. Yet, one must listen to people like the great saint Dorothy Day. She wrote in her book *The Long Loneliness*,

> The only answer in this life to the loneliness we are all bound to feel is community. The living together, working together, sharing together, loving God and loving our brother (and sister) and living close (to them) in community so we can show our love for (them).[164]

I wanted to keep that quote in mind as we sold our house and moved into The Cypress of Raleigh.

We are, thankfully, traveling less, and one of our trips away was to Cumberland Island, Georgia, where I performed the wedding service for Margaret Graves (Hart and Joe Graves's daughter) and Jeff Hallos. It was fun to see Cumberland again and to stay at Greyfield where the wedding was held. They were married on the steps and about 150 people sat on the lawn under the live oaks. A harp and a flute and an unscheduled mockingbird provided the music, and an old golden retriever dozed on one of the lower steps. A number of the couple's friends were from New York, and one of them, at the reception after the wedding said to me, "Geez, this reception musta cost a bundle! Just bringing in all that moss and hanging it on the trees musta cost a fortune!"

The Carnegie family had helped preserve Cumberland Island as a National Seashore.

We've been there a number of times. I had another Graves wedding there for Elizabeth Estill Graves and Matt Gooding outside of the

---

164. Dorothy Day, *The Long Loneliness, Autobiography of the Legendary Catholic Social Activist* (New York: Harper Collins, 2009).

Grange, where wild horses came up and looked on and left a few wedding presents during the service.

I was asked to join the Sphinx Club (a men's social club), and at their annual Christmas Feast I sat next to Senator Jesse Helms. He won me over, partially, by asking how Bobby was and added that he always enjoyed watching his sports show on TV when he was in Raleigh. He told a story about his doctor, who asked him to "walk briskly" for his health. He said he was walking briskly in the Capitol to cast a vote when someone passed him as though he were standing still. It was Strom Thurmond!" Having lunch with the senator was a big contrast to my morning, spent with some Salvadorian farmworkers near Newton Grove where our diocese has a farmworker ministry.

Another of our outreach efforts was to help organize a group called People of Faith Against the Death Penalty. It will be a long fight, but I am convinced that we must abolish the death penalty. I believe that a sentence of life in prison without parole should take its place. We are the only civilized country in the world that still has the death penalty. My involvement in this effort has consisted of meeting with the governor to ask for him to commute each case and joining those who marched on his mansion and demonstrated outside Central Prison the night of an execution. Neither effort seems to make any difference. Professor John Boger (UNC law school professor) told me, as we were standing outside the prison, of a quote from the playwright Paul Green. Green replied to a man who asked him as he stood outside the prison, "Do you think you can change the world?"

"No," Green replied. "Probably not, but I am here so the world won't change me."

After one vigil in a cold rain, after the execution had taken place (they always do it in the middle of the night as though they are ashamed) I was making my way back to my car when a state policeman took his flashlight and shined it at a puddle of water and said, "Watch your step, Reverend."

"Watch your step, Reverend."

It was a little touch of humanity—a moment of grace at the end of a cold, wet, and sad night.

Our diocese, while I was bishop, had what it called a companion relationship with a diocese in another country. We joined with Belize and later Honduras. I made a number of visits, and their bishops, clergy, and laypeople came to us. At one point the bishop of Belize's son, who attended St. Augustine's, was married at Christ Church, and since we were away at Quogue, the bishop and his family stayed at our house and used our car. At least for a while our neighborhood was integrated!

Belize was relatively peaceful, English speaking, and didn't even have an army. Honduras was another story, and their bishop never seemed to trust us or go out of his way to show us his diocese. Jim Lewis was one of our visitors, as was I, and we by-passed the bishop and went into the interior to visit the real Hondurans in their villages. I remember sleeping in a hammock with a pig and some chickens sleeping beneath me on the mud floor of the hut. At the end of our visit we stopped at the American embassy and got a cool reception. The words was that our ambassador was tied up in meetings. I told his secretary who we were and that I thought I had gone to school with the ambassador. That opened the door, and he kept looking at me with a puzzled expression.

Arthur Miller, in *Timebends* (1987), told of Smedley D. Butler, a retired Marine Corps general. The general wrote, "I helped make Mexico and especially Tampico safe for American Oil interests. I helped make Haiti one of our companies and Cuba a decent place for National City Bank to collect revenues in. I helped make Honduras right for American fruit companies."

No wonder our ambassador was a little cautious in the presence of our group, which had asked him some questions about native land restoration.

To his credit, General Butler saw this naked use of his troops jeopardizing American lives for private profit, which turned him around totally.

In January 1996 Joyce and I were a far cry from Honduras and Belize. With Bill and Mary Swing (he was the bishop of California) we were in a cottage in Carmel, California, for the AT&T Pebble Beach Golf Tournament. Bill was one of the amateurs playing, and he had asked me to be his caddy for the pro-am segment. What a thrill!

It was great fun to rub shoulders with all the great pro golfers and celebrities like Clint Eastwood and Bill Murray. I was taken for Jack Lemmon four or five time (with a golf hat on, I do resemble him a little). One woman actually asked for my autograph!

I had the great pleasure of playing the famous Cypress Point Golf Course with a friend of my cousin Al Shands

What a thrill to caddy at Pebble Beach.

named Chuck Winston. It is a magnificent layout. You can hear and see sea lions and seals on the rocks below. I shot 90, which wasn't too bad, and won three dollars on the course until we came behind a foursome. They signaled for us to play through.

So we hit our shots toward the green, with mine landing about four feet behind a bunker at the side of the green. When we reached the foursome, it turned out that Chuck knew all of them and introduced them to me. "This is John McCloy [the CEO of our bank]," and then another couple of equally impressive men and then finally, Arnold Palmer! His ball was near mine, and as I stood over my shot in the presence of this company, I prayed I wouldn't chunk it into the trap. "Just this one, Lord!"

And so it was. The chip was right on the money, and the ball rolled within gimme range of the hole. The great Arnie Palmer said, "Nice shot, Bob!" This was my greatest golf moment without a doubt. "Thank you, Jesus!"

On July 27, 1996, I took part in the consecration and ordination of Gary Gloster as suffragan bishop of North Carolina. Funny enough, I had known Gary since he was a young boy. His grandparents were active in my first parish in Middlesboro. In fact, his grandfather was senior warden. They celebrated their fiftieth wedding anniversary, and all the Gloster clan, including Gary—then a preteenager—came for the big

day. Gary served as crucifer. Now, many years later, I helped make him a bishop. He and Judy had served in our diocese the whole time I had been bishop.

I remember the consecration service took a strange turn since Gary had been a clown in the growing clown ministry. So, at the offertory, several of his clown colleagues ran about putting red noses on the participants, including the presiding bishop, Ed Browning, who looked surprised and embarrassed. Thankfully, I was at the back of the group and they

They planted a clown's nose on the Presiding Bishop!

had run out of noses. I thought the whole thing was in bad taste and out of place in the stately confines of Duke Chapel.

I had been elected to the Duke Marine Lab Advisory Board. The Marine Lab is near Beaufort, and since we have a condo at Atlantic Beach (next door), I'm glad to be involved. We often meet with the big board of the Nicholas School of the Environment, which has some heavy hitters on it. Among them are Sally Kleberg, who is kin to us through Alice Estill King (the King Ranch); Peter Stroh, the Stroh's Beer man; Watts Hill Jr. from Durham; Elizabeth "Boots" Thrower, who knows our friends Mary and

Teddy Cross—neighbors on Nantucket; Gilbert Grosvenor, chairman of the board of the National Geographic Society; and Bill Wrigley Jr., whose Chicago Cubs break everyone's heart each season. Gilbert Grosvenor, in an address at Duke, said, "The future quality of life on planet earth will depend upon our ability to stabilize the environment and to live within sustainable consumption of our natural resources." He gave that address in 1997, and other voices were raised before his, such as those of Rachel Carson; Orrin Pilkey, professor of earth science at Duke; Aldo Leopold; and Stewart Udall.

Joe Graves, in his excellent book *Cumberland Island Saved*, quotes Kurt Vonnegut's poem "Requiem[165]":

When the last living thing
Has died on account of us
How poetical it would be
If earth could say,
In a voice floating up
Perhaps
From the floor
Of the Grand Canyon,
"It is done."
People did not like it here....

Our summers supplying the summer chapel, the Church of the Atonement, have made us part-time New Yorkers and introduced us to a host of new friends and acquaintances. For a number of years I've also preached at the Dune Church in Southampton, either before or after our month at

165. Kurt Vonnegut, "Requiem" from *A Man Without a Country* (New York: Seven Stories Press, 2010)

Quogue. They have a different visiting preacher each Sunday. The church is unique in that it sits right on the dunes facing the ocean. Unlike Quogue, the ushers wear white pants, neckties, dark-blue jackets, and no socks.

As usual we had lunch after the service at the Dune Church at the Beach Club with the same couple, since he is the equivalent of a senior warden. That Sunday, the ninth of September, 2001, our host asked if we minded if their daughter joined us since she was leaving for a new job in New York that was to begin on Monday the tenth. She was a lovely, bright honors graduate and eager to begin her new job Monday morning.

Joyce and I packed up and left for North Carolina after lunch, arriving in Virginia late that evening, where we often stayed. The next morning we drove down I-95 and noticed a gigantic traffic jam heading the other way into Washington. People were even getting out of their cars and standing in the road. We turned on the car radio and heard the dreadful news of 9/11. Our friends' daughter was one of those killed in her new office in the World Trade Center. We had been less than a mile away from the Pentagon in our motel.

One of the many good things that come with retirement is the time to do some things you really want to do. I started helping with a therapeutic riding program for physically and mentally challenged children. It's called Helping Horse in its literature because no one could spell "therapeutic." I volunteer each Tuesday. I get there early in the afternoon, curry, pick feet, clean some stalls, put out hay, check water buckets, and finally, tack the horses we'll be using. We have two classes—one at 5 p.m. and the other at 7 p.m., and six students make up the early class and about ten come at seven.

My job is to lead the horse while two volunteers walk (and trot!) on each side of the rider. Our horses are as old as I am in horse years, and I have developed a special friendship by bringing peppermints to hand out before and after each class. I'm the oldest volunteer, and while I

think feeding mints is against the
rules, the instructors are afraid to
stop me. Age has its benefits, and
because of an article and picture
in the paper having to do with the
death penalty, my cover was broken
and they know I'm a bishop. I
almost never miss a Tuesday, and
it's a great treat to be able to com-
bine work with the children and
hands-on time with horses.

"Walk on, Bob!"

We teach the children to give
commands to the horses and to know their names. One little boy (who has
been blind from birth) gets mixed up and sometimes says, "Walk on, Bob!"

In celebrating the birth of Absalom Jones, the first black priest in the
Episcopal Church (1746–1818), I represented the diocese at St. Augustine's
College and was asked to "bring greetings."

I did so by quoting Justice Clarence Thomas. While I think he is a
flop as a Supreme Court Justice, he had made a talk at Tuskegee that hit
the point of the day's celebration of Absalom Jones, which is that power
sometimes comes from unexpected people and who come, as Justice
Thomas does, from very limited beginnings. In his speech at Tuskegee
College he said,

> The real reason I'm here is the dream Booker T. had for all of us.
> Many of you are the first in your family to go to college. I was there.
> Some of you have grown up in rural areas. I was there. Some of you
> were raised by one or neither parent. I was there; some of you have
> barely or never seen your fathers. I was there. Some of you only have
> one pair of shoes. I was there. Some of you will be heavily in debt

when you leave college. I was there. Some of you may be frustrated; some of you may be angry; some of you may be confused. I was there.

Then he concluded, "I'm coming back today on a mission of love."

As I write these memoirs I'm reminded of a cartoon in the *New Yorker*, titled, "Low Self-Esteem." It shows a man at his desk writing, "Dear diary: sorry to bother you again."

These recollections may be a bother, but still I hope my children and grandchildren will at least find them to be part of their heritage. Frances Mayes (*Under the Tuscan Sun*) quotes a Chinese poet who noticed that to re-create something in words is like being alive twice.

I'm doing a lot of drawing, in addition to some paintings for various church art shows. I illustrate a literary journal called *The New Harmony Journal* that comes out of Chapel Hill and is edited by my friend Claudius Miller. I've done a number of illustrations for the Christ Church Cookbook and did the drawing on the aprons they sold along with the books. Dr. George Edwards asked me to illustrate his book *Man's Chief End*, which is the story of his life. After it was published, I went into our locally owned book store Quail Corners, and asked for a copy. The clerk told me their supply had sold out and that they had ordered more copies. I asked, "How many did you sell?" and she replied, "All eight copies!"

I'm the cartoonist-in-residence at our assisted-living home and produce a cartoon each month. I drew cartoons, beginning with Christ Church, Lexington, for the weekly bulletin at all the churches where I served. They often helped soften issues that were divisive, and yet I have even had two people leave the church (in Washington, DC) over what I thought was a pretty tame depiction of then president Richard Nixon. (I have to admit I was glad to see one of them move along!) At least no one shot me or burned down the church or the rectory. So far I haven't offended anyone that badly! Here are some more:

"Our people really love the new Prayer Book."

Honk if you love Jesus.

"A lot of folks just show up for Easter."

"Next year remind me to use palm crosses!"

"I think it's called subliminal advertising."

"It's that widow with her mite again."

So many of my friends and contemporaries have died. Sometimes I wonder why I'm left. Joyce and I are so fortunate to have each other and to have these last years together after sixty-four years of marriage. Our children are nearby, too, with Helen and Elizabeth and their spouses in Raleigh, and Bobby an hour and a half away in Wilmington. Like the Psalmist put it, "We have lived to see our children's children." They are spread about the country but are often back in Raleigh. I thank God every night before I get in bed and I ask him to "Guide me, waking and guard me sleeping, that awake I may watch with Christ and asleep I may rest in peace." I want to be alert to the opportunities that come each day to serve (and meet) the Lord in serving others.

Lancelot Andrews wrote, "Each day has its evening, and so also has life." Here in the evening of our lives, Joyce and I are so blessed.

One of the nice things we have together is time to have a drink before going to dinner. It is quality time and not something we had when I was actively bishoping. Even Lent doesn't get in our way. We are like Evelyn Waugh's mother, Laura, about whom he wrote[166], "During Lent she restricted herself to one glass of drink a day. She found a receptacle which others might have identified as an exceptionally large flower vase." "But," Waugh added, "it saw her through."

We are still traveling, and early in 2000 we were in Montego Bay, Jamaica, visiting our Raleigh friends Joe and Cynthia Hardison at their place in Round Hill. Round Hill is a gated community, and when one enters the gate, the place becomes an Eden before the fall. Outside, there is abject poverty, anti-American feelings, lots of crime, and sometimes violence.

I asked Joe if there was a jogging trail, and he was quick to say, "Yes, but stay on the path and don't go down into the valley below. There are darkies there and they'll bite and kick you!" I thought I was talking to a Ku Kluxer. "Darkies?" Then I realized Joe has a thick southern accent that I have trouble understanding at times. He was saying, "donkeys"! The help came via donkey each morning and kept them tethered down in that valley. It turned out that they were quite docile and friendly, especially when I began to bring them apples and carrots from the kitchen. The only danger I encountered was from the cook, who probably wanted to kick and bite me for using up her supplies.

Feeding the donkeys.

---

166. Auberon Waugh, *Will This Do* (Carroll & Graf Pub. 1998)

While bishop, I was chair of the board at our diocesan retirement home, the Penick Home, named for one of my predecessors and located in Southern Pines. Joyce and I drove to Southern Pines to call on Joe and Margie Cheshire. Joe was my chancellor and a close friend and colleague. He also served as parliamentarian at diocesan conventions. At one convention a man was going on and on about some social action legislation that he opposed. He accused me of not reading the Bible and intimated that Jim Lewis (our social action chair) was a communist! I finally turned to Joe and, with my hand covering the microphone, asked what I could do by the Rules of Order to cut him off. Joe's legal and canonical advice was, "Just tell the SOB to sit down and shut up!"

In May 2001 Joyce and I were in Louisville for the 127th running of the Kentucky Derby. We have been to lots of Derbies (we were there for the 100th), but this one was special in that Monarchos—who was trained by young John Ward, the nephew of one of my oldest Lexington friends, Junie Roberts—won. What a thrill! We were the guests of Joyce's best friend Dottie Herrman's husband, Louis. He is the grandson of Colonel Matt Winn, who put the Derby on the map. We hosted a brunch before the races at the Louisville Country Club where we were members while living in Louisville. Our guests were the Herrmans, the John Speeds and John's sister Sue, Al and Mary Shands, and the Tafels and Stoughs.

One of my retirement experiences was an invitation to be the preacher at the Sunday service at St. James Church in Wilmington. The occasion was the triennial meeting of the Society of the Cincinnati.

At the formal dinner on Saturday night before my one appearance as preacher the next day, one of the old members, bedecked in ribbons and in tails, came up to me and said, "Your talk this morning was one of the best I've heard at the meeting of our society!" He wandered off before I had a chance to say anything. Later I asked someone who the speaker had been that morning and found they had someone read a paper George Washington had written on education!

Despite an occasional talk or sermon, I'm enjoying being a pew sitter on Sundays and am learning a lot about preaching— some very good, some not so much. John Pollock, rector of St. Andrews Church in Morehead City, which is our parish when we're at the beach, used a great illustration in one of his sermons. A man was in the business school at Harvard and on the final exam of the semester, the last question was, "What is the name of the woman who cleans the classroom and the rest of the building?" The student said to

Your talk this morning was one of the best I've heard at this Society.

the professor, "Is this a trick question or a joke?" Then he realized that it was an important one. The next day he went to the professor and said, "Her name is Eva Gonzalas, and she has three children."

John used this while preaching on the Gospel story of the rich man and Lazarus.

Our diocese helped start the People of Faith Against the Death Penalty, and at their annual awards banquet I received the award for "exemplary leadership in educating and mobilizing faith communities to act to abolish the death penalty."[167]

Poor Joyce had to sit through twenty short talks by men who had been on death row after being falsely accused and eventually having their sentences dropped. They were very moving stories, but each went way over the time allotted. We still have a long way to go in abolishing the death penalty in North Carolina.

In mid-November 2007 we were in Dallas for the Celebration of a

---

167. For Rev. James Lewis's account of the founding and early history of the movement in North Carolina see www.pfadp.org/about-topmenu-110/history-topmenu-46.

New Ministry for my friend of long standing who was in our diocese, the Reverend Robert S. Dannals. He is an excellent choice, and I think they will love him and his family. The Enholms had organized some "friends of the Estills" to have a portrait painted of me as the fourth rector of St. Michaels and All Angels. They had an unveiling and a lovely reception afterward at the Enholms' home. Joyce commented that I looked twenty-seven years younger in the portrait, and that's what they wanted, since we left there twenty-seven years ago. I preached at the grand service and again at the 8:45 and 11:00 a.m. services on Sunday, all of which, I'm certain, made them glad to have a new preacher.

Our moving day from Landor Road to the assisted-care facility at The Cypress of Raleigh was July 8, 2008.

I met the movers at Cindy Estill's residence and supervised their packing and moving the breakfront that Bobby had left, along with nearly everything but his clothes, when he walked out of their marriage. I had to buy back the breakfront for three thousand dollars! Everything had to be packed and placed in storage until our apartment at The Cypress was ready in September. In the meantime we'd be camped out in our condo at Atlantic Beach.

My beloved Digby—our springer spaniel—on the last Sunday morning at Landor Road broke his cruciate ligament again. His former break involved a long and painful operation and recovery, and I just couldn't put him through that again. He was getting weak in his hind legs as well, and it was difficult for him to get up and down, especially on his trips to the beach. He always loved to run out into the ocean and sit down just before the break in the waves and then face the beach and let the waves roll over him. People would stop walking and watch him.

So I had to make the awful decision to have him put to sleep, and as they led him away at the vet's he looked up with his wonderful eyes as though he was saying, "It's alright—you're doing the right and loving thing." I buried his ashes in our pet cemetery in the ivy in the upper part of the backyard at Landor Road. He always loved that part of the yard and the forest of trees.

My good friend Bill Sigmon's son bought our house and proceeded to take down forty-one trees from the part of the yard where our pet cemetery was located. He then removed truckloads of dirt and leveled the area into a grass lawn. Our former neighbor asked him if he could have some of that dirt for his front yard, and lo and behold, our pet cemetery is now front and center. I told him that someday a beanbag I'd buried another dog in would probably surface. Digby's ashes will help the grass grow. So, in that sense, he's recycled there, just as he is in my heart.

After we sold our house and before The Cypress was ready for us, we moved to our place at the beach, Dunescape.

Our two months at Dunescape were really fine once we established better phone service and a post office box, and moved in some things in addition to the furnishings already there.

We celebrated being in our new home at The Cypress with sixteen of us (all family) having Thanksgiving dinner in our apartment. What a blessing to all—all our children and grandchildren together. We've achieved the biblical wish, "May you live to see your children's children."

The Cypress is a gated community and very aware of safety for all the residents. We have a blinking red light that—if we don't walk around and activate it every now and then—will call to see if we're alright. We've never been safer, though I wonder who would want to steal us!

My favorite security story is about Studs Turkel. He was reading to his wife, who was sick and lying on the sofa in the living room. After she had gone to sleep, he turned off the light and sat for a few minutes to be sure. Suddenly, the window opened, and a thief, thinking no one was in the room, came in. Turkel turned on the light, and the surprised thief demanded money. Turkel told him all he had was two twenties and gave them to the thief. But then Turkel said he needed money to get his sick wife some medicine in the morning. The man gave back one of the twenties, and Turkel said, "Thank you," and the man said, "You're welcome," and turned to climb back out the window. Turkel said, "You don't have to do that," and ushered him to the front door. He opened the door, and the man said, "Thank you," and Turkel replied, "You're welcome."

A sequel to the story is that apparently the story got out and the Turkels' house was burglarized two more times! He finally made a sign, "Beware of the Dog," and posted it in the yard. "I'm the dog," Studs would say with a chuckle.

On New Year's 2009 at Dunescape on one of my beach walks, I came across a dead seabird, partly covered by the sand. If it is true that God knows when the smallest sparrow falls, and I believe it to be true, then the great seabird is no exception. As I was thinking that, one of the feathers blew up in the wind and scurried off along the beach and back into the sea. "May the souls of all God's creation rest in peace, and may light perpetual shine on them."

Later in February we flew to Fort Lauderdale and spent the night with Revell and Barrie. She was eighty-five, and he was ninety. Of course we didn't know it at the time, but it was the last time we would see Barrie, who died two years later. He had been a Marine Air Corps pilot in a fighter jet and had served for nearly six years during World War II. Twice he was the only survivor of his air-wing and had ended the war flying cargo planes over the hump. He was a clinical psychologist, and in addition to a private practice, he interviewed prospective executives for several corporations.

We drove from Fort Lauderdale to Palm Beach and visited my cousin (on my mother's side) Jane Carolyn Rosebury, now known as "Kitchie" and married and widowed twice. Her first husband was an heir to the Avon estate and dropped dead on the street in New York. Her second husband, Roy Tolleson, also died last year.

It was good to be back in touch with Kitchie. We both laughed over the fact that when we were children, her mother (they lived in Paris, Kentucky) would bring her to our house in Lexington. She was a fat little girl and enough younger that I did not look forward to a day with her. One time, to my shame, I climbed a tree, and when she found me, spit down at her. Little did I know she would develop into an extremely bright and interesting adult.

I spit down on her.

We had a great visit; were welcomed in her lovely Florida home at a forty-person sit-down dinner; reunited with a good friend from Quogue, Gee Gee Maxwell, who has a place in Palm Beach; and toured the area's Norton Museum[168] with Gee Gee's daughter Graham, who is one of the museum executives. Gee Gee's husband, Hamish Maxwell, was a good friend as well and headed the giant corporation of Philip Morris. At Quogue on one occasion I asked him if he got tired of the commute to and from the City. He said he didn't mind because he could catch-up on his reading or even take a nap after a busy week. While he didn't mention it, I found out that he had a limo and driver! After one of the nor'easters took down a large tree at the entrance of our little church, the Maxwells donated another—almost as large.

---

168. The Norton Museum of Art was founded in 1941 by Ralph Hubbard Norton (1875–1953) and his first wife, Elizabeth Calhoun Norton (1881–1947). Norton, the former head of the Chicago-based Acme Steel Co., moved to West Palm Beach upon retirement and decided to share his sizable collection of paintings and sculpture. The late Art Deco / Neoclassical building designed by Marion Sims Wyeth opened its doors to the public on February 8, 1941. Its mission statement is "to preserve for the future the beautiful things of the past."

The next day we lunched at the Gulf Stream Club and had dinner at the former ambassador to the Court of St. James's big estate on the ocean. The last day, Pete Dye, the famous golf course architect and a friend and neighbor of Kitchie's, came by and gave me an autographed copy of his new book with pictures and descriptions of his courses. My! I'm certainly sorry I spit on Kitchie long ago.

When we were high school age, guests would come to visit, and since I didn't have a steady girl, I often became the blind date. Lucy Gay, whose father, Gus, was a distant cousin, had several of her friends from her boarding school for the Derby. Lucy was a year ahead of me in school because of the war.

Bobby Brewer, Billy Hays, and I were invited to go to Louisville for the Derby as dates. We had the Gays' station wagon and a driver. It was a grand way to see the Derby, and it turned out the guests were good company. On the way back, my date and I were in the very back seat of the wagon with our feet propped up on the back of the seat in front of us. Everyone was half asleep after the exciting day and the long trip home. Suddenly, out of the quiet, my date broke wind loudly. I'm sure all thought I was the culprit, and my three male friends were choking back their laughter. It was a very memorable day to say the least, and it certainly ended with a bang.

Moving ahead in time, Joyce and I celebrated our fifty-ninth wedding anniversary with a cruise on the American/Canadian line, which took us to Nantucket, Martha's Vineyard, Block Island, and Newport, sailing out of Warren, Rhode Island. This time we were regular paying passengers. When we returned, I found that my old friend and fellow priest Claudius Miller had died and I was invited to take part in the service with the rector of the Chapel of the Cross in Chapel Hill. My close friend Bill Brettmann preached.

Claudius wrote his own obituary, in which he said the four most cherished things in his life after his family were the Episcopal Church, the *New York Times*, the *New Yorker*, and the Democratic Party. One of Claudius's sons read a final word from Claudius which he read at the grave. "He suggested," his son said, "that any of you Republicans who might be at the service might want to choose that occasion to repent and join the Democratic Party."

We rejoiced at President-Elect Barack Obama's election and his choice of Joe Biden as vice president. Looking back beyond George W. Bush's disaster as president, I'm reminded of Arthur Schlesinger recalling Gore Vidal's old joke about President Reagan's library fire: "Reagan is sad because his library burned down, and he lost both of his books, and he hadn't even finished coloring one of them."

On the way home to North Carolina we visited Lexington and, as we always do, stopped at the Estill Lot in the Lexington Cemetery. We stood at Julian's grave, which is next to my mother's and father's graves. He would have been forty-seven years old by then (May 2001). Joyce and I will join his grave there one day. It is a lovely spot.

Part of my heart will always be in Kentucky, but we love North Carolina, and with our children and grandchildren there, that is where we have retired.

Claudius's death ended the publication of the *New Harmony Journal* and the weekly lunches at the equivalent of the *New Yorker*'s Algonquin Round Table, which all of us enjoyed. It also ended my contributions as illustrator and cartoonist of the *NHJ*.

Mary Cross, a longtime friend from Louisville now living in Princeton, called to tell us of Teddy Cross's death. They planned a memorial service in the Princeton University Chapel. I performed their wedding years ago in Louisville. Recently I had included some cartoons of "What It's Like to Live at The Cypress." Teddy wrote back and sent us his new book,

Waterbirds (2009), which is a magnificent collection of photographs of birds all over the world. As the reviewer in the *New York Times* said, "The pictures convey deep empathy with the natural world.... It is as though his pictures are sharing intimate moments with good friends."

Teddy was deeply involved in civil rights work, marched in Selma, advised Presidents Johnson and Nixon on economic development opportunities for black Americans, wrote two books on black empowerment, and published the *Journal of Blacks in Higher Education*. Teddy wanted his epitaph to read:

> *He passed on*
> *To a better World*
> *Still waiting for*
> *a perfect picture*
> *of a reddish egret.*

Ted and Mary came for a weekend with us at Quogue one summer. They had an engagement in East Hampton, so they said they'd meet us after lunch at the Quogue Beach Club. We were sitting on the beach with what was known at Quogue as "the hairnet crowd" when the Crosses arrived. We introduced them around, and everyone was most cordial. Someone asked where they had been since they had missed lunch. Teddy said, "We were at a fundraiser in East Hampton for Bella Abzug" (!). Slowly each couple began to leave, suddenly remembering a tennis date or the need to go to the Quogue market and before long we were alone and laughing with Ted and Mary.

Another of my close friends, John C. Williams, died in early December 2009. Cancer finally got him after a long, hard battle. Jim Adams, our new rector at Christ Church, and I had the service, and I was asked to give the homily. John C. loved boats and especially his boat, so I quoted Kenneth Grahame's *Wind in the Willows*, where Water Rat says to cap

Mole , "There is nothing, absolutely nothing half so much worth doing as simply messing about in boats ... or with boats. In or out of them it doesn't matter, that's the charm of it."

Joyce and I went out on John C's boat many times. One of my last trips with him was during one of our golf outings. We had played all day, and when we came in, we got on his boat and simply messed about. He was much better as the skipper of his boat than he had been that day on the golf course. We miss him greatly.

On one of the golf outings, five of us stayed in John C's cottage. John C.'s wife, Margaret, came by to apologize for interrupting our "men's retreat" but explained that she had to give one of their two black Labs a shot each night. I told her that while we would be glad to see her, I could give the dog her shots and explained my experience in the navy. She seemed relieved, gave me the equipment, pointed out which one was Belle, and left. That night, after drinks with the twenty or so golfers and a big dinner at a local restaurant, we came in and tumbled into bed. I said my prayers, rolled over, and just as I was dropping off, remembered my duty to Belle.

The two Labs were sleeping on the porch just outside my room, so I got my equipment, filled the syringe and went out on the porch. Both labs looked exactly alike: I tried calling Belle's name, and both wagged their tail and looked up at me with friendly faces. Finally, all I knew to do was play "eenie, meenie, miney, moe," and shoot away. I got back in bed, praying that I'd shot the right dog, and

Eenie, meenie, miney moe.

that if I had not, the victim would not die. She didn't, and the next day Margaret forgave me.

Those golf outings each fall and spring were valuable ways to meet new people and have quality time with old friends. We'd play a course on the way to the beach, drive afterward to one of our several hosts' places, gather on a porch overlooking the sea, and go to one of the local eating places, where I seemed to be the designated Grace sayer. We'd play golf the next day at one of the courses at Atlantic Beach and head back to our host's homes and the next day play another course and leave afterward for Raleigh.

One year and three months after John C's death, another close friend, Bill Sigmon, died. Bill and Martha Ann were almost the first couple we met. Lucille McKee (my assistant Bill Clarkson's mother-in-law) arranged a series of Thursday night suppers at the Carolina Country Club for us to meet people. Bill admitted later that he was somewhat apprehensive in meeting the new bishop. "Did this guy drink? What would he think if the rest of us ordered drinks? Should I order a Coke? Wine? What?" Apparently the waiter came to me first, and I said, "I'd like a vodka martini, up with a twist." Bill said he thought to himself. *I'm going to like this bishop, he's alright.* Neither he nor I had any idea how close a friendship we would have and that, finally, I would give the homily at his funeral.

I'm still surprised at the extent of pastoral care I'm called upon to do here at The Cypress and in the Raleigh community and even in the diocese. I make almost weekly hospital calls, often on good and old friends. Jack Hofler was one of those and had been quite ill and was still a little fuzzy. On one of my calls, we had a nice chat and then I said I didn't want to tire him out and added, "Let's have a prayer before I leave." I took his hand, bowed my head, and said, "O Lord," and Jack interrupted by saying, "You have bumps on your head!" I stopped the prayer, and we talked for a few minutes about sun spots and skin cancer. I said again, "Let's get back to our prayer," and began, "O Lord," only to have him say,

"Your face is red, too!" That did it. I assured him I had high color and bid him good-bye. He never got his prayer!

Reeve Lindbergh, in her Introduction to the sixth and final collection of her mother's diaries and letters[169], writes, "[We] have to meet old age and the certainty of death. First the death of those we love and cannot bear to lose, family and friends, young and old, and then one's own old age and inevitable death—the end of life." That is so true and it is a privilege and challenge to minister to people at those times.

Sid and Nancy Sanders were at Virginia Seminary, where he was chaplain, when he was elected bishop of East Carolina. They were good friends, and we attended his consecration. Later, when I became bishop, we saw a lot of them, and he and I played golf together at meetings and when we were able to get together.

One Sunday when we were at our place at the beach we went to Saint Francis-by-the-Sea and discovered it was the Bishop's Visitation Sunday. Sid preached a fine sermon, but at the announcement time he welcomed "the bishop and his wife from the Central [sic] Diocese." That was sort of a dig, but then he went on to say, "Bob and Joyce are a world-renown gospel singing team, and I'm sure that after the service they'll sing for you if you ask them." People looked around and smiled expectantly. Neither Joyce nor I can carry a tune, so after the announcements, she whispered, "Let's leave after we take communion!"

Actually we stayed and not a soul asked us to sing. Sadly, I was able to get back at Sid in preaching the homily at his funeral. His ashes were buried at Sanders Point, overlooking the sound at Trinity Center. I miss him every time we go to East Carolina.

My cousin Sam Shoemaker made the title of one of his last books, *I Stand by the Door.*

---

169. Reeve Lindbergh's introduction to *Against Wind and Tide: Letters and Journals, 1947-1986* (New York: Pantheon, 2012).

I realize that at age eighty-six, I stand by the door. As I've written before, many of my friends and contemporaries are dead. Some were close friends and former clergy in our diocese. I've preached nearly a dozen homilies and taken part in over a dozen services. Some wrote before they died specific instruction for the service, including hymns, prayers, and a request for a homily. I wish everyone would do that, although a homily may not be necessary. One friend years before his death wrote up his wishes for his funeral. Among other things, he wrote, "If the priest wants to give a homily, find another priest!"

Despite all those "standing by the door" thoughts, I recall it was Horace (65–8 BC) who wrote, "Seize the day, put no trust in the morrow" (*Odes*, XI, last line). "Carpe diem" (seize the day) has become the theme phrase for the Cursillo movement, but I doubt anyone would have attributed it to Horace. Still, it is an excellent daily motto for people in retirement.

At this writing, one of the favorites to win the 2015 Derby is a horse named Carpe Diem.

Speaking of endings, it is probably time to bring this to a close. Despite the fact that I haven't reached the time to pass through that symbolic door, I certainly am standing right beside it. I find the words in the General Thanksgiving in the Prayer Book to be relevant, and each new day I say with gratitude, "We bless thee for our creation, preservation, and all the blessings of this life" (*Book of Common Prayer*, page 58). Truly, I have been blessed. As the Psalmist points out, "My boundaries enclose a pleasant land; indeed, I have a goodly heritage" (Psalm 16:6).

My prayer is that our children and their children in the generations yet to come will find and live with the assurance that "nothing, not even death, shall separate us from the love of God which is in Christ Jesus our Lord."

I don't believe my generation should be called "The Greatest Generation." My generation, myself included, has failed in so many of life's challenges. There are still wars, segregation, climate change, and the growing gap between the haves and the have nots. Of all these, I think the conservation of our earth is probably the most urgent problem our generation is leaving behind.

I want tomorrow for those who will come after me. I want those who come after me to live their lives full of blessings, light, and hope.

One of the benedictions in the Episcopal Service that offers more inclusive language is, I think, especially fine. I use it whenever I can. "May the blessing of the God of Abraham and Sarah and of Jesus Christ, born of our sister Mary, and the Holy Spirit, who broods over creation as a mother over her children, be with you always. Amen."

Appendix

Curriculum Vitae: Robert Whitridge Estill

MOTHER | Elizabeth Pierpont Whitridge, daughter of Sarah Wilson Whitridge and Victor Whitridge

FATHER | Robert Julian Estill, son of Robert Christopher Estill and Naomi Wierman Sheffer Estill

1927 SEPTEMBER 7 | Born, Lexington, Kentucky, 471 West Second Street

1929 JANUARY 13 | Baptized in Christ Church Cathedral, Lexington, Kentucky, by the Right Reverend Lewis W. Burton (1986–1928) and the Reverend Charles Stuart Hale, Rector.

1933 | Hamilton Grammar School

1937 | Move to Robin Hill, Eastin Road, Lexington, Kentucky

1939 NOVEMBER 19	Confirmation at Christ Church, Diocese of Lexington, Bishop Henry Pryor Almon Abbott (1929–1945), Christopher Philip Sparling, Rector
1941– MARCH 27, 1944	Episcopal High School, Alexandria, Virginia
1944 MAY– 1945 MAY 29	Kavanaugh High School, Lawrenceville, KY
1945	US Navy
1946–1949	University of Kentucky, Bachelor of Arts degree, Spring 1949
1949 JANUARY	Christ Church, Richmond, Kentucky
1949 MAY 10	Licensed Lay Reader by Bishop William Robert Moody, Diocese of Lexington
1949– 1950	First year at Episcopal Theological School, Cambridge, Massachusetts
1950	Postulant for Holy Orders, in charge of Christ Church, Richmond Organized the Seabury Club
1950 JUNE 17	Robert Whitridge Estill and Joyce Haynes were married at St. Mark's Episcopal Church, Louisville, Kentucky

1950 SUMMER	Fieldwork at St. John's, Otter Lake, Michigan
1950–1951	Second year at ETS, Cambridge
1951	Summer at St. Mary's, Middlesboro, Kentucky
1951–1952	Senior year at ETS and graduation with a Bachelor of Divinity degree
1952 JUNE 27	Ordination to the diaconate, Church of the Good Shepherd, Lexington, Kentucky, June 27, 1952, by the Right Reverend William R. Moody, Bishop of Lexington
1952–1955	St. Mary's Church, Middlesboro, Kentucky
1952 OCTOBER 10	Death of father, Dr. Robert Julian Estill
1953 FEBRUARY 11	Ordination to the Priesthood, Christ Church, Lexington, Kentucky, February 11, 1953, by the Right Reverend William R. Moody, Bishop of the Episcopal Diocese of Lexington
1953 OCTOBER 10	Birth of daughter Helen Haynes Estill
1954	Birth and death of Robert Julian Estill II
1955	Death of mother, Elizabeth Pierpont Whitridge

1955–1964   Rector, Christ Church, Lexington, Kentucky, from
                   December 1, 1955.

                   Births of Robert Whitridge Estill Jr. (February 26,
                   1957) and Elizabeth Rodes Estill

                   Youth Conferences

1956 DECEMBER   To: Our Riding Rector
                   A parson should have a "good seat"
                   And "light hands," and an order complete
                   For riding to hounds
                   Where clean sport abounds
                   May no spill that parson delete!
                   —H, Dec '56

1958   IX Lambeth Conference, London, Chaplain for
                   Bishop Moody

1959–1963   Commission on Human Rights, appointed by
                   Gov. Bert Combs (1959–1963)
                   Reappointment to the Kentucky Human Rights
                   Commission Association with Governor Ned
                   Breathitt (1963–1967)

1960 SPRING   The University of the South, Sewanee, Master of
                   Sacred Theology

1963 NOVEMBER 11   JFK assassination

1964–1969	Dean of Christ Church Cathedral, Louisville, Kentucky
1966	Civil Rights Activities 1966 Kentucky Civil Rights Bill Passed Worked with Bert Combs, Ned Breathitt, MLK Jr. President, Kentucky Council of Churches Meeting RFK at Binghams, worked for him
1967–1979	Appointment to the Standing Liturgical Commission Church of the Atonement, Quogue, New York, for the summers for thirty-five years
1968 APRIL 4	Martin Luther King Jr. assassination
1968 JUNE 5	Robert Fitzgerald Kennedy assassination
1969-1973	Rector, St. Alban's Church, Washington, DC
1973-1976	Virginia Theological Seminary, Director of Continuing Education. Started the DMin program
1976-1980	St. Michaels and All Angels, Dallas, Texas (June 1, 1976) Helen at the University of Arizona, Bobby at TCU, and Elizabeth at Highland Park High School

1979 SPRING	University of the South, Sewanee, and Vanderbilt University, Doctor of Ministry
1980 SPRING	Virginia Theological Seminary, Doctor of Divinity (Honorary)
1980–1994	Bishop of the Diocese of North Carolina
1980 MARCH 15	Consecration in Duke Chapel
	House of Bishops Chairman of Board for Theological Education Editorial Chairman of the Standing Liturgical Commission The 1979 *Book of Common Prayer* approved President of the North Carolina Council of Churches
1984 SPRING	University of the South, Sewanee, Doctor of Divinity (Honorary) 14 Years as Bishop, retired, with Bob Johnson as successor
1988	XII Lambeth Conference Queen's Garden Party Sabbatical Bought Dunescape
1992 SPRING	St. Augustine's College, Doctor of Humane Letters (Honorary)

1994	Retired May 14
	Cruises
	Retired from Quogue after thirty-five summers
	Interim in Lexington, Kentucky, for four months
2001 JULY 18	Hall of Fame, Kentucky Commission on Human Rights
2008	Moved into The Cypress of Raleigh

THE SUN
SHINES
BRIGHT